A TO Z OF ARABIC-ENGLISH-ARABIC TRANSLATION

Ronak Husni and Daniel L. Newman

A to Z of
Arabic-English-Arabic
Translation

SAQI

ISBN 978-0-86356-885-5
eISBN 978-0-86356-756-8

A full CIP record for this book is available from the British Library
A full CIP record for this book is available from the Library of Congress

Printed and bound by Bookwell, Finland

SAQI

26 Westbourne Grove, London W2 5RH

www.saqibooks.com

Contents

Introduction

Rationale behind the book

This book is the result of many years of teaching university-level courses on translation between Arabic and English by the authors to both native English and Arabic speakers.

It is important to state from the outset what this book is *not*. It is *not* a grammar book or composition manual. Nor is it a treatise on translation theory or a historical overview of Arabic-English translation. Rather, it is intended to explain and illustrate various questions that are of relevance to the translator who works between these two languages. It focuses on common errors made by students and translation practitioners in general, with an emphasis on the microstructural linguistic elements of the translation process. The clear practical intent, however, does not mean that the *A to Z* is devoid of theory or that it does not play a part in translation. In fact, theory is everywhere and the way in which the translation mechanisms and processes are discussed is rooted in a solid theoretical basis.

One of the questions that any author needs to ask is whether their book fills an existing gap in the market. The answer in the case of the *A to Z* is that it fills several.

Firstly, it is a much-needed addition to the field of Arabic/English translation where there is a dearth of resources.

Secondly, while the overwhelming majority of existing works concentrate on one translation direction, the *A to Z* is – very much like the scripts that are used in it – *bidirectional* inasmuch as it addresses problems relating to both Arabic-English and English-Arabic translation. Naturally, the inevitable consequence is that some entries may be more relevant to native speakers of either Arabic or English. However, it would be wrong to presume that this is a misguided attempt to be all things to all people. Indeed, even if the native speaker of the language may not need assistance with the correct usage of this or that idiomatic expression, s/he will benefit from guidance on how to translate it into the Target Language. What is more, the aim is never to discuss grammatical points *per se*, but only in relation to their difficulty in translation. Indeed, there are plenty of grammar books available for those whose appetite has been whetted for more detail on grammatical items.

Thirdly, rather than dealing with themes or processes, the *A to Z* focuses on specific translation problems, each of which is carefully contextualized and illustrated for the most part by authentic examples culled from contemporary literature and the media from various Arab countries.

Fourthly, the approach is one of comparative analysis, with a discussion of grammatical, lexical and semantic aspects being viewed through the prism of translation in order to offer the reader guidance on correct and idiomatic usage.

Translation is all about making choices, and there is rarely only one solution; usually, the same idea may be expressed in a variety of ways. Hence, the examples in the book often contain multiple translations of a given source text.

Target readership and aims of the book

The intended readership of the *A to Z* are university-level students of translation and professional translators, alike. And while it was originally designed for those whose mother tongue is either Arabic or English and who possess advanced proficiency in their non-native language, it can be used by others who have attained the required aptitude in both these languages.
More specifically, the book is aimed at:

- developing and honing users' ability and skills in translating between Arabic and English;
- enhancing idiomatic expression in both languages;
- raising awareness of the pitfalls specific to Arabic/English translation;
- increasing competency by providing the appropriate strategies for effective translation.

How to use the book

The design and layout of the book are in keeping with the overall aims and the alphabetic arrangement of all entries in the *A to Z* ensures ease of use both as a manual and as a reference work for the practice of Arabic-English-Arabic translation.

Whereas the reader is expected to have a basic knowledge of grammatical concepts, specialized linguistic terminology has been kept to a minimum. The practical pedagogic aim of the *A to Z* also underlies the fact that all examples are fully vowelled whereas the imperfect stem vowels are added in brackets to Form I verbs. e.g. هَتَفَ (i).

Naturally, any selection is, to some degree, subjective, as well as being limited by practical constraints and some readers may lament the absence (or inclusion) of this or that point. Valid though such criticism may be, it is important to stress that in choosing the entries, the authors were guided by their classroom experience.

Although, in theory, readers may decide to work their way through the book from beginning to end, the layout is conducive to it being used as a reference work for specific issues, or to 'dip into'. As such, it is eminently suited for both independent and classroom use. In the latter context, teachers may, for instance, choose to concentrate on certain items that may be relevant to a text that is being discussed in class.

Finally, a word about language variety. When dealing with a diglossic language such as Arabic, the question that arises is, of course, *which* kind of Arabic. This is not the place to enter into this highly complex issue; suffice it to say that the language exemplified in this book is Modern Standard Arabic, i.e. the formal normative variety of the language as it is used today in formal writing by educated native speakers. As a result, we have eschewed dialectisms and regionalisms. The English variety employed in the book is formal British English, though relevant comments are provided regarding North American usage when necessary.

In addition to our students, both past and present, many of whose challenging questions we have attempted to answer, the authors would like to thank Jack Wesson for his meticulous feedback on the manuscript.

Durham, Sharjah, January 2013

List of abbreviations and symbols

AE	American English
AP	active participle (فاعل)
DEM	demonstrative adjective
f. pl.	feminine plural
f. s.	feminine singular
imp.	Imperfect (المُضارِعُ المَرْفوعُ)
intrans.	Intransitive (verbs)
m.s.	masculine singular
MSA	Modern Standard Arabic
perf.	perfect (الماضي)
pl.	plural
POS	part of speech
PP	prepositional phrase
PRON	pronoun
sg.	singular
SL	Source Language
ST	Source Text
subj.	subjunctive (المُضارِعُ المَنْصوبُ)
VN	verbal noun (مَصْدَرٌ)
VSO	Verb-Subject-Object
/	marks alternative translations
*	precedes erroneous forms

Abbreviations/acronyms

In English, it is common to abbreviate words. One generally makes a distinction between **abbreviations** and **acronyms** in that the latter can be read as words. Consider the difference between 'ETA' (expected time of arrival) and 'NATO' (North Atlantic Treaty Organization). In the former, each letter is pronounced separately (/i: -ti: -ei/), whereas the latter is read as /neitou/. Whilst acronyms are generally capitalized, abbreviations tend to be in lower case, except if they involve proper nouns or technical terms. e.g. 'FAO' (Food and Agricultural Organization'), 'DNA' (deoxyribonucleic acid).

In some cases, **acronyms** become so 'naturalized' in the language that their acronymic origins have been forgotten and, consequently, they appear in lowercase. e.g. 'laser' (< 'LASER', Light Amplification by Stimulated Emission of Radiation), 'radar' (< 'RADAR', Radio Detection And Ranging).

Acronyms are often added with suffixes. e.g. *yuppie* ('young upwardly mobile professional'), *dinky* ('double income with no kids [yet]').

A particular type of abbreviation is so-called 'clipping', which is also known as 'truncation', and involves the cutting of one or more syllables from a word (usually at the end). Whilst some are part of informal usage (e.g. *doc*, 'document'), several have gained independent status. e.g. *ad* (advertisement), *lab* (laboratory), *sub* (submarine), *deli* (delicatessen <shop>), *demo* (demonstration), *zoo* (zoological gardens), *fax* (facsimile), *cab* (cabriolet), *bus* (omnibus).

In principle, abbreviations are unknown in Classical Arabic, even if there are some examples like حَوْقَلَ (to say لا حَوْلَ ولا قُوَّة إلا بالله), بَسْمَلَ ('to say بسم الله'), or صلعم (صَلَّى اللهُ عَلَيْهِ وَسَلَّم, 'God bless him and grant him salvation'), which is added after a mention of the Prophet Muhammad. Western-style abbreviations and acronyms are a very recent invention under the influence of English. e.g. ص. ب. (صُنْدُوق البَريِد, 'PO Box'). They remain quite rare and are generally restricted to media Arabic. e.g. أ.ف.ب ('AFP', the news agency *Agence France Presse*), أوبيك

(OPEC), ناتو (NATO), آر بي جي ('RPG', rocket-propelled grenade'). As a result, when translating English acronyms into Arabic, it is always safer to give the full form.

There are no examples of 'clipping' in Arabic.

Above/over

Although both mean *higher than*, they cannot be used interchangeably; **above** tends to refer to a position along a vertical scale, with **over** denoting movement, while also being used with numbers, expressions of quantity or measurement. In Arabic, the preposition فَوْقَ and the comparative أَكْثَرُ مِنَ (for numbers and quantities) are the usual translations of these terms. e.g.

"She is **above** suspicion."

إِنَّها فَوْقَ الشُّبُهاتِ

"We're standing 200 metres **above** the ground."

نَقِفُ عَلَى اِرْتِفاعِ 200 مِتْرٍ فَوْقَ سَطْحِ الأَرْضِ

"His intelligence is **above** average."

ذَكاؤُهُ فَوْقَ العَادةِ

"His success was **above** all expectations."

كانَ نَجاحُهُ فَوْقَ كُلِّ التَّوَقُّعاتِ

"She is **over** sixty (years old)."

إِنَّها فَوْقَ السِّتِّينَ مِنَ العُمْرِ

"He weighs **over** 75 kilograms."

وَزْنُهُ أَكْثَرُ مِنْ 75 كِيلوغْراماً

"The aircraft flew **over** our house."

حَلَّقَتِ الطَّائِرَةُ فَوْقَ بَيْتِنا

"This dress cost me **over** three hundred pounds."

كَلَّفَني هذا الفُسْتانُ أَكْثَرَ مِنْ ثَلاثِمِئَة جُنَيهٍ

"Throw (f. sg.) the ball **over** the wall!"

إِرْمِي الكُرَةَ فَوْقَ الحائِطِ

> ☞ **NOTE**: the following figurative expressions: 'to rise/be above (some-thing)' and 'get over (something/someone), meaning 'to disregard' and 'overcome (e.g. problems, crisis), respectively. e.g.
>
> "We **got over** our our difficulties and made it through the exams."
>
> تَغَلَّبْنا عَلَى صِعابِنا وَنَجَحْنا في الامْتِحاناتِ
>
> ... قَهَرْنا/ذَلَّلْنا/اجْتَزْنا صِعابَنا
>
> "You have to **rise above** his insults if you want to work here."
>
> يَنْبَغي لَكَ تَجاوُزُ إِهاناتِهِ إذا أَرَدْتَ العَمَلَ هُنا

Adverbs

As English and Arabic have different linguistic structures, it stands to reason that it is nigh-on impossible to expect a one-to-one correspondence in the translation of various grammatical categories and/or parts of speech.
Arabic 'adverbs' can come in the following forms:
1. particles. e.g. فَقَطْ, 'only';
2. indeclinable nouns ending in –*u*. e.g. قَطُّ;
3. indefinite accusative nouns: جِدّاً, 'very', كَيْفَ, 'how'.

When talking about the translation of adverbials[1], the following issues are of importance:

- the type of adverbial;
- the composition of the adverbial (one or several words);
- the equivalent in the other language;
- the position of the adverbials in the sentence.

Types

The most frequent types of adverbs are:

1. Adverbs of Manner

These express the way in which something is done. e.g.

"You must leave **quickly**."

يَجِبُ أَنْ تُغَادِرَ بِسُرْعَةٍ

"They were working **efficiently**."

كَانُوا يَعْمَلُونَ بِكَفَاءَةٍ

English adverbs of manner generally end in '-(ic)(al)ly', whereas they are placed after the Direct Object or after the verb (if there's no Object).

In Arabic, English **adverbs of manner** can be rendered in a variety of ways:

- Indefinite noun in the accusative;
- Indefinite adjective in the accusative;
- Prepositional phrases introduced by بِ or فِي, followed by an indefinite noun (often a verbal noun);
- The following compound prepositional phrases (followed by an indefinite noun):
  - بِصُورَةٍ ('in the manner of').
  - بِشَكْلٍ/عَلَى شَكْلٍ ('in the form of').
  - بِطَرِيقَةٍ ('in the method of').
  - بِصِفَةٍ ('in the quality of').

---

1. "adverbial" is used in preference to "adverb" if it involves phrases, rather than a single word.

فَعَلْناهُ مَعاً

"We did it **together**."

ذاكَرْتُ/اسْتَذْكَرْتُ دُرُوسِي جَيِّدا

"I studied my lessons **well**."

لا أُحِبُّ السَّفَرَ بِالطَّائِرةِ بِشَكْلٍ عامٌ

"**Generally** (speaking), I don't like to travel by plane."

هذه مُشْكِلةٌ في دُوَلِ الخَلِيجِ بِصِفةٍ خاصَّةٍ

"This is a problem, **particularly** in (Arabian) Gulf countries."

كَانُوا يَتَظاهَرُونَ ضِدَّ الحُكُومةِ بِطَرِيقةٍ عَلَنِيَّةٍ

"They were demonstrating **openly** against the government."

خَرَجَتِ الأُستاذَةُ عَلَى عَجَلٍ/بِسُرْعَةٍ

"The teacher left **in a hurry**."

قَرَأْتُ الكِتابَ بِاهْتِمامٍ

"I read the book **with interest**."

> ☞ **NOTE**: Arabic adverbs of manner are placed after the Direct Object or after the verb (in the absence of an Object).

The most typical and traditional method to express manner in Arabic is, however, through a **circumstantial clause** (الحال) or **cognate accusative** (المَفْعُول المُطْلَق).

A. The circumstantial clause (الحالُ)

Deriving its name from the fact that it describes the state (حال) of the subject as an action is performed, the *ḥāl* is most often formed with an indefinite participle in the accusative case. Alternatively, the same idea can be rendered through وَ (the so-called واو الحال), which is followed either by a **pronoun** (if it involves a nominal sentence[1]), or وَقَد with a perfect[2] tense (verbal sentences). e.g.

"He sat down **despondently**."

جَلَسَ مُكْتَئِباً

جَلَسَ وهُوَ مُكْتَئِبٌ

جَلَسَ وَقَد كَئِبَ

اِسْتَمَعَ إلى المُوسِيقى وَهوَ يَرقُصُ

"He listened to music **while he was dancing**."

B. The cognate accusative (مَفْعولٌ مُطْلَقٌ)

This involves a construction containing the verbal noun (مَصْدَرٌ) of the main verb, which is further modified adjectivally (with the adjective agreeing in gender and number with the verbal noun). e.g.

"I protested **vehemently**"

لَقَدْ اِحْتَجَجْتُ اِحْتِجاجاً شَديداً

[لَقَدْ اِحْتَجَجْتُ بِشِدَّة/بِقُوَّة =]

"The party wants to participate **fully** in secular society."

يُريدُ الحِزْبُ أَنْ يُشارِكَ مُشارِكةً كامِلةً في المُجْتَمَعِ العِلْمانيِّ

2. Place adverbials

These express where something takes place and in English are usually found after the object, otherwise after the verb. If it co-occurs with an adverb of manner in the sentence, the adverb of place should follow that of manner. e.g.

"He was killed **with a knife** [MANNER] in **London** [PLACE]."

قُتِلَ بِسِكّينٍ في لَنْدَنَ

---

1. "nominal sentence" here refers to its use in Arabic grammar, i.e. a sentence/clause that begins with a noun, rather than a finite verb.

2. In this book, "perfect" will be used to denote المَاضي, "imperfect" for المُضارِعُ, "subjunctive" for المُضارِعُ المَنصوبُ and "jussive" for المُضارِعُ المَجزومُ.

Unlike adverbs of manner, those of place can also be placed in sentence-initial position – usually for emphasis. e.g.

"**In Beirut**, the Prime Minister met with the other members of the Alliance."

قابَلَ رَئِيسُ الوُزَراءِ أَعْضاءَ الائْتِلافِ الآخرينَ في بَيْرُوتَ

In Arabic, place adverbials occur only rarely in sentence-initial positions; most frequently they are found in **medial** positions, i.e. after the verb or after the subject when it is explicit. e.g.

"Last year, Mansur was **in France**."

كانَ مَنْصُورُ في فَرَنْسا السَّنةَ الماضِيةَ

"Fatima was living **here**."

كانَت فاطَمةُ تَعِيشُ هُنا

"The President arrived **at Marrakech airport** yesterday."

وَصَل الرَّئِيسُ أَمْسِ إلى مَطارِ مَرّاكُشٍ

"Nesreen waited for him **at the station gate**, but he was in the arrivals hall."

انْتَظَرَتْهُ نِسْرِينُ على بابِ المَحَطَّةِ بَيْدَ أَنَّهُ/إلاَّ إِنَّهُ كانَ في صالةِ الوُصُولِ

3. Time adverbials

These express when an action or event takes place and are usually found in the same places as the adverbs of place, i.e. either at the very beginning of the sentence or at the end, with the former position being the one used in case of emphasis. e.g.

"My aunt was there **before the war**."

كانَتْ خالَتِي هُناكَ قَبْلَ الحَرْبِ

"He **yesterday** arrived in Paris."

وَصَلَ إلَى بارِيس أَمْسِ

21

When time adverbials co-occur with adverbials of manner and place, the usual order is: MANNER + PLACE + TIME. e.g.

"He sent the message **by post** [MANNER] **from Brussels** [PLACE] **two weeks ago** [TIME]."

أَرسَلَ الرِّسالةَ بِالبَرِيدِ مِن برُوكسِل مُنْذُ أُسْبُوعَيْنِ

"Ahmed will travel **to Baghdad tomorrow**."

سَيُسافِرُ أَحْمَدُ غداً إلى بَغْدادَ

In Arabic, **time adverbials** usually occur after the verb or the subject (if it is explicit). e.g.

أَلْقَى الوَزِيرُ أَمْس مُحاضَرةً في القاهرةِ

"The minister delivered a speech **yesterday** in Cairo."

However, they can equally be found after the object or in sentence-final position. e.g.

قَرَّرَتْ وزارةُ البُنْيةِ التَّحْتِيّةِ رَفْعَ أَسْعارِ النَّفْطِ بِنِسْبَةِ 6% (اعتباراً) مِنْ مُنْتَصَفِ لَيْلَةِ الأَحَد

"The Ministry of Infrastructure decided to raise petrol prices by 6% as **from midnight on Sunday**."

When time adverbials co-occur with adverbials of manner and place in Arabic, the usual order is: VERB/explicit SUBJECT + TIME + PLACE. e.g.

تُنَظِّمُ الأُمَمُ المُتَّحِدَةُ اليَوْمَ في مُنْتَجَع العَقَبةِ الأُرْدُنِّيِّ المُؤْتَمَرَ الاقْتِصاديَّ

"The UN today organizes the Economic Conference in the Jordanian resort of Aqaba."

When adverbs of time co-occur with adverbs of manner and place in Arabic, the usual order is: VERB/explicit SUBJECT + TIME + PLACE + MANNER

وَصَلَ الوَزِيرُ اليَوَم إِلَى القَاهِرةِ حَامِلاً رِسالةً مُهِمَّةً

"The minister today arrived in Cairo carrying an important letter."

خَرَجَ اِبْنِي صَبَاحاً إِلَى الْجَامِعَةِ لِحُضُورِ الْمُحَاضَرَةِ الاِفْتِتَاحِيَّةِ لِلأُسْتَاذِ الْجَدِيدِ

"My son left this morning for University to attend the inaugural lecture by the new professor."

☞ Also see 'Still/Yet'

4. Adverbs of frequency

These express how many times the action conveyed by the verb takes place and in English are usually found between the subject and verb, except in the case of the verb '**to be**', which they follow. If the verb is complex, i.e. consists of an auxiliary or modal, and a main verb, the adverb of frequency is placed after the first verb form. e.g.

"They **regularly** eat out."
إِنَّهُمْ يَأْكُلونَ خَارِجَ الْبَيْتِ بِاسْتِمرارٍ/عَلَى الدَّوام

"I was **always** honest with you."
كُنْتُ دائماً صادقًا مَعَكَ
كُنْتُ صادقًا مَعَكَ عَلَى الدّوام

"You should **never** have agreed to this."
ما كانَ يَنْبَغِي أَنْ تُوافِقَ عَلَى هذا قَطُّ

☞ **NOTE**: when the auxiliary is '**used to**' or '**have**' used as a main verb the frequency adverb is usually placed after the verb/explicit subject. e.g.

"I **never** used to worry."
لَمْ أَكُنْ أَقْلَقُ في السَّابِقِ قَطُّ

"She **always** treats her friends gently."
إِنَّها دائماً تَعامِلُ أَصْدقائَها بِلُطْفٍ

The Arabic adverbs of frequency are usually found after the verb or the subject (if it is explicitly stated). e.g.

أَذَهَبُ أَحْياناً إلى المَتْحَفِ في وَسَطِ المَدِينَة

"I **sometimes** go to the museum in the centre of town."

☞ For **adverbs of degree**, see separate entries on 'Nearly', 'Quite', 'Hardly/Scarcely/Barely/Just'

Advise/advice

Note the difference in spelling between the verb **to advise** and the noun **advice**, which is uncountable in English and, therefore, there is no "advices"! The usual Arabic word for "advice", نَصِيحَة (pl. نَصائِحُ) is countable, which may lead to mistranslations of a sentence such as:

أَوَدُّ تَقْدِيمَ بَعْضِ النَّصائِح لَكُمْ

"I'd like to give you some **advice**." (NOT *advices!)

Of particular interest are cases which involve numbers. e.g.

وَجَّهَ لي خَمْسَ نَصائِحَ قَبْلَ مُغادَرَتي

"He gave me five **pieces of advice** (NOT *advices!) before I left."

The verb *advise* is followed by **OBJ+TO+INF** in English, while the Arabic counterpart, نَصَحَ (i), is followed by the complementizer أَنْ. e.g.

بِمَ تَنْصَحُني أَنْ أَشْرَبَ بَعْدَ العَشاء؟

"What would you **advise** (or recommend) me to drink after supper?"

Affect/effect

To affect is "*to have an* **effect** *on*". Confusingly, there is also a verb **to effect**, which means "*to bring about*", "*to achieve*". The former should be rendered in Arabic by أَثَّرَ في/عَلَى, the latter by قامَ(u) + ب + VN. e.g.

"The economic crisis severely **affected** many European countries which will suffer from its effect in many areas."

أَثَّرَتِ الأَزْمَةُ الإِقْتِصادِيَّةُ عَلَى دُوَلٍ أُورُبِّيَّةٍ عِدَّةٍ، سَتُعاني مِنْ تَأْثيراتِها في مَجَالاتٍ مُتَعَدِدَةٍ

"The new manager **effected** basic changes in this company."

قامَ المُديرُ الجَديدُ بِإِجْراءِ تَغْييراتٍ أَساسِيَّةٍ في هذِهِ الشَّرِكةِ

> ☞ **NOTE: to affect** (+ NOUN) also has another, less commonly used meaning of 'to feign, pretend', which can be rendered in Arabic in one of two ways:
>
> 1. **Form VI** (تَفاعَلَ) verb. e.g.
>
> "She **affects** (= feigns) ignorance of his mistakes."
> تَتَجاهَلُ غَلَطاتِه
>
> 2. the following verbs: تَكَلَّفَ or تَصَنَّعَ، تَظاهَرَ، ادَّعَى. e.g.
>
> لَقَدْ تَظاهَرَ بِالصُّداع كَيْ لا يَذْهَبَ إلى الحَفْلة
> "He **affected** a headache in order not to go to the party."
>
> تَكَلَّفَتِ/تَصَنَّعَتِ الضُّعْفَ حَتَّى خَرَجْتُ مِنَ الغُرْفة
> "She **affected** weakness until I (had) left the room."
>
> يَدَّعي فِقْدان الذَّاكِرة
> "He **affected/feigned** loss of memory."

After/afterwards

This set may pose some confusion in translation as a result of contrastive usage in English and Arabic. "**After**" is a preposition which means "*following the appointed time, event, ...*", whereas "**afterwards**" is an adverb meaning *'subsequently'*. In Arabic, however, both may be rendered by بَعْدَ or بعدَ ذلكَ e.g.

"The accident happened after his arrival."
حَصَلَتِ الحادِثَةُ بَعْدَ وُصُولِه

"When will he meet you? Before the meeting or **afterwards** (NOT *after!)?" (OR: "Before or after the meeting?")
مَتَى سَيُقابِلُكَ، قَبْلَ الاِجْتِماعِ أَمْ بَعْدَهُ؟

"I'll see you **afterwards** (NOT *after!)."
سَأراكَ بَعْدَ ذلكَ

"**Afterwards**, we spent two weeks in the capital."
بَعْدَ ذلكَ أَمْضَيْنا أُسْبُوعَيْنِ في العاصِمَةِ

Another cause of negative interference is the fact that بَعْدَ is used in Arabic where English requires **in**. e.g.

"We will go there **in** (NOT *after!) two hours' time."
سَنَذْهَبُ إلى هُناكَ بَعْدَ ساعَتَيْنِ

Agreement

This word denotes the way some words change when they occur with others; for instance, when a feminine singular noun is modified by an adjective in Arabic, the latter normally must also be put in the feminine, as a result of which it is said to 'agree' with the noun. We are concerned here with some special cases involving verb-subject agreement and noun-adjective agreement.

Verb-subject agreement

As there is no gender in English, verbs agree with their subjects only in **number**, i.e. whether it is singular or plural. Whilst this is pretty straightforward in the majority of cases, there is one important group of exceptions: **collective** nouns referring to groups of people. In this instance, both singular and plural are possible, depending on the meaning, of course.

In practice, the verb agrees with the **logical** subject (the actual or implied referents), rather than the **grammatical** subject (the grammatical form).

Consider, for instance, the following two sentences:

"The police **are** chasing the criminals."

تُطارِدُ الشُّرْطَةُ المُجْرِمِينَ

"The police **is** a fine body of men."

إِنَّ الشُّرْطَةَ جِهازٌ يَتَكَوَّنُ مِن خِيرَةِ الرِّجَالِ
إِنَّ جِهازَ الشُّرْطَةِ يَتَكَوَّنُ مِنْ خِيرَةِ الرِّجَالِ
الشُّرْطَةُ مِنْ خِيرَةِ الرِّجَالِ

In both cases, the subject is the same ('the police'), but in the first sentence the stress is on the constituent components, that is, the individual policemen who do the chasing. In the second, the emphasis is on the organization.

The same applies to other words which refer to groups of people, such as *government, committee, group, family, company, family, government, jury, school, staff, team, union*. e.g.

"The **government have** agreed upon a new tax increase."

لَقَدْ وافَقَتِ الحُكَومةُ عَلَى زِيادَةٍ جَدِيدَةٍ فِي الضَّرائِبِ

"The **government consists** of ten ministers."

تَتَكَوَّنُ الحُكَومةُ مِنْ عَشَرَةِ وُزَرَاءَ

"The average **family spends** a quarter of the income on food."

تُنْفِقُ العائلةُ المُتَوَسِّطَةُ رُبْعَ دَخْلِها عَلَى الأَكْلِ

إِنَّ العَائِلَةَ المُتَوَسِّطَةَ تُنْفِقُ ما يُعادِلُ رُبْعَ دَخْلِها السَّنَوِيِّ عَلَى الأَكْلِ

"His **family have** invited us for dinner."

دَعَتْنا عَائِلَتُهُ لِلْعَشاء

"The committee **was** set up twenty years ago amidst a crime wave."

أُسِّسَتِ اللَجْنَةُ قَبْلَ عِشْرِينَ عَاماً وَسَطَ مَوْجَةٍ مِنَ الجَرائِمِ

"The committee **have** put forward new proposals to reduce crime."

قَدَّمَتِ اللَجْنَةُ اقْتِراحاً جَدِيداً لِلتَّقْلِيلِ مِن الجَرائِمِ

"The United Nations **have** sent in relief aid."

لَقَدْ أَرْسَلَتِ الأُمَمُ المُتَّحِدَةُ مَعُونَةً ماليَّةً/غِذائيَّةً

"The United Nations **is** a charitable organization."

الأُمَمُ المُتَّحِدَةُ مُنَظَّمَةٌ خَيْرِيَّةٌ

Occasionally, misuse may lead to ambiguity. e.g.

"The **team is** coming to our city." [= The team come to our city to play]

يَأْتِي الفَرِيقُ إلى مَدِينَتِنا

"The **team are** coming to our city." [= the members of the team are coming to the city.]

يَأْتِي (أَعْضاءُ) الفَرِيقِ إلى مَدِينَتِنا

The same emphasis on the logical subject also explains why clearly plural nouns take a singular verb if they refer to one single entity. e.g.

"The United States **has** decided to pull out of the Kyoto Protocol."

قَرَّرَتِ الوِلاياتُ المُتَّحِدَةُ أَنْ تَنْسَحِبَ مِن مُعاهَدةِ كِيُوتُو

"The Netherlands **is** a big country."

هُولَندا دَوْلَةٌ كَبِيرَةٌ

In Arabic, there is always agreement with their **grammatical subject**, except with collectives that refer to nationalities, which are always masculine plural, such as العَرَبُ ('the Arabs') and, الانْكليزُ ('the English'). e.g.

"In the pre-Islamic period, the Arabs spoke many dialects."

العَرَبُ كانُوا يَتَكَلَّمُونَ لَهْجاتٍ كَثيرةٍ في عَصْرِ الجاهليّةِ

"The English considered themselves important after Faisal ascended the throne of Iraq."

كانَ الإنْكليزُ يَعْتَبِرُونَ أَنْفُسَهُم أَصْحابَ الفَضْلِ في وُصُولِ فَيْصَلَ إلى عَرْشِ العِراقِ

In some cases, generic collective nouns are rendered idiomatically as plurals in Arabic. e.g.

"The opposition stressed that the country needs to reform itself."

لَقَدْ أَكَّدَ المُعارِضُونَ أَن البِلادَ مُضطَرَّةٌ إلى إصْلاحِ نَفْسِها

"The intelligentsia have played a key role in the revolution."

لَعِبَ المُثَقَّفُونَ دَوْراً أَساسِيّاً/هامّاً في الثَّوْرةِ

"The poor and the rich are bracing themselves for the worst."

يَتَحَسَّبُ الفُقَراءُ والأَغْنياءُ للأَسْوَءِ

Some English nouns (many of them denoting sciences) with a plural form are always regarded as a **singular** grammatically. e.g.

athletics	أَلْعابُ القُوى
economics	اقْتِصاد
mathematics	رياضِيات
news	أَخْبار
measles	حَصْبة
politics	سِياسة
physics	فيزياء
statistics	إحْصاء/إحْصائية/إحْصائيات

"Athletics is very useful for people."

الرِّياضَةُ مُفِيدَةٌ جِدًّا لِلإِنْسانِ

"**Economics was** among my favourite subjects at University."
كَانَ الاِقْتِصادُ أَحَدَ الْمَواضِيعِ الْمُفَضَّلةِ لَدَيَّ في الْجامِعَةِ

"The **news** about the front **was** not very good."
إِنَّ الأَخْبارَ عَنِ الْجَبْهَةِ غَيْرُ جَيِّدَةٍ/غَيْرُ سارَّةٍ

"**Measles is** easily cured in children these days."
إِنَّ عِلاجَ مَرَضِ الْحَصْبَةِ عِنْدَ الأَطْفالِ سَهْلٌ في هذِهِ الأَيَّامِ

"**Politics is** very often not logical."
لَيْسَتِ السِّياسَةُ في مُعْظَمِها مَنْطِقِيَّةً

"The **physics** of speech **is** essential knowledge for every linguist."
إِنَّ مَعْرِفَةَ فيزِياءِ الأَصْواتِ ضَرُورِيَّةٌ لِكُلِّ عالِمٍ لُغَوِيٍّ

"**Statistics is** not often used in literature."
لا تُسْتَخْدَمُ الإِحْصائِياتُ عادةً في الأَدَبِ

BUT:

"The unemployment **statistics** (= figures) **are** extremely bad as a result
of the credit crunch."
كانَت نِسْبَةُ الْبَطالةِ سَيِّئَةً جِدًّا بِسَبَبِ الأَزْمَةِ الاِقْتِصادِيَّةِ/أَزْمَةِ الاِئْتِمانِ/الاِنْكِماشِ

A related case is that of so-called **summation plurals**, i.e. nouns that exist only in
the plural and typically denote an item of clothing or an instrument consisting of
two parts: e.g. 'scissors' (مِقَصٌّ), 'pliers' (مِقْراضٌ), 'trousers' (سِرْوالٌ). In English,
they always agree with a plural verb, whereas in Arabic they tend to correspond
to singular nouns, as the respective translations of the above nouns. e.g.

"These scissors are very sharp."
هذا الْمِقَصُّ حادٌّ جِدًّا

The unit nous of summation plurals is usually formed with 'a pair of': e.g. 'five
pairs of trousers', خَمْسَةُ سَراوِيلَ.

Measurements and figures may be singular when the quantity referred to is a unit. Otherwise, the plural is used. e.g.

"Three years **is** a long time."

إِنَّ ثَلَاثَ سَنَوَاتٍ وَقْتٌ طَوِيلٌ

"Three-fifths of people **drive** recklessly."

إِنَّ ثَلَاثَةَ أَخْمَاسٍ مِنَ النَّاسِ يَقُودُونَ سَيَّارَاتِهِم بِتَهَوُّرٍ

As the translations of the above sentences reveal, Arabic verbs agree in number with the **grammatical subject**, albeit with the following exceptions:

i.   plural nouns referring to non-human entities are feminine singular grammatically; e.g.

البُيُوتُ كَانَتْ/كَانَتْ البُيُوتُ نَظِيفَةً

"The houses were clean."

ii. when the verb precedes the subject, as it usually does in formal writing, the former is always in the singular, even if the subject is in the **dual** or **plural** (but agrees with it in **gender**). e.g.

خَرَجَ الأَسَاتِذَةُ وَاتَّجَهُوا إِلَى المَطَارِ

"The lecturers (m.) left and headed for the airport."

سَافَرَتِ البِنْتَانِ إِلَى فَرَنْسَا
البِنْتَانِ سَافَرَتَا إِلَى فَرَنْسَا

"The two girls travelled to France."

This rule also applies to complex verb forms, that is, when an auxiliary verb is used, such as كَان, in which case the latter is in the singular, but the main verb is in the plural (or dual) as it **follows** the subject. e.g.

كَانَتِ البَنَاتُ يَأْكُلْنَ فِي الصَّفِّ

"The girls were eating in class."

Dual

One of the frequent mistakes when translating between Arabic and English arises from the mistranslation of the dual, either by using a plural for an English dual reference, or, conversely, by 'overspecification' in English. e.g.

"The men walked into the restaurant; one had a beer, whilst the other ordered a sandwich."

دَخَلَ الرَجُلانِ المَطْعَمَ، فَطَلَبَ أَحَدُهُما كَأْساً مِنَ العَصيرِ في حينِ طَلَبَ الآخَرُ شَطيرةً

In this example, the translator is, of course, tempted to translate the first 'men' by رجال; however, as it becomes clear later on in the sentence that there are only two, the dual must be used in Arabic.

On the other hand, when translating from Arabic into English, the overuse of **'the two…'** or **'both'** often results in a repetitive and awkward style. In English, it is more idiomatic to use a plural when there is a succession of duals in Arabic. e.g.

وَصَلَ العامِلانِ إلى الفُنْدُقِ لِيُسافِرا بَعْدَها إلى المَصْنَعِ، وَفي اليَوْمِ التّالي اسْتَلَما عَمَلَهُما الجَديدَ

"The two workers arrived at the hotel and then **they** went to the factory. The next day **they** started their new jobs."

'Covert gender'

Despite having a feminine form, i.e. ending in ة, some Arabic words denote males. In addition to masculine proper nouns (e.g. أسامة), there are a number of so-called 'cryptomasculine' nouns, such as خَليفة ('caliph'), عَلّامة ('great scholar') and رَحّالة ('inveterate traveller'). In these cases, **logical** agreement prevails over the grammatical one. e.g.

قَدْ يَفوزُ العَلّامَةُ بالجائِزةِ العالَمِيّةِ

"The great scholar may win the world prize."

The rule applies to:

i. masculine nouns that take a feminine-marked plural. e.g. طَلَبَة ('students'). This is particularly relevant for borrowings from European languages, many of which take sound feminine endings. e.g. لُورْدات ('Lords') بَرْلَمَانات ('Parliaments'). e.g.

خَرَجَ اللُّورْداتُ/اللُّورْداتُ خَرَجُوا مِنَ الوَلِيمةِ ورَجَعُوا إلى المَجْلِسِ

"The Lords left the banquet and returned to the House."

☞ **NOTE**: the plural of borrowings ending in ـو such as اِسْتُودِيُو / اِسْتُودِيُوهات، كازِينُو/كازِينُوهات، بِيانُو/بِيانُوهات، فِيدِيُو/فِيدِيُوهات، سِينارِيُو/ سِينارِيُوهات، كِيلُو/كِيلُوهات.

ii. feminine words that are not marked for gender, i.e. that do not have ة. These include:

- Female proper nouns. e.g. حَنان، زَيْنَب، سُعاد، هِنْد، مَرْيَم، نَوال;
- nouns denoting females: أُمّ, 'mother'; عَرُوس, 'bride'; بِنْت, 'daughter'; أُخْت, 'sister';
- parts of the body that come in pairs. e.g. يَد ('hand'), أُذُن ('ear'); e.g.

كانَتْ رِجْلُهُ بَجْرُوحةً

"His leg was wounded."

☞ **NOTE** the following that are masculine, despite being part of a set of two body parts:

مِرْفَق (pl. مَرافِقُ), 'elbow'; صُدْغ (pl. أَصْداغ), 'temple'; خَد (pl. خُدُود), 'cheek'; حاجِب (pl. حَواجِبُ), 'eyebrow';

- names of cities (both Arab and non-Arab!) and tribes as the words مَدِينة and قَبِيلة, respectively, are considered to be implied; e.g.

إزْدَهَرَتْ تُونُسُ خِلالَ العُصُورِ الوُسْطَى

"**Tunis** flourished during the Middle Ages."

اِنْتَشَرَتِ الشَّمَّارُ في جَنُوبِ العِراق

"The **Shammar** (tribe) spread across southern Iraq."

- names of countries (notable exceptions being: المَغْرِب، الأُرْدُنّ، السُّودان،
e.g. ;(لُبْنان، العِراق)

تُعاني مِصْرُ مِن أَزْمةٍ اِقْتِصاديّةٍ حادّة

"Egypt is suffering from an acute economic crisis."

إنَّ لُبْنانَ شَهِدَ تَغَيُّراتٍ كَثيرةً في تاريخِهِ الطَّويل

"Lebanon witnessed many changes in the course of its long history."

The following miscellaneous set of words:

أَرْض (pl. أَراضٍ), 'Earth';	إِسْت ([pl. أَسْتاه]), 'backside;
بِئْر (pl. آبار، بِئار), 'well';	حَرْب (pl. حُرُوب), 'war';
خَمْر (pl. خُمُور), 'wine';	دار (pl. دِيار), 'house';
دَلْو (pl. أَدْلٍ، دِلاء، أَدْلاء), 'bucket';	رَحِم (pl. أَرْحام), 'uterus';
سِنّ (pl. أَسْنان), 'tooth';	شَمْس (pl. شُمُوس), 'sun';
ضَبُع (pl. ضِباع، أَضْبُع), 'hyena';	عَصا (pl. عُصِي، أَعْص), 'stick';
فَأْس (pl. فُؤُوس), 'axe';	كَأْس (pl. كُؤُوس، كِئَاس), 'cup';
كَرْش (pl. كُرُوش), 'paunch';	نَعْل (pl. نِعال), 'sandal';
نَفْس (pl. نُفُوس، أَنْفُس), 'soul';	نار (pl. نِيران), 'fire'

e.g.

كانَتِ الدَّارُ قَذِرةً

"The house was dirty."

اِنْدَلَعتِ الحَرْبُ الأَهْلِيّةُ قَبْلَ سَنَتَيْنِ

"The civil war started two years ago."

سَتَغْرُبُ الشَّمْسُ بَعْدَ ساعَة

"The sun will set in an hour's time."

اشْتَعَلَت النَّارُ بِدُونَ أَيَّةِ ذَرِيعَةٍ/سَبَبٍ

"Fire broke out without any reason."

Some Arabic nouns can have **either** masculine or feminine gender. e.g.

حال (pl. أَحْوال): 'state, condition'   رُوح (pl. أَرْواح): 'spirit'

أَرْنَب (pl. أَرانِبُ): 'rabbit'   إِصْبَع (pl. أَصابِعُ): 'finger'

سِكِّين (pl. سَكاكِينُ): 'knife';   سُلَّم (pl. سَلالِمُ): 'stairs'

سَبيل (pl. سُبُل، أَسْئِلة): 'road'   دُكّان (pl. دَكاكِينُ): 'shop'

سَماء (pl. سَماوات): 'sky'   سُوق (pl. أَسْواق): 'market'

طَريق (pl. طُرُق، طُرُقات): 'road'   عُقاب (pl. أَعْقُب، عِقْبان): 'eagle'

عَقْرَب (pl. عَقارِبُ): 'scorpion'   عُنْق (pl. أَعْناق): 'neck'

عَنْكَبُوت(pl. عَناكِبُ): 'spider'   كَبِد (pl. أَكْباد): 'liver'

كِيس (pl. أَكْياس): 'bag'   لِسان (pl. أَلْسُن، أَلْسِنة): 'tongue'

مَرْكَب (pl. مَراكِبُ): 'ship'   مِلح (p. أَمْلاح): 'salt'

> ☞ **NOTE**: Technically, بَلَد ('town', 'country') can also be masculine or feminine but in practice it occurs almost solely as masculine. Its plural بلاد can also function as a singular in its own right and denote 'country' (with بُلْدان as the plural), but its grammatical gender tends to be feminine:
>
> حَقَّقَت البِلادُ مُسْتَوَىً عالِياً مِنَ النُّمُوِّ
> "The country attained a high level of development."
>
> تَتَفَوَّق البُلْدانُ العَرَبِيَّةُ بِأَدائِها التَّعْليمِيُّ عَلَى جَميع المَناطِق النّامِيَّة بِاسْتِثْناء أَمْريكا اللاتينِيَّة
> "Arab countries excel at educational performance in the developing world, second only to Latin America."

Some nouns have a 'double' gender, linked to specific meanings. e.g.

عَجُوز (pl. عَجائِز), 'old woman/man'. e.g.

"The old man/woman is on a hunger strike to death."

تُضْرَبُ/يُضْرَبُ العَجوزُ عَنِ الطَّعامِ حَتَّى المَوْتِ

' (عُرُس .pl) groom/(عَرائس .pl) bride', عَرُوس

In contemporary usage, however, عجوز tends to be treated as a masculine, while عَرُوس generally denotes 'bride', with عَريس being the common word for 'bride-groom'.

Another set of 'double-gendered' noun-adjectives are those patterned on فَعيل. e.g.

قَتيل (قَتْلى .pl), 'dead/death';

أَسير (أَسْرَى، أَسَراءُ، أَسارَى .pl), 'prisoner';

جَريح (جَرْحَى .pl), 'wounded'

When there is contextual ambiguity, the feminine marker ة, or a feminine noun may be added. e.g.

وَقَعَتِ المَرْأَةُ القَتيلةُ عَلَى الأَرْضِ

وَقَعَتِ القَتيلةُ عَلَى الأَرْضِ

"The dead woman fell to the ground."

Quantifiers

With words denoting an amount, i.e. **quantifiers** such as كُلّ، أَغْلَبُ، غالِب، أَغْلَبِيّة، and أَكْثَر، أَكْثَرِيّة، جُلّ، مُعْظَم and بَعْض, the verb agrees with the quantified noun in gender and number, except when there is a pronominal suffix, in which case (masculine singular) agreement occurs with the quantifier (except كُلّ if its meaning is '**all of**', rather than 'every'). In English, a **plural verb** is necessary in all cases. e.g.

كُلُّ الطُّلابِ سَيَحْضُرونَ المُحاضَرةَ

الطُّلابُ كُلُّهُم سَيَحْضُرونَ المُحاضَرةَ

سَيَحْضُرُ كُلُّ الطُّلابِ المُحاضَرةَ

"**All** students will attend the lecture."

تَعْتَرِضُ النِّساءُ كُلُّهُنَّ عَلَى القانُونِ الجَديدِ

النِّساءُ كُلُّهُنَّ يَعْتَرِضْنَ عَلَى القانُونِ الجَديدِ

"**All** women oppose the new law."

يَجِبُ أَنْ يَحْتَوِيَ كُلُّ جَدْوَلٍ عَلَى أَمَاكِنِ الأُمْتِحَانات
"**Every** table must include the examination venues."

كُلُّ صَفْحَةٍ تَشْتَمِلُ عَلَى أَسْماءِ الْمُوَظَّفِينَ
"**Every** sheet contains the names of the employees."

كُلُّهُم يُسافِرُونَ غَداً/يُسافِرُ كُلُّهُم غّداً
"**All** of them will travel tomorrow."

بَعْضُهُنَّ لَسْنَ تُونِسِيَّاتٍ
"**Some of them** (fem.) are not Tunisian."

أَغْلَبُهُم/أَكْثَرُهُم/مُعْظَمُهُم/جُلُّهُم لا يُشارِكُ في الانْتِخابات
"**Most of them** do not take part in the elections."

'Number'

In English, the word '**number**' is plural if it is preceded by "**a**", and singular when preceded by "**the**". In Arabic, agreement is with the modified noun. e.g.

"A **number** of students **are** working here."
عَدَدٌ مِنَ الطُّلابِ يَعْمَلُونَ هُنا
يَعْمَلُ هُنا عَدَدٌ مَنَ الطُّلابِ

"The **number** of people in debt in this country **is** very large."
إنَّ عَدَدَ الأَشْخاصِ الَّذِينَ عَلَيْهِم دُيُونٌ في هذِهِ الدَّوْلَةِ كَبِيرٌ جِدًّا

The translations of the above examples reveal that in Arabic the **grammatical subject** once again prevails.

'Or/nor'

In English, if the parts of subjects joined by '**or**' or '**nor**' are singular, then the verb is singular. When they are all plural, then the verb is also plural. However, if there is a mixture of plural and singular forms, then the verb agrees with that which is clos(er) (est). With personal pronouns, the latter rule also applies. e.g.

"Neither John nor I **am** late."

لَمْ أتَأَخَرْ وَلَمْ يَتَأَخَرْ جون أيضاً

أنا وجون لَمْ نتأَخَرْ

"Peter or Mary **should** do it."

يَنْبَغِي لِبِيتر أوْ ماري أَنْ يَعْمَلَهُ

"The teacher or the administrators **have** to notify students of any changes to the examination time-table."

يَجِبُ عَلَى الأُسْتاذِ أَوْ الإِدارِيِّينَ إِعْلامُ الطُّلابِ بِأَيِّ تَغْيِيرٍ في مَواعِيدِ الامْتِحاناتِ

"Either she or you **are** late."

لَقَدْ تَأَخَّرَ أَحَدُكُما

In some cases, this may give rise to some awkward constructions, and careful users of English would probably rephrase the last sentence to:

"Either she is late, or you are."

Similarly, if the second/last element is the only singular one, most English-speakers would have the verb agree with the plural(s) in practice. e.g.

"The children or their teacher **have** left the keys."

تَرَكَ الأَطْفالُ أَوْ أُسْتاذُهُم المِفْتاحَ

In Arabic the above sentences do not pose any grammatical problems for the most part in view of the VSO order, i.e. the sentence-initial verb is in the singular, agreeing in gender with the **first** subject.

Noun-adjective agreement

Most of the elements mentioned above in relation to verb-agreement apply to noun-adjective agreement, which, too, is essentially determined by whether or not the noun refers to humans or non-humans, though, of course position does not have an effect since in Arabic the adjective always *follows* the noun it modifies.

Covert gender

The issue of covert gender mentioned in respect of verb agreement rules also, of course, has an impact on noun-adjective agreement. e.g.

السُّوقُ الحُرَّةُ,	Duty Free market
الدَّارُ الآخِرةُ,	the Afterlife
الحَرْبُ العالَمِيَّةُ,	World War
إطلاق نار كثيف	fierce (gun) fire
الأَرْضُ المُقَدَّسَةُ,	the Holy Land
تُونُسُ الخَضْراءُ,	Tunis 'the Verdant'
حَلَبُ الشَّهْباءُ,	Aleppo 'the Grey'
دِمَشْقُ الفَيْحاءُ,	Damascus 'the Fragrant'

> ☞ **NOTE:** القُدْسُ القَدِيمَةُ, Old Jerusalem, **BUT** القُدْسُ الشَّرِيفُ, Jerusalem 'the Noble'!

Some adjectives agree with either masculine or feminine verbs and nouns. e.g.

لَدُودٌ,	'dogged'
شَكُورٌ,	'grateful'
صَبُورٌ,	'patient'

عمِّي/عمَّتِي صَبُورٌ جِدًّا
"My uncle/aunt is very patient."

Others in a number of fixed expressions remain unmarked for gender. e.g.

أُمّ حَنُونٌ/رَؤُومٌ: 'doting mother'

حَرْبٌ ضَرُوسٌ: 'fierce war'

Arabic has a number of adjectives that are inherently feminine, i.e. they can only apply to women, yet are masculine in form, and thus never take the feminine marker ة. e.g. حامِل ('pregnant'), حائِض ('menstruating'), عَقيم ('barren, sterile'), عاقِر ('barren'), عانِس ('spinster'), طالِق ('divorced'). e.g.

اِمْرَأَةٌ عاقِرٌ, 'a barren woman'

اِمْرَأَةٌ حامِلٌ, 'a pregnant woman'

> ☞ **NOTE:**
> 1. نِساءٌ حَوامِلُ, 'pregnant women'(!)
> 2. the other word for '**pregnant**' only has a feminine form:
> حُبْلى (pl. حَبالى ,حَبْلانة) e.g. اِمْرَأَة حُبْلى /نِساءٌ حَبالى

Quantifiers

When a quantifier is used, there is agreement with the specified **noun**, rather than with the quantifier. e.g.

جَميعُ الكُتُبِ الجَديدَةِ اِشْتَمَلَت عَلَى صُوَرٍ (تَوضيحِيّة)
"All the new books contained illustrations."

شاهَدْنا بَعْضَ الأفْلام الأجْنَبِيّةِ
"We watched some foreign films."

> ☞ **NOTE:** The issue of logical vs. grammatical subject also affects possession. Whereas in English students may be asked 'to leave their **bags** outside', their Arabic counterparts will be told to leave شَنْطَتَهُم. The difference is based on the fact that in English, the fact that each student has a bag necessitates a plural, whereas in Arabic the emphasis is on the fact that each student has one bag, with the use of the plural implying that they have several bags (at least more than one) each.

"They had a funny look on their **faces**."

عِنْدَهُم نَظْرَةٌ مُضْحِكَةٌ عَلَى وَجْهِهِم

"They will go to the final negotiation round with presents in their **suitcases**."

سَيَذْهَبُونَ إِلَى مُفَاوَضَاتِ المَرْحَلةِ النِّهائِيَّة وَفِي حَقيبَتِهِم هَدايا

All (of)/each/every

In English, '**all**' can be followed either by an indefinite or definite plural noun, whereas '**all of**' can only be followed by a definite noun. When '**all**' means *the entirety, totality*' or is used with a pronoun, it is followed by '**of**' + **definite noun**. e.g.

"**All** (of) (the) students protested against the new law."

اِحْتَجَّ جَمِيعُ/كُلُّ الطُّلاب عَلَى القانُونِ الجَديدِ

"**All** workers who were there voted against the strike."

صَوَّتَ كُلُّ/جَمِيعُ العُمَّالِ الَّذِينَ كانُوا هُناكَ ضِدَّ الإِضْرابِ

"**All** the wood had been burnt."

اِحْتَرَقَ الحَطَبُ كُلُّهُ

"**All of** us attended the lecture by the Dean of the Faculty."

حَضَرْنا كُلُّنا/جَميعاً المُحاضَرَةَ الّتي أَلْقاها عَميدُ الكُلِّيَّة

Note the use of 'all' as a noun, as in the following example:

"**All** he could do was admit to the crime, and accept the punishment."

كُلُّ ما كانَ عَلَيْهِ/بِوُسْعِهِ هُوَ أَنْ يَعْتَرِفَ بالجَريمَةِ ويَتَقَبَّلَ العِقابَ

This is mirrored in Arabic, where '**all**' is usually expressed by the noun كُلّ, which, too, can be followed by a preposition, i.e. مِنْ. Note that when كُلّ means 'all (of)', it is always followed by a **definite plural noun** (or a pronoun). e.g.

تَكَلَّمَ مَعَ كُلِّ المُشْتَرِكينَ/المُشْتَرِكينَ كُلِّهِمْ
"He spoke with all of the participants."

يَجِبُ أَنْ تَحْضُرُوا كُلُّكُم المُؤْتَمَر
"**All of** you have to attend the conference."

كُلُّ الطُّلابِ الَّذينَ يُعانُونَ مِن إعاقَةٍ في التَعليم هُمْ مِن أَفْرادِ المُجْتَمَعِ الَّذينَ يَجِبُ عَلَيْنا جَميعاً مُساعَدَتُهم
"**All of** the students with learning disabilities are full members of society and have to be helped by **all of** us."

> ☞ **NOTE** that when كُلّ is the subject of a subsequent verb, the latter is in the plural if the quantified noun is human (also see AGREEMENT). e.g.
>
> "All the demonstrators rejected the government demands and are calling for civil disobedience."
> رَفَضَ كُلُّ المُتَظاهِرينَ المَطالِبَ الحُكومِيَّةَ ويُنادُونَ بالعِصْيانِ المَدَنيّ

In addition to كُلّ, Arabic also employs the following to express totality or entirety:

* جَميع, 'all, total' is a noun which occurs in an إضافة construction. e.g.

جَمِيعُ الطُّلابِ, 'all students'

☞NOTE: جَمِيع is also used with the article to denote 'all people' – الجَمِيعُ – whereas in the indefinite accusative it means 'all together', جَمِيعاً. e.g.

الجَمِيعُ يَعْلَمُ ذلِكَ, 'everyone knows that.'

يَحْمِي أَبْناءَنا جَمِيعاً, 'he protects all of our sons.'

• أَجْمَعُ (note the superlative form!) denotes 'whole', 'in its entirety' (fem. جَمْعاءُ; pl. أَجْمَعُونَ, جُمَع). It is used as an adjective and is thus found in post-modifier position. e.g.

العالَمُ الغَرْبِيُّ أَجْمَعُ, 'the whole Western world'

☞NOTE: بِأَجْمَعِه, 'in its entirety'. e.g.

يُسافِرُونَ بِأَجْمَعِهِم/جَمِيعاً
'All of them are travelling.'

بَغْدادُ أَجْمَلُ مَدِينَةٍ في العالَمِ بِأَجْمَعِه/أَجْمَع/بِأَسْرِه
'Baghdad is the most beautiful city in the whole world.'

• كافَّة (note the feminine form!) occurs as the first element in an إضافة. e.g.

كافَّةُ الأَنْحاءِ, 'all areas'

☞NOTE: the adverb كافَّة means 'all without exception', 'collectively'. e.g.

يَشْمَلُ هذا القانُون الطُّلابَ كافَّةً/جَمِيعَ الطُّلابِ
"This law includes all students."

- قاطِبةً, *'all together'*, *'all without exception'*, *'every single one'*. e.g.

أَضْخَمُ/أَكْبَرُ جَيْشٍ في الأَرْضِ قاطِبةً
"The biggest army in the **whole** world"

- بِأَسْرِه, *'entirely'*, *'all (of)'*, *'every single one'*. e.g.

ذَهَبُوا إلى المُتْحَفِ بِأَسْرِهِمْ
"**All of** them went to the museum."

- بِرُمَّتِه: *'in its entirety'*. e.g.

فَرَنْسا بِرُمَّتِها قالَت لا لِلرَّئِيسِ
"**All (of)** France said 'No' to the President."

- بِقِلِّيَتِه, *'completely'*, *'wholly'*. e.g.

أَكَلَ الأَسَدُ الغَزالَ بِقِلِّيَتِه أَيّ بِعِظامِه وجِلْدِه
"The lion **completely** ate the gazelle, with hide and hair."

- بِحَذافِيرِه, *'all of it'*, *'without exception'*. e.g.

سيُطَبَّقُ القانُونُ بِحَذافِيرَهُ
"The law will be applied **in its entirety**."

☞ **NOTE**: the use and translations of the following expressions with 'all':

All in all (= '*in general*'): بِالجُمْلَة، بِشَكْلٍ عامٌّ ، عُمُوماً، عَلَى العُمُومِ،
عَامَّةً، عَلَى نَحْوٍ عامٍّ. e.g.

"**All in all**, I think we're better off without him."
عَلَى العُمُومِ نَحْنُ في وَضْعٍ أَفْضَلَ بِدُونِهِ

all along (= '*throughout*')

e.g. 'All along, they thought that we wouldn't agree.'
كانُوا يَعْتَقِدُونَ دائماً بِأَنَّنا لَنْ نُوافِقَ
كانُوا يَعْتَقِدُونَ طَوالَ الوَقْتِ أَنَّنا لَنْ نُوافِقَ

one and all (= '*every single one*'). e.g.

"It is important to make this clear to **one and all**."
مِنَ المُهِمِّ أَنْ نُوَضِّحَ هذا لِكُلِّ واحِدٍ مِنْهُم
مِنَ الأهْمِيَّةِ بِمَكانٍ أَنْ نُوَضِّحَ هذا لِكُلِّ واحِدٍ مِنْهُم

all alone (= '*all by –self*'). e.g.

"He was left there **all alone/all by himself**."
تُرِكَ هُناكَ وَحْدَهُ
تُرِكَ هُناكَ وَحِيداً

all the better (= '*so much the better*'). e.g.

"**All the better**, if she doesn't tell him the truth."
إنَّ مِنَ الأفْضَلِ ألاَّ تُخْبِرَهُ بِالحَقِيقةِ

☞ Also see 'Agreement'

Allow/permit/let

All three verbs imply the *giving of consent* for something. The difference centres mainly on grammatical usage:

(1)   both **to allow** (more common) and **to permit** can be followed by **OBJECT + TO+INFINITIVE**, and take an **-ING FORM** when there is no personal object;

(2)   In case of an **impersonal passive**, only **to permit** is used;

(3)   only **to allow** can be used with adverb particles;

(4)   **To let**, which is also the least formal of the three, is followed by an **object + bare infinitive** (never **-ING!**) and cannot be used in the passive, in which case it is replaced by **to allow**.

In Arabic, however, all three are generally rendered by سَمَحَ (u). e.g.

(1)
"We do not **allow/permit** people to smoke."
لا نَسمَحُ للنَّاسِ بالتَّدخِينِ

"We do not **allow** smoking."
لا نَسمَحُ بالتَّدخِينِ
التَّدْخِينُ مَمنوعٌ

(2)
"It is not **permitted** to eat on the premises."
لا يُسمَحُ بالأَكْلِ في المَبْنَى

"The rules do not **permit** cheating."
لا تَسمَحُ القَوانِينُ بالغِشِّ

(3)
"The dog was not **allowed** out after 6 p.m."
لَمْ يُسمَحْ للكَلْبِ بالخُرُوجِ بَعْدَ السَّاعةِ السَّادِسةِ مَساءً

(4)

"I cannot **let** this happen to the company."

لا أَسْمَحُ/لَنْ أَسْمَحَ أَنْ يَحْدُثَ هذا للشَّرِكَةِ

"This cannot **be allowed** to happen."

لا يُمْكِنُ السَمَاحُ لِهذا بِأَنْ يَحْدُثَ
لا يُمْكِنُ أَنْ نَسْمَحَ لِهذا بِأَنْ يَحْدُثَ
لا يُمْكِنُ لِأَحَدٍ أَنْ يَسْمَحَ لِهذا بِأَنْ يَحْدُثَ

Already/just/yet

These adverbs often cause problems to translators from English to Arabic since the rendering of the concepts they convey is often achieved through periphrastic constructions rather than adverbs, as is the case in English.

The tenses used with these adverbs pose another problem. In English they tend to be used with the **present perfect**. e.g.

"I have **already** done this."

لَقَدْ سَبَقَ وَأَنْ فَعَلْتُ هذا

"He **has** just arrived." (US: 'He just arrived')

لَقَدْ وَصَلَ تَوًّا

"We have not been on holiday **yet**."

لَمْ نَذْهَبْ إِلى العُطْلَة بَعْدُ
لَمْ نَحْصَلْ عَلى إِجازَتِنا/عُطْلَتِنا بَعْدُ

Yet is the equivalent of **already** in **negative** and **interrogative** sentences. e.g.

"Have you seen her **yet**?"

هَلْ رَأَيْتَها بَعْدُ ؟

"I have not read the book **yet**."

لَمْ أَقْرَأ الكِتَابَ بَعْدُ/لَحَدِّ الآنَ/إلى الآنَ

If the sense is '*earlier than expected*', **already**, rather than **yet**, should be used. e.g.

"Have you **already** finished the dishes?"

هل اِنْتَهَيْتَ مِن غَسْلِ الأَطْباقِ؟

In Arabic, no distinctions are made whether the sentence is negative or interrogative, whereas the tense tends to be the perfect. The constructions are as follows:

'already':	(لَقَد) سَبَقَ لَه + VERBAL NOUN
	(لَقَد) سَبَقَ لَهُ أَن + PERFECT
'just':	لِتَوِّه
	الآنَ
	في الحال
'not yet':	بَعْدُ + **jussive** + لَمْ

e.g.

لَقَدْ سَبَقَ لَها زيارةُ المُتْحَفِ
لَقَدْ سَبَقَ لَها أَنْ زارَتِ المُتْحَفَ
"She has **already** visited the museum."

لَمْ يَأْتِ بَعْدُ
"He has not come **yet**."

وَصلوا لِتَوِّهم
"They have **just** arrived."

بَدَأَتْ هَجَمَاتُ تَحالُفِ المُعارَضَة تَوَّاً فَانْسَحَبَ الحِزْبُ الحاكِمُ مِن الاِنْتِخابات
"The attacks from the opposition coalition have (only) **just** started and the ruling party has withdrawn from the elections."

خَرَجَ مِنْ المَكْتَبِ الآنَ

"He has **just** (now) left the office."

In some cases, no adverbial is used in the translation of **already**. e.g.

سَيَكُونُونَ قَدْ زارُوا المَتْحَفَ (في الوَقْتِ الَّذي نَصِلُ فِيه)

"They will have **already** visited the museum [by the time we arrive]."

رُبَّما/يُمْكِنُ أَنْ يَكُونُوا قَدْ زارُوا المَتْحَفَ (لأَنَّهُمْ وَصَلُوا أَمْسِ)

"They could **already** have visited the museum [because they arrived yesterday]."

مِنَ المُؤَكِّدِ أَنَّهُمْ زارُوا المَتْحَفَ (لأَنَّهُمْ كانوا عَلَى عِلْمٍ بِمكانِه)/(لأَنَّهُمْ كانوا يَعْلَمُون مكانَهُ)

"They must **already** have visited the museum [since they knew where it was]."

When **already** means 'previously', the Arabic translation is **either** قَبْلَ الآنَ, قَبْلاً or سابِقاً. e.g.

"They have **already** visited the museum (e.g. during their first visit)."

قَدْ زارُوا المَتْحَفَ سابِقاً (أَثْناءَ زِيارَتِهِم الأُولى)

Note that **just** can be added with **only**, in which case it conveys a sense of reluctance or defence. e.g.

"She's **only just** set foot in the company; you can't expect her to know everything yet!"

لَقَدْ بَدَأَتِ العَمَلَ لِتَوِّها/تَوّا في الشَّرِكةِ فَلا تَتَوَقَّع مِنْها أَنْ تَعْرَفِ كُلَّ شِئٍ

Also note the following idiomatic non-temporal uses of **just**:

"She's **just** as intelligent as her brother."

إِنَّها ذَكِيَّةٌ كَأَخِيها

"The coffee's **just** right – neither too hot, nor to cold."

القَهْوَةُ مُمْتازَةٌ فَهِيَ لَيْسَتْ حارَّةً ولا بارِدَةً

"That's **just** [= exactly/precisely] what I wanted to say."

هذا بِالضَّبْطِ ما أَرَدتُّ قَوْلَهُ

"I'm **just** so tired."

أَنا تَعْبانُ فَقَطْ

"**Just** imagine!"

تَخَيَّلْ فَقَطْ!

"**Just** don't let him get to you!"

لا تَدَعْهُ يُثِيرَ أَعْصابَكَ!

لا تَدَعْهُ يُغْضِبكَ!

"That takes **just as** long."

هذا يَأْخُذُ/يَسْتَغْرِقُ المُدَّةَ نَفْسَها

"**Just because of** what you said I won't do it!"

نَظَراً لِما قُلْتَه فإنَّني لَنْ أَفْعَلَ ذلكَ

لَنْ أفْعَلَ ذلِكَ لا لِشَئٍ إلا لأَنَّكَ قُلْتَ بِهِ (قُلْتَه)

Although/though/albeit

Although and **though** both mean **despite**, but the former can never appear at the end of a sentence. **Though** is more informal, and is often found with **even**. It can also appear at the end of a sentence (= *however*). **Albeit** means *even though*, and only occurs in the middle of the sentence. e.g.

"Cold **though** it was, we still managed to finish the football game."

بِالرَّغْمِ مِنَ البَرْدِ تَمَكَّنَّا مِن إِكْمالِ/إِتْمامِ مُباراةِ كُرةِ القَدَم

"He is a successful, **albeit** arrogant, young man."

إنَّهُ شابٌ نَاجِحٌ عَلَى الرَّغْمِ مِن تَكَبُّرِه

"**Although** they were poor, all the kids all got an excellent education."

بِالرَّغْمِ مِن فَقْرِهِم فَقَدْ تَعَلَّمَ الأَطْفالُ جَمِيعاً تَعْلِيماً مُمْتازاً

"Even **though** I arrived on time, there was nobody else there."

بِالرَّغْمِ مِن أَنَّنِي وَصَلْتُ في المَوْعِدِ المُحَدَّدِ إلاّ أَنَّهُ لَمْ يَكُنْ هُناكَ أَحَدٌ غَيْرِي

Depending on the context, these are rendered in a variety of ways in Arabic:

Pronoun Preposition Negative particle perfect (قَدْ +) imperfect + إنَّ هُناكَ سَ/سَوْفَ	فَ*	Noun +	بِالرَّغْمِ مِنْ أَنَّ
		Noun +	بِرَغْمِ أَنَّ
		Noun +	رَغْمَ أَنَّ رَغْمَ
		Noun +	لَكِنَّ
		Noun +	مَعَ أَنَّ
Pronoun +	إلاّ أَنَّ +		
Demonstrative +		Noun +	عَلَى الرَّغْمِ
Accusative noun +			
*Note: فَ is optional in all cases **except** before قَدْ and إنَّ			

e.g.

بِالرَّغْمِ مِنْ أَنَّ ظُرُوفَهُ كانَتْ صَعْبَةً إلاّ أَنَّهُ اسْتَطاعَ التَّفَوُّقَ في مَهَمَّتِهِ
"**Despite** his difficult circumstances, he was still able to excel in his duties."

بِرَغْمِ أَنَّ الأمْتِحانَ كانَ صَعْباً إلا أَنَّني أَجَبْتُ عَلَى جَميعِ الأَسْئِلَة
"**Even though/although** the exam was difficult, I answered all the questions."

عَلَى الرَغْمِ مِنْ مَرَضِهِ فَقَدْ قَرَّرَ أَنْ يَحْضُرَ الاجْتِماعَ
"**Despite** his illness he decided to attend the meeting."

مَعَ أَنَّني لَمْ أُوَفِّرِ الكَثيرَ مِنَ المالِ، فَسَوْفَ أَسْتَطيعُ السَّفَرَ إلَى الشَّرْقِ الأَوْسَطِ
"**Even though/although** I did not save a lot of money, I will be able to go to the Middle East."

"**Even though/although** he loves his country, he emigrated to America."

رَغْمَ حُبِّهِ لِوَطَنِهِ إلا أَنَّهُ هاجَرَ إلَى أَمْريكا
يُحِبُّ وَطَنَهُ وَلكِنَّهُ هاجَرَ إلَى أَمْريكا

Among/between

A distinction is made between these two words, depending on the number of parties involved: **between** is restricted to two people, with **among** referring to three or more, or to a whole group. In Arabic, the same word, بَيْنَ (sometimes preceded by مِنْ، ما or فيما), can be used for both meanings, with '**among**' being also rendered by the preposition ضِمْنَ ('*within*', '*inside of*'). e.g.

"She was sitting **between** John and Mary."
كانَتْ تَجْلِسُ بَيْنَ جون وَماري

"I was walking **among** the crowd, trying desperately to find my daughter."
كُنْتُ أَمْشِي بَيْنَ حُشُودِ النَّاسِ أحاوِلُ جاهِداً أَنْ أَجِدَ ابْنَتِي

"Sarah will be **among** the contestants in the race."
سَتَكُونُ سارة بَيْنَ المُشارِكينَ في السِّباق

"The President was **among** those present at the reception held at the Royal Palace."

كانَ الرَّئيسُ مِنْ بَيْنَ الحاضِرينَ في حَفْلَةِ الاسْتِقْبالِ الْمُنْعَقِدَةِ في القَصْرِ المَلَكِيِّ

"The team was selected from **among** their midst."

تَمَّ انْتِقاء الفَريقِ مِنْ بَيْنِهِم

"You can find it somewhere **among** those papers."

سَتَجِدُهُ في مَكانٍ ما بَيْنَ هذهِ الأَوْراقِ

☞ **NOTE**: only 'between' can be used in expressions involving time and numbers, and is translated into Arabic as (في) ١. e.g. ما بَيْنَ ,بَيْنَ

"I visited him **between** the 10th and 15th of March of last year."

زُرْتُهُ بَيْنَ العاشِرِ وَالخامِسِ عَشَرَ مِنْ شَهْرِ مايو من العامِ الماضي

"We received **between** $200 and $300 for those old books."

تَسَلَّمْنا ما بَيْنَ 200 وَ300 دُولارٍ أَمْريكيٍّ لِهذهِ الكُتُبِ القَديمَةِ

"Direct Foreign Investment in Egypt increased by 41.4% **between** 1994 and 1998."

قَدْ حَقَّقَتِ الاسْتِثْماراتُ الأَجْنَبِيَّةُ المُباشِرَةُ في مِصْرَ زِيادَةً قَدْرُها 41.4% فيما بَيْنَ العامَيْنِ المالِيَيْنِ 1994 و 1998

"They sold **between** ten and fifteen shirts at that shop on Saturday."

باعُوا ما بَيْنَ عَشَرَةِ وَخَمْسَةِ عَشَرَ قَميصاً في ذلِكَ المَحَلِّ

Amount/number

Though these two nouns are increasingly used interchangeably, it is important to note that **amount** can only be used with uncountables (mass nouns), while **number** applies to countables. This is largely mirrored in Arabic, with عَدَد being used for **number** and كَمِّيَّة for **amount**. e.g.

"The **number** of cars on the road has increased dramatically over the past ten years."

اِزْدادَ عَدَدُ السَّيَّاراتِ كَثيراً في السَّنَواتِ العَشَرِ الأَخيرَةِ

"People in the UK consume five times the **amount** of tea, milk and sugar that is used in the rest of the European Union."

يَسْتَهْلِكُ النَّاسُ في بريطانيا خَمْسَةَ أَضْعافِ كَمِّيَّةِ الشَّايِ وَالحَليبِ وَالسُّكَّرِ الَّتي يَسْتَهْلِكُها النَّاسُ في بَقيةِ الاتِّحادِ الأُوروبِّيِّ

An (أَنْ)/anna (أَنَّ)/in (إِنْ)/inna (إِنَّ)

The above particles have a number grammatical peculiarities that cause problems in translation.

إِنَّ and أَنَّ are part of a set known as 'إِنَّ and her sisters' (the others are كَأَنَّ, 'as if'[1] and لَعَلَّ, 'perhaps'[2]) because they share a number of features, most important of which is the fact that they turn the subject noun accusative, whereas a pronoun must be added if the subject is not overt; in other words, they cannot be followed immediately by a verb.

إِنَّ: in Classical Arabic, it was used to introduce sentences that did not start with a verb; in MSA, it tends to be used as a sentence-initial intensifier – either with a noun or pronoun – and is then often translated as 'indeed'. From a grammatical

---

1. See As If/As Though.
2. See Maybe/May Be.

ERRATUM

To be placed on page 55

	English	Arabic
NOUN/PRON + أَنَّ +	to prove	أَثْبَتَ
	to feel	أَحَسَّ بِـ
	to announce	أَعْلَنَ
	to deny	أَنْكَرَ
	to agree on	اِتَّفَقَ عَلَى
	to believe, think	اِعْتَقَدَ
	to recognize	اِعْتَرَفَ بِـ
	to suppose	اِفْتَرَضَ
	to show	بَيَّنَ
	to imagine	تَخَيَّلَ
	to remember	تَذَكَّرَ
	to imagine	تَصَوَّرَ
	to tell	حَكَى (i)
	to dream	حَلَمَ (u)
	to mention	ذَكَرَ (u)
	to see	رَأَى (a)
	to tell, report	رَوِيَ (i)
	to allege	زَعَمَ (u)
	to hear	سَمِعَ (a)
	to feel	شَعَرَ (u)
	to assert	صَرَّحَ
	to think	ظَنَّ (u)
	to know	عَرَفَ (i)
	to learn	عَلِمَ (a)
	to understand	فَهِمَ (a)
	to observe	لاحَظَ
	to find	وَجَدَ (i)

	to be able to	اِسْتَطاعَ
	to be able to	أَمْكَنَ
	to love	أَحَبَّ
	to want	أرادَ
	to insist on	أَصَرَّ عَلَى
	to swear	أَقْسَمَ
	to order	أمَرَ (u)
	to deny	أنْكَرَ
	to wait	اِنْتَظَرَ
	to expect	تَوَقَّعَ
	to happen	حَدَثَ (u)
	to happen	حَصَلَ (u)
	to swear	حَلَفَ (i)
	to fear	خافَ (a)
SUBJUNCTIVE + أَنْ +	to fear	خَشِيَ (a)
	to be satisfied	رَضِيَ (a)
	to desire	رَغِبَ (a) فِي
	to refuse, reject	رَفَضَ (u)
	to help	ساعَدَ
	to ask	سَأَلَ (i)
	to doubt	شَكَّ (u) فِي
	to request	طَلَبَ (u)
	to accept	قَبِلَ (a)
	to be able to	قَدَرَ (u, i)
	to decide	قَرَّرَ
	to hate	كَرِهَ (a)
	to intend	نَوَى (يَنْوِي)
	to be necessary	وَجَبَ (يَجِبُ)
	to wish	وَدَّ (a)

point of view, the مُبْتَدَأ becomes اِسْم (in the accusative), whereas the خَبَر remains in the nominative. e.g.

إِنَّهُم يَعْتَقِدُونَ أَنَّ الغايَةَ تُبَرِّرُ الوَسِيلةَ

"They indeed believe that the end justifies the means."

إِنَّ البَابَ مَفْتُوحٌ

"The door is open."

> ☞ **NOTE**: that when the subject is separated from the particle by a place adverbial, it remains in the ACCUSATIVE. e.g.
>
> "There is a driver in the train."
> إِنَّ في القِطارِ سائقاً

إِنْ: this particle introduces if-clauses in **CONDITIONAL SENTENCES**

أَنْ/أَنَّ: both are complementizers, that is to say, they introduce clauses and are the equivalent of the English 'that'. One of the problems when translating that-clauses from English to Arabic is the fact that the choice of أَنْ and أَنَّ depends on the verb with which they occur, unlike in English where 'that' is used with all verbs. Generally speaking, أَنَّ tends to occur with verbs of perception (e.g. 'to believe', 'to feel', 'to hear', 'to know', 'to read', 'to think'), while أَنْ is found after verbs expressing ability, hope, expectation. Unfortunately, in many cases things are not as simple or predictable as that, as can be seen from the following list which contains some of the frequently encountered verbs that collocate with each:

In some cases, verbs collocate with both أَنْ and أَنَّ. e.g. عَسَى ('it could be that'). The difference in usage between أَنْ and أَنَّ also affects prepositional phrases. e.g.

أَنْ	مِن المُمْكِنِ ('it is possible that')
	مِن المُتَوَقَّع ('it is hoped that')

55

| | أَنَّ | مِن الـمَعْرُوف (‘it is known that’) |

☞ Also see ‘Can/May/Might’

☞NOTE:

1. The verb following أَنْ is in the SUBJUNCTIVE, the verb with أَنَّ is in the IMPERFECT. e.g.

عَلِمْتُ أَنَّهُ مُشْتاقٌ إلى رُؤْيَتِها
"I knew that he was eager to see her."

أَقْسَمَ أَنْ يَسْحَبَ شَكْواه
"He swore that he would withdraw his complaint."

2. إِنَّ can also be used as a complementizer, but **only** with the verb قَالَ (‘to say’), in which case it introduces indirect speech. e.g.

قالَ الوَزِيرُ إِنَّ البَلَدَ مُعَرَّضٌ لِهَجَماتٍ فُلُولِ الكَتائِبَ للنِّظامِ السابِقِ
"The Minister said that the country was under attack by the remnants of the militia belonging to the former regime."

3. When the verb is negated, the negative particle لا and أَنْ are often contracted to أَلّا. e.g.

يَجِبُ أَنْ لا/أَلّا تُدَخِّنَ
"You must not smoke."

4. Some of these verbs require a preposition before أَنْ/أَنَّ. e.g.

كانَتْ تَشُكُّ في أَنْ يَصْدُقَ في/يَفِي بِوَعْدِه
"She doubted whether he would fulfil his promise."

اِعْتَرَفَ رَئِيسُ الْوُزَرَاءِ بِأَنَّ الْحُكُومَةَ فَشَلَتْ فِي تَأْدِيةِ وَاجِبِها

"The Prime Minister recognized/acknowledged that the government had failed in its duty."

5. The same complementizer can govern several items. e.g.

"We have to recognize our mistakes, correct them and learn from them."

يَجِبُ أَنْ نَعْتَرِفَ بِغَلَطَاتِنا وَنُصَحِّحَها وَنَتَعَلَّمَ مِنْها

"He said that the meat, vegetables and coffee were cold."

قَالَ إِنَّ اللَّحْمَ والْخُضَرَ والْقَهْوَةَ بارِدَةٌ

6. Some Arabic verbs allow for a construction with a verbal noun (with إِحَالة) as an alternative to the أَنْ/أَنَّ: clause. e.g.

سَوْفَ يَسْتَطِيعُ كِتَابَةَ الرِّسَالةِ فِي الْمَطار

"He'll be able to/can write the letter at the airport."

7. While in English 'that' can often be left out, it must always be included in Arabic. e.g.

أَنْكَرَ أَنَّ هَزِيمَةَ الْفِرْقةِ سَوْفَ تُطِيحُ بِفُرَصِها فِي الْوُصُولِ لِلدَّوْرِ النِّهائِيِّ

"He denied (that) the team's defeat would ruin their chances in the final."

8. The Arabic clause introduced by أَنْ/أَنَّ often needs to be translated by an infinitive in English. e.g.

أَرَدتُّ أَنْ أَقُولَ لَها إِنَّهُ يُحِبُّها

"I wanted **to tell** her that he loved her."

اِتَّفَقْنا عَلَى إِعَادَةِ بِنَاءِ مِصْرَ عَلَى أُسُسٍ سَلِيمَةٍ

"We agreed **to rebuild** Egypt on a solid basis."

قَرَّرَ أَنْ يُلْغِيَ القانُونَ الجَدِيدَ الَّذِي أَثارَ الْجَدَلَ

"He decided to abolish the new controversial law."

9. English subordinate clauses sometimes need to be rendered by a prepositional phrase including a verbal noun in Arabic. e.g.

أَكَّدَتْ لِي إِخْلاصَها

"She assured me that she was sincere [of her sincerity]."

Like إِنَّ، لكِنَّ ('but'), which marks contrast between two clauses, must also be followed by a noun or pronoun, while its variant, لكِنْ, is the form used with a verb. e.g.

أَعْرِفُ أَنَّهُ لِصٌّ وَلكِنِّي غَفَرْتُ لَهُ جَرائِمَهُ

"I know he is a thief **but** I forgave him his crimes."

Anymore/no more/no longer/any longer

All three adverbials denote cessation of an activity or non-availability of something and the difference between them is primarily one of grammatical usage: **anymore** (or **any more**) and **any longer** should only be used with negatives, whereas **no more** and **no longer** occur only with affirmative verbs. The usual Arabic construction is through the negative of the verb عادَ, i.e. لَمْ يَعُدْ. e.g.

"Polio is **no longer** a deadly disease."
لَمْ يَعُد شَلَلُ الأَطْفالِ مَرْضاً قاتِلاً

"You (m. pl.) are **no longer** responsible for our actions."
لَمْ تَعُودوا مَسْئُولِينَ عَنْ أَعْمالِنا

"She is **no longer** interested in going on the trip with us."

لَمْ تَعُدْ تَرْغَبُ في الذَّهابِ مَعَنا إلى الرِّحْلةِ

"We couldn't stand it **any longer**."

لَمْ نَعُد نَتَحَمَّلُ/نُطيقُ هذا

"I **no longer** have anything left in life."
[= "I don't have anything left in life (any more)."/
"I have nothing left in life any more."]

لَمْ يَعُدْ لي شَيْئٌ في الْحَياةِ
لَمْ يَبْقَ لي شَيْئٌ في الْحَياةِ

In some cases, however, the same meaning is conveyed in Arabic by a content verb or adverbial. e.g.

"She will not be able to get my help anymore."

لَنْ تَتَلقَّى مُساعَدَةً مِنِّي بَعْدَ الآنَ/لَنْ أُساعِدَها أَكْثَرَ مِنْ هذا

"She won't be able to do it **any more** in three years' time."

لَنْ تَسْتَطيعَ أَنْ تَفْعَلَ ذلِكَ بَعْدَ ثلاثِ سَنَواتٍ

"There is **no more** milk left in the fridge."

لَمْ يَبْقَ أَيُّ حَليبٍ في الثَّلاجةِ

"He can't look at her **any longer**."

لا يَسْتَطيعُ النَّظَرَ إلَيْها بَعْدَ اليَومِ/بَعْدَ الآنَ

"I can't take his ridiculous behaviour **anymore**."

لا أَسْتَطيعُ قُبُولَ سُلُوكِهِ السَّخيفِ بَعْدَ اليَومِ/بَعْدَ الآنَ

> ☞ **NOTE: TO BE + no more/longer** means 'to die'. e.g.

"He is **no more**."

تُوُفِّيَ/مات

Only **no more** can also be used to express **degree**. e.g.

"You have **no more** claim to the truth than anybody else, so get off your high horse."

لا يُمْكِنُكَ أَنْ تَدَّعِي الصِّدْق أَكْثَرَ مِن غَيْرِكَ ، فَدَعْكَ مِن هذا الغُرُور/فَكَفاكَ تَعَالِياً

"She isn't **any more** interested in pyramids than I am in gardening!"

إنَّ حُبَّها للأَهْرامات كَحُبِّي لِلبَسْتَنَة
إنَّ اهْتِمامَها بالأَهْرامات لا يَفُوقُ اهْتِمامِي بِالبَسْتَنَة

any more (always written in two words!) can also mean '*not more of something*'. e.g.

"We do not need **any more** regulations; we've got too many already!"

لا نَحْتاجُ إلى أَنْظِمَةٍ وَقَوانِينَ أُخْرَى فَعِنْدَنا ما يَكْفِي/أَكْثَرُ مِن اللازِم

Appeal/appal

Despite being similar in form, these two verbs actually mean almost the direct opposite: **to appeal** refers to an attraction, while **to appal** denotes shock. e.g.

"This idea rather **appeals** to me."

تَرُوقُ لِي هذه الفِكْرةُ
تُعْجِبُنِي هذه الفِكْرةُ

"We were **appalled** at/by what we found out."

ما عَرَفْناهُ أزْعَجَنا/رَوَّعَنا
ما اكْتَشَفْناهُ صَدَمَنا

"They were **appalled** to discover what she had done."

صُدِمُوا بِما اكْتَشَفُوا عَنْها

In terms of translation, the following points merit mention:

1. The usual Arabic verb to render '**appeal**' is أَعْجَبَ. Note that it requires an object pronoun suffix. e.g.

   تُعْجِبُني الأَهْرامُ

   ['The Pyramids are pleasing to me.']
   "The Pyramids appeal to me."
   "I find the Pyramids appealing."
   "The Pyramids are appealing (to me)."

2. In English, '**to appal**' tends to appear only in the passive voice, whereas the usual Arabic translation involves the participles مُرَوِّع، مُرْعِب or مُريع, or adjectives such as هائل or فَظيع. e.g.

   كان سُلوكُهُ مُريعاً

   "His behaviour was appalling."
   "We were appalled at/by his behaviour."

Appreciable/appreciative

This set is often confused for obvious reasons. They should, however, be carefully distinguished: when you are **appreciative** (or **appreciatory**) of something, it means that you appreciate it, i.e. think highly of it. As for **appreciable**, this is, in fact, synonymous with 'noticeable', 'clear'. e.g.

"Whenever I've spoken to her, she was always very **appreciative** of what I'd done for her."

كُلَّما تَحَدَّثْتُ مَعَها وَجَدتُها مُمْتَنَّةً لِما فَعَلتُهُ مِن أَجْلِها

كانَت كُلَّما تَقَابَلْنا/الْتَقَيْنا نُعَبِّرُ عَنْ امْتِنانِها لِما فَعَلْتُهُ مِنْ أَجْلِها

"There is an **appreciable** difference in the analysis of the data".

هُناكَ اخْتِلافاتٌ جَلِيَّةٌ في تَحْليلِ البَياناتِ

هُناكَ اخْتِلافاتٌ لا يُسْتهانُ بِها في تَحْليلِ البَياناتِ

Approval/disapproval

There are a number of idiomatic expressions in which approval/disapproval is expressed in English. However, these are not always easily translatable in Arabic, not least because of cultural reasons. For instance, in English it is customary to couch a negative point in a vaguely positive-sounding construction, which in many cases cannot be translated literally into Arabic, where approval is often expressed much more succinctly. The following are some of the commonly used expressions and phrases that may be encountered.

Approval

Medium

"That seems a good idea."

يَبْدُو أَنَّ هَذِهِ فِكْرة جَيِّدةٌ

"I think we can go along with these arrangements."

نَسْتَطيعُ المُوافَقَةَ عَلَى هَذِهِ التَّرْتيبات

نَسْتَطيعُ قَبُولَ/المُوافَقَةَ/تَطْبيقَ هَذِهِ التَّرْتيباتِ

"I'm happy to leave it to you."

لا مانِعَ لَدَيَّ مِنْ تَرْكِ الأَمْرِ لَكَ

سَأَتْرُكُ الأَمْرَ لَكَ

"We're in agreement on this issue."

نَحْنُ مُتَّفِقُونَ عَلَى هَذِهِ المَسْأَلَة

نَحْنُ عَلَى اتِّفَاقٍ حَوْلَ هَذِهِ المَسْأَلَةِ

"There seems to be a consensus on this point."

يَبْدُو أَنَّ هُنَاكَ اتِّفَاقاً شَامِلاً حَوْلَ هَذِهِ النُّقْطِة

Strong

"I'm in complete agreement."

أَنَا مُتَّفِقٌ مَعَكَ تَمَاماً

أَنَا أَتَّفِقُ مَعَكَ تَمَاماً

أَنَا مُوَافِقٌ عَلَى مَا تَقُولُ تَمَاماً

أَنَا أُوَافِقُكَ الرَّأْي تَمَاماً

أُوَافِقُ عَلَى مَا تَقُولُ تَمَاماً

"I couldn't agree more."

أَنَا مُوَافِقٌ عَلَى مَا تَقُولُ تَمَاماً

"I'm with you all the way on this."

أَنَا مَعَكَ عَلَى طُولِ الخَطِّ

أَنَا أُؤَيِّدُكَ في هذا الأَمْرِ

"You're right there."

أَنْتَ مُحِقٌّ في هَذِهِ النُّقْطِةِ

"You've hit the nail right on the head."

لَقَدْ أَصَبْتَ عَيْنَ الحَقِيقة

لَقَدْ أَصَبتَ المَحَزَّ

"I'm completely in favour of that."

أَنَا أُؤَيِّدُ ذَلِكَ تَمَاماً

"I've absolutely no objection."

لَيْسَ لَدَيَّ أَيُّ اِعْتِرَاضٍ

Disapproval

Introducing Disapproval

"I don't want/wish to be negative, but ..."

لا أُرِيدُ أَنْ أَكُونَ سَلْبِياً وَلكِنَّ ...

"I accept the need for ..., but ..."

... أَنا أَقْبَلُ بِأَنَّ هُناكَ حاجةً إلى ... ولكِنَّ

... أَنا أَعْتَرِفُ بِحاجةٍ إلى ... ولكِنَّ

... أَنا أُقَدِّرُ بِأَنَّ الوَضْعَ/المَوْقِفَ/الأَمْرَ يَحْتاجُ إلى ... ولكِنَّ

"I appreciate your point of view, but ..."

أَنا أُقَدِّرُ وُجْهةَ نَظَرِكَ وَلكِنَّ ...

It's not that I've got anything against it, but ..."

لَيْسَ لَدَيَّ شَيءٌ ضِدَّهُ/لَيْسَ عِنْدِي أَيُّ شَيءٍ ضِدَّهُ وَلكِنَّ ...

"I appreciate that, and while I don't agree with it, I'll take it into account."

أَفْهَمُ ذلِكَ وَسَوْفَ أَنْظُرُ إلَيْهِ/آخُذُهُ بِعَيْنِ الاعْتِبارِ بِالرَّغْمِ مِن أَنَّنِي لا أُوافِقُ عَلَيْهِ

لا أُوافِقُ عَلَيْهِ وَلكِنِّي سَأَنْظُرُ في الأَمْرِ مَرَّةً أُخْرَى

أَنا أُقَدِّرُ وُجْهةَ نَظَرِكَ بِالرَّغْمِ مِن أَنَّنِي لا أُوافِقُكَ عَلَيْهِ وَأَعِدُكَ بِأَنِّي سَأَنْظُرُ في المَسْأَلةِ مَرَّةً أُخْرَى

"I agree up to a point, but ..."

أَنا أَتَّفِقُ مَعَكَ/ أَنا مَعَكَ إلى حَدٍ ما وَلكِنَّ ...

"I see your point but ..."

أُقَدِّرُ وُجْهةَ نَظَرِكَ وَلكِنَّ ...

"I see what you're getting at but ..."

أَعْرِفُ ما تُرِيدُ الوُصُولَ إلَيْهِ وَلكِنَّ ...

"I suppose/presume you're right but ..."

لَعَلَّكَ عَلَى حَقٍّ ولكِنَّ ...

لَرُبَّما كُنْتَ مُحِقّاً وَلكِنَّ ...
أَظُنُّكَ عَلَى حَقٍّ وَلكِنَّ ...

"I fail to see the relevance."
لا أَسْتَطِيعُ أَنْ أَرَى صِلةً/ارْتِباطاً
لا أَرَى أَنَّ هُناكَ ارْتِباطاً/صِلةً بَيْنَ هذا وذاكَ

"Although there's a lot to say for it ..."
مَعَ أَنَّنا نَسْتَطِيعُ أَنْ نَقُولَ الكَثِيرَ بشَأْن ذلِكَ ولكِنَّ ...
هُناكَ إِيجَابِياتٌ كَثِيرةٌ في هذا المَوْضُوع ولكِنَّ ...

"I'm sorry, but I really don't think that's such a good idea."
آسِف فَأَنا لا أَعْتَقِدُ أَنَّ هذِهِ فِكْرةٌ جَيِّدةٌ

"I understand the motive for broaching the subject, but ..."
أَفْهَمُ الدَّافِعَ وَراءَ التَّطَرُّق لهذا المَوْضُوع وَلكِن ...

Mild

"I'm sorry, but that's not really practical."
أَنا آسِفٌ لكِنَّ هذا في الواقِع غَيْرُ عَمَلِيٍّ

"I think you're missing the point."
لا أَعْتَقِد أَنَّك فَهِمْتَني
أَعْتَقِد أَنَّكَ لَمْ تَفْهَم الأَمْرَ
لا أَعْتَقِد أَنَّكَ تَفْهَمُ ما أَقُول

"That's quite debatable."
هذا أَمْرٌ مُثِيرٌ للنِّقاش
هذا مَوْضُوعٌ جَدَلِي جِدّاً
هذا المَوْضُوعُ قابِلٌ للجَدَل/مُثِيرٌ للجَدَل

"I'm afraid I'm not very happy about that."
آسِفٌ لا يُمْكِنُني قُبُولَ هذا

"I'm sorry, but I have reservations about that."

أَنا آسِفٌ وَلكِنَّ لَدَيَّ تَحَفُّظاتٍ حَوْلَ هذا الأَمْرِ/الشَّأْنِ

"I suspect that we're faced with a moot point."

يُخَيَّل إِلَيَّ/يَبْدُو لي/يَخْطُرُ بِبالي أَنَّنا نُواجِهُ مَوْضوعاً مُثيراً لِلجَدَلِ

"Don't get me wrong, but ..."

لا تَفْهَمْني خَطَأً وَلكِنَّ ...

لا تُسِئْ فَهْمي وَلكِنَّ ...

"Don't misunderstand me, but ..."

لا تَفْهَمْني غَلَطاً/لا تُسِئْ فَهْمي وَلكِنَّ ...

"I'm sure we both want to avoid a situation where ..."

أنا مُتَأَكِّدٌ أَنَّ كِلَيْنا يُريدُ أَنْ يَتَحاشى/يَتَجَنَّبَ مَوْقِفاً يَكُونُ ...

أنا مُتَأَكِّدٌ أَنَّ كِلَيْنا يُريدُ أَنْ يَتَحاشى/يَتَجَنَّبَ مَوْقِفاً ... حَيْثُ/يَكُونُ فيهِ

"I appreciate your position, but I'm afraid we cannot go along with this."

أَفْهَمُ مَوْقِفَكَ وَلكِنَّنا لِلأَسِفِ لا نَسْتَطيعُ أَنْ نُوافِقَ عَلى هذا

"If you look at it closely, you will see that it must be reviewed."

لَوْ نَظَرْتَ إِلَيْهِ عَنْ/مِنْ كَثَبٍ لَرَأَيْتَ أَنَّهُ يَجِبُ أَنْ يُراجَعَ

لَوْ تَمَعَّنْتَ فيهِ لَوَجَدتَ أَنَّهُ يَجِبُ أَنْ يُراجَعَ

لَوْ دَقَّقْتَ فيهِ لَوَجَدتَ أَنَّهُ يَحْتاجُ إِلى مُراجَعةٍ

"I'm afraid that this kind of thing is not my cup of tea."

لِلأَسِفِ لَيْسَ هذا مِن الأُمُورِ المُحَبَّبةِ إِلَيَّ

لِلأَسِفِ لا أُحِبُّ مِثْلَ هذا الشَّيءِ

لِلأَسِفِ أَنا لا أُحِبُّ هذهِ الأَشياءَ

"We mustn't jump to conclusions."

يَجِبُ أَلاَّ نَتَسَرَّعَ في الحُكْمِ

لا يَجِبُ التَّسَرُّعُ في الحُكْمِ

"We shouldn't rush into anything."

يَجِبُ أَلاَّ نَتَسَرَّعَ في هذهِ الأُمُورِ

"I can't say I'm (very) impressed."

لا أَسْتَطِيعُ القَوْلَ بِأَنَّنِي مَبْهُورٌ (جِدّاً)

لا أَسْتَطِيعُ القَوْل بِأَنَّ هذا الأَمْرَ يَسُرُّنِي/يَرُوقُ لِي (كَثِيراً)

لَمْ يُعْجِبْنِي ذلكَ

لا يُعْجِبُنِي الأَمْرُ أَبَداً

Strong

"I really can't accept that."

فِي الحَقِيقةِ أَنا لا أَسْتَطِيعُ قُبُولَ ذلكَ

"I'm absolutely/completely against that."

أَنا ضِدُّ ذلكَ تَماماً

"That's out of the question."

هذا الأَمْرُ غَيْرُ قابِل لِلنِّقاش

هذا غَيْرُ وارِدٍ

"That's just not on!"

هذا غَيْرُ مُمْكِنٍ أَبَداً

لا يُمْكِنُ قُبُولُ هذَا أَبَداً

هذا غَيْرُ مَقْبُول

لا يُمْكِنُ هذا أَبَداً

"I disagree completely."

أَنا لا أَتَّفِقُ مَعَ ذلكَ أَبَداً

أَنا أَخْتَلِفُ مَعَكَ تَماماً

"You've got it all wrong!"

أَنْتَ مُخْطِئٌ تَماماً

لَقَدْ أَسَأْتَ فَهْمَ الأُمورِ

Arab/Arabic/Arabian

'**Arab**' is a noun which refers to someone of Arab origin; as an adjective it de̶
notes things referring to Arabs. '**Arabic**' can only denote the language, whereas
'**Arabian**' refers to things (not people!) related to the Arabian Peninsula (Arabian Gulf). In Arabic, however, the same form عَرَبِي is used in all three cases,
though for *Arabian* the adjective خَلِيجِيّ ('Gulf') is often used, as in الخَلِيجُ العَرَبِيُّ
(NOT * الخَلِيج الفارِسِيّ, just as in English the phrase 'Persian Gulf' should be
avoided!). e.g.

"**Arab** history is very rich in powerful rulers."
إِنَّ التَّارِيخَ العَرَبِيَّ حافِلٌ بِأَسْماءٍ قادَةٍ (حُكَّامٍ) أَشِدَّاءَ/أَقْوِياءَ

"I bought an **Arabic** book on Islamic Spain."
اِشْتَرَيْتُ كِتاباً بِاللُّغة العَرَبِيَّة عَن الأَنْدَلُس/اِسْبانيا المُسْلِمة

"**Arabian** horses are famous all over the world for their speed and grace."
تَشْتَهِرُ الخُيُولُ العَرَبِيَّةُ في العالَم أَجْمَع بِسُرْعَتِها وَرَشاقَتِها (بِحُسْنِ قَوامِها)
إِنَّ الخُيُولَ العَرَبِيَّةَ عُرِفَت في كُلِّ العالَم بِسُرْعَتِها وِبِرَشاقَتِها

"The remaining part will be exported to **Gulf** markets, especially to Oman
and Kuwait."
سَيَتِمُّ تَصْدِيرُ الجُزْءِ الباقِي إِلى الأَسْواق الخَلِيجِيَّة خُصُوصاً إِلى عُمانَ وَالكُوَيْتِ

Note that a phrase like هُوَ خَلِيجِي is most correctly translated as "He comes/is
from the (Arabian) Gulf."

When it comes to architecture, عَرَبِي can still be used in Arabic, but should in
most cases be rendered by 'Islamic' in English for idiomatic reasons. e.g.

اِنْتَشَرَت هَنْدَسةُ المِعْمارِ العَرَبِيَّةُ/العِمارةُ الإِسلامِيَّةُ في القُرُونِ الوُسْطَى
"**Islamic** architecture spread in the Middle Ages."

As/because/since/for

The following conjuncts introduce **reason clauses** in English;
   - **as**
   - **because**
   - **since**
   - **seeing that** (in view of the fact that ...)
   - **now that** (it being the case that ...)
   - **for**
   - **in as much as**

All either *precedes* or *follows* the main clause, while **for** usually follows the main clause.

In Arabic, the following reason clause introductors are used:

إذْ

قَرَّرَتِ الحُكومَةُ إِلْغاءَ سِياسَتِها إِذِ النَّتائِجُ عَلَى المِنْطَقَةِ سَتَكُونَ خَطِيرةً جِدّا
"The government decided to abandon its policy **because** the impact on the region was going to be very dangerous."

بِسَبَب + إضافة/pronoun suffix/demonstrative. e.g.

تَأَخَّرْتُ عَن الإِمْتِحانِ بِسَبَبِ المَطَرِ
"I was late at the exam **because** of the rain."

لَقَدْ أَصْبَحَ التَّنَقُّلُ بَيْنَ الدُّوَلِ سَهْلاً بِسَبَبِ تَوفِيرِ وَسائِلِ المُواصَلاتِ
"Moving between countries has become easy **because** of the availability of means of transport."

فَشَلَتْ في مَهَمَّتِها بِسَبَبِه
"She failed in her assignment **because** of him."

لا أَسْتَطِيعُ السَفَرَ الْيَومَ بِسَبَبِ هذا الجَوِّ البارِدِ
"I can't travel today **because** of this cold weather."

بِفِعْلِ + إضافة/pronoun suffix/demonstrative. e.g.

"The Euro fell back against the dollar **because** of fears regarding the Italian debts."

تَراجَعَ اليُورُو أَمامَ الدُّولارِ بِفِعْلِ مَخاوِفَ مِن الدُّيُونِ الإِيطالِيَّةِ

لِأَنَّ + NOUN/PRON. e.g.

لَنْ يُسافِرَ غَداً لِأَنَّهُ مَريضٌ
"He won't travel tomorrow **because/seeing that** he's ill."

لا يُمْكِنُهُم الدُّخُولَ لِأَنّا غَيْرُ مُهَيَّئِينَ/مُسْتَعِدِّينَ بَعْدُ
"They can't come in **as/since** we're not ready yet!'

"She doesn't want to come in **since/as/because** she feels that you insulted her."

لا تُريد الدُّخُولَ لِأَنَّها تَشْعُرُ بِأَنَّكَ قَدْ أَهَنْتَها

"Don't blame me, **for** it wasn't my decision to come to this hotel."

لا تَلُمْني لِأَنَّ اِخْتِيارَ هذا الفُنْدُقِ لَمْ يَكُنْ قَراري

حَيْثُ أَنَّ/إِنَّ + NOUN/PRON. e.g.

حَكَمَ القاضي عَلَى المُتَّهَم حَيْثُ أَنَّ الجَرائِمَ المَنْسُوبَةَ إِلَيْهِ قَدْ ثَبَتَتْ
"The judge sentenced the accused since the crimes against him had been proved."

إِنّ التَّعَرُّضَ لِلشَّمْسِ مُهِمٌّ جِدّاً وَلكِنْ يَجِبُ أَنْ يَكُونَ لِفَتْرَةٍ قَصيرَةٍ حَيْثُ إِنَّها سِلاحٌ ذو حَدَّيْنِ
"Exposure to the sun is very important, but it must be limited **inasmuch as** it is a double-edged sword."

إِذْ إِنَّ + NOUN/PRON. e.g.

أَعْرِفُ ما حَصَلَ لَهُم (أَخْبارَهُم) إِذْ أَنَّهُم يُراسِلُونَني بِاسْتِمْرار
"I know what's been happening to them, **because** they're always writing to me."

بِمَا أَنَّ ... فَ + NOUN/PRON. e.g.

بِمَا أَنَّهُ مَرِيضٌ جِدًّا فَلَنْ يَحْضُرَ الاجْتِمَاعَ غَداً
"**As** he's very ill, he won't attend the meeting tomorrow."

بِمَا أَنَّ الجَوَّ جَمِيلٌ فَسَأَذْهَبُ إِلى الحَدِيقَة
"**As** the weather is nice, I'll go to the park."

بِمَا أَنِّي هُنا فَدَعْنِي أُساعِدُكَ في إِعْداد العَشاء
"**Now that/since/as** I'm here, I might as well help you prepare dinner."

نَظَراً لـ ... فَ/فَقَدْ + NOUN/PRON. e.g.

نَظَراً لِسُوءِ الأَحْوالِ الجَوِيَّةِ فَقَدْ قَرَّرْتُ تَأْجِيلَ سَفَري
"I decided to postpone my departure **because** of the bad weather conditions."

عَلَى ذلك. e.g.

لَقَدْ إِزْدادَ عَدَدُ الفُقَراءِ في الدُّوَلِ النَّامِيَّةِ وَعَلَى ذلكَ يَنْبَغي عَلَى الدُّوَلِ الغَنِيَّةِ زِيادَةُ المُساعَدَاتِ الإِنْسانِيَّة
"The number of poor people in developing countries has risen and, **as a result**, rich countries have to increase their humanitarian assistance.

لِذلكَ. e.g.

تَأَخَّرَ القِطارُ وَلِذلكَ كانَ عَلَيَّ أَنْ أَسْتَقِلَّ الحافِلَةَ
"The train was late and **because of this/as a result** I had to take the bus."

مَنْ جَرَّاءِ (أَنَّ). e.g.

قالَتْ مَصادِرُ إِعْلامِيَّةٌ إِنَّ مَوْتَ السُّجَناءِ كانَ مِن جَرَّاءِ تَعَرُّضِهِم إِلى تَعْذِيبٍ وَحْشِي
"According to media sources, the prisoners died **because** of fierce torture."

نَظَراً لِـ + NOUN/PRON. e.g.

"**Seeing that/as/since** you have helped me in the past, I'll not tell the boss that you didn't show up for work this morning."

نَظَراً لِمُساعَدَتِكَ لِي في الماضي فَإِنَّني لَنْ أُخْبِرَ الرَّئيسَ بِعَدَمِ مَجِيئِكَ/حُضُورِكَ إلى العَمَلِ هذا الصَّباحَ

عَلَى ذِمَّةِ + NOUN/PRON. e.g.

"The court decided to jail the defendant for four days for the purpose/ because of the investigation."

قَرَّرَت المَحْكَمةُ حَبْسَ المُتَّهِمِ 4 أَيَّامٍ عَلَى ذِمَّةِ التَّحْقِيقاتِ

☞ Also see 'Since/For/During'

As for

For reasons of style or emphasis, the subject of a verb is put in sentence-initial positions and is often introduced by '**as for**'. In Arabic, the *topic* (the fronted object) is introduced by أمَّا, whereas the *comment* (the part of the sentence commenting on it) is preceded by فـ, which is not translated into English. e.g.

"**As for** the security services, they crushed the revolution without hesitation."

أمَّا قُوَّات الأمْنِ فَقَمَعَت الثَّوْرَةَ بِدُونِ تَرَدُّدٍ

"**As for** her, she will never go against her father's wishes."

أمَّا هِيَ فَلَنْ تُعارِضَ رَغْباتِ أبِيها أبَداً

Note that one can also achieve the same effect without the connective أمَّا by preposing the subject with the addition of a resumptive pronoun affixed to the verb. In English, the translation of this construction often includes the use of **'only'**. e.g.

"You encounter a man as generous as he (is) **only** rarely in life."

نادِراً ما تَجِدُ رَجُلاً سَخِيًّا مِثْلَهُ في الحَياة/لا تَجِدُ رَجُلاً سَخِيًّا مِثْلَهُ في هذا العالَم إلا نادِراً

As if/as though

Both **'as if'** and **'as though'** mean as it would be if, and are often (though not exclusively) used with past tenses to denote present meaning. In Arabic, both are rendered by وَكَأَنَّ. e.g.

"It's **as if/though** she didn't want me to leave."

كانَتْ وَكَأَنَّها لا تُريدُني أَنْ أَذْهَبَ

In 'unreal' comparisons, the subjunctive form of the verb **'to be'**, i.e. **were**, is used instead of the past tense **was**, with the latter being reserved for **real** comparison. In practice, this means that you use the simple past form when the comparison is not contrary to fact. The usual Arabic construction here is كَما لَوْ كانَ ..., though كَأَنَّ is also found. e.g.

"They were talking about him **as if/though** he were present. [he died]

كانُوا يَتَكَلَّمُونَ عَنْهُ كَما لَوْ كانَ حاضِراً

"They looked at me **as if/though** I were a criminal." [I'm not a criminal]

كانُوا يَنْظُرُونَ لي وَكَأَنَّني مُجْرِمٌ

"She was talking to him **as if/though** she was about to hit him." [she could hit him]

كانَتْ تَنْظُرُ إلَيْهِ وَكَأَنَّها عَلَى وَشْكِ أَنْ تَضْرِبَهُ

As/like

In a number of contexts, these two adverbs may be used interchangeably in English; however, with a finite clause (one containing a verb) only **as** should be used, with **like** being restricted to nouns. A similar phenomenon may be observed in Arabic where كَـ and مِثل are used only with nouns, and كَما (أَنّ) with verbs. e.g.

"**Like** you, I love travelling to Middle Eastern countries."

أَنَا مِثْلُكَ أُحِبُّ السَّفَرَ إِلَى دُولِ الشرقِ الأوسَطِ/الشَّرقِ الأَوْسَطِ

"**As** my mother said, you should go to the hairdresser's."

يَجِبُ أَنْ تَذْهَبَ إِلى الحَلاَّقِ كَما قالَت أُمِّي

"Do **as** you're told."

إِفْعَلْ كَما أُمِرْتَ/إِفْعَل ما أُمِرْتَ بِهِ

"**As** it is, they have been studying for five hours and they still have a lot to do.

حَسَبَ الوَضْعِ الحَالِي فَقَدْ أَمْضُوا خَمْسُ سَاعاتٍ في المُذاكَرَةِ، وما زالَ أمامَهُم الكثيرَ (لِيَفعَلُوهُ).

"The Member of Parliament was appointed **as** the new manager of the company."

عُيِّنَ عُضْوُ مَجْلِسِ النُّوابِ مُديراً جَديداً للشَّرِكةِ

Sometimes, they can be used contrastively. Consider, for instance, the difference in meaning between these two contexts, which is also reflected in the choice of words in Arabic. e.g.

"He works **as** a painter." [it is his job]

إِنَّهُ يَعْمَلُ رَسّاماً

"He works **like** a painter." [his method of working is like that of a painter]

يَعْمَلُ مِثْلَ الرَّسامِ

As long as

In Arabic this is rendered by ما دامَ which can be followed either by a verb, noun, or adverb, ... with the continuation clause often being introduced by فَ. e.g.

"**As long as** he doesn't resign, the protest will continue."

ما دامَ رئيساً فَإنَّ الاحْتِجاجاتِ مُسْتَمِرَّةٌ

"**As long as** he works for this company, his financial situation will improve."

ما دام يَعْمَلُ في هذه الشَرِكة، فَإنَّ حَالَتَهُ الماديةَ سَتَتَحَسَّنُ

"**As long as** there is work there, our dreams will not be shattered."

ما دامَتْ هُناكَ فُرَصٌ لِلعَمَلِ فَإنَّ أحْلامَنا لَنْ تَتَبَخَّرَ

"**As long as** they are in power, they are entitled to issue laws."

ما دامُوا في الحُكْمِ يَحِقُّ لَهُم إصْدارُ قوانِينَ جَدِيدةٍ

"Muslims shouldn't be blamed for taking care of themselves, **as long as** they strive towards justice to others."

لا يَنْبَغِي أَنْ يُلامَ المُسْلِمُونَ إذا اهْتَمُّوا بِمَصالِحِهِم ما دامُوا حَرِيصِينَ عَلَى تَحْقِيقِ العَدالةِ لِغَيْرِهِم

As much as

This expression means *in the same measure as* or *to the same extent as* and is rendered in Arabic by the prepositional phrases بِقَدْرِ ما or قَدْرَ ما, which are usually followed by a verb (in the perfect or imperfect), or بِقَدْرِ + noun. e.g.

إنَّ اللهَ يَأْخُذُ بِقَدْرِ ما يُعْطِي

'God takes **as much as** He gives.'

بِقَدْرِ ما أُحِبُّكِ أَكْرَهُكِ

'I hate you **as much as** I love you.'

> ☞ **NOTE:** When the noun is a countable, the expression becomes **as many … as.** e.g.
>
> هُناكَ إيجابِياتٌ بِقَدْرِ السَّلْبِيات
> "There are **as many** positive **as** negative aspects."

As soon as

This expression is subject to a number of constraints in terms of the tenses that can be used in English:

i.	PRESENT SIMPLE … FUTURE SIMPLE
ii.	PRESENT SIMPLE … PRESENT SIMPLE (intention, narrative)
iii.	PAST SIMPLE … PAST SIMPLE

In Arabic, it is rendered by the following:

		+ SUBJ.	بِمُجَرَّدِ أَن
		+ IMPERF./ PERF.	حالَما
+PREF.	+ حَتَّى	+ SUBJ.	ما كادَ أَن
		+ IMPERF.	لَمْ يَكَدْ
		+ PERF.	ما إِنْ

e.g.

"**As soon as** they finished unpacking, they left to explore the city."

بِمُجَرَّدِ أَنْ أَفْرَغوا حَقائِبَهُم ذَهَبُوا لِلاسْتِكْشاف/لِلاسْتِطْلاعِ عَلَى المَدينة

"**As soon as** he gives me the money, I'll give him the keys to the house."
سَأُعْطيهِ مِفْتاحَ البَيْتِ حالَما يُعْطِيني المَالَ

"He came in and **as soon as** he saw me there, he fled through the garden."
دَخَلَ البَيْتَ ولكِنَّهُ ما كادَ أَنْ يَراني حَتَّى هَرَبَ عَن طَريقِ الحَديقة

"**As soon as** they'd finished work, they packed their bags and left."
لَمْ يَكادُوا يَنْتَهُونَ مِن العَمَلِ حَتَّى حَزَمُوا حَقائِبَهُم وغادَرُوا

"**As soon as** I read the letter, I realized its importance."
ما إنْ قَرَأْتُ الرِّسالةَ حَتَّى أَدْرَكْتُ خُطُورتَها

As well as

This phrase is synonymous with *in addition to* or *not only*. When it is used with a verb, the -ING form is usually used. It is placed either before or after the additive noun. The Arabic translations include the following:

إلى جانِب، فَضْلاً عَنْ، كَذلكَ، أيضاً، بالإضافةِ إلى، إضافةً إلى
e.g.

"**As well as** learning how to swim, he has been taking Dutch lessons"
بالإضافةِ إلى تَعَلُّمِهِ السِّباحَةَ فإنَّهُ بَدَأَ بِأَخْذِ دُرُوسٍ لِتَعَلُّمِ اللُّغة الهُولَنْدِيَّة

"John passed the driving test, **as well as** Duncan."
(= "John passed the driving test, and Duncan did as well."
"Both John and Duncan passed the driving test."
"John passed the driving test, as did Duncan."
"John passed the driving test, and Duncan did, too.")
نَجَحَ جُون في امْتِحانِ السِّياقةِ/القِيادةِ وَكَذَلِكَ دُنْكَن

نَجَحَ جون في امْتِحانِ السِّياقةِ/القِيادةِ ونَجَحَ دنكن أَيْضاً
نَجَحَ كلٌّ مِن جون ودنكن في امْتِحانِ السِّياقةِ/القِيادةِ
نَجَحَ جون في امْتِحانِ السِّياقةِ/القِيادةِ كما نَجَحَ جون
نَجَحَ جون في امْتِحانِ السِّياقةِ/القِيادةِ وَنَجَحَ دنكن كَذلِكَ

☞ **NOTE**: observe the difference in meaning between:

"She writes, **as well as** acting on the stage." [she writes, whereas she

also works as an actress.]

إنَّها تَكْتُبُ وتُمَثِّلُ عَلَى المَسْرَحِ أَيْضاً

and

"She writes **as well as** she acts." [her writing is as good as her acting]

إنَّها بارِعَةٌ في الكِتابةِ وفي التَّمْثِيلِ كَذلِكَ

As well can also mean 'too', but is used only post-nominally. e.g.

"You shouldn't be angry with him, everyone else forgot to do it **as well**."

يَجِبُ أَنْ لا تَغْضَبَ مِنْهُ لأَنَّ الآخَرِينَ نَسُوا أَنْ يَفْعَلُوهُ (ذلك) أَيْضاً

However, when preceded by 'may' or 'might', **as well** means 'with the same effect', in which case it is rendered in Arabic as مِن المُسْتَحْسَنِ أَنْ. e.g.

"You **might as well** give him the photographs since I don't need them anymore."

مِن المُسْتَحْسَنِ أَنْ تُعْطِيَهُ الصُوَرَ لأَنَّنِي لَمْ أَعُدْ أَحْتاجُ إِلَيْها

☞ **NOTE**: Do not confuse the above phrase with the comparative as well, meaning 'as good as':

"She plays tennis just **as well**." (= she is as good a tennis player as she is, for instance, an ice-skater.)

إنَّها بارِعةٌ في لُعْبَةِ التَّنِسِ كَذلِكَ
تَلْعَبُ التَّنِسَ بِبَراعةٍ مُماثِلةٍ لـ ...

Auxiliary verbs

Arabic has a series of 'auxiliary' verbs, which, though not behaving exactly like, for instance, the English **'do'** or **'have'**, do share some of the latter's 'helper' role in the sense that they tend to co-occur with other verbs and very rarely by themselves. In some cases, these verbs have a completely different meaning when used as a main verb. e.g. أَخَذَ, 'to begin to' (auxiliary)/'to take'. In terms of construction, they have in common that the subject tends to be placed between the auxiliary and 'main' verb. The verbs may be divided into a number of categories, according to meaning:

1. Inchoative verbs

These verbs denote the start of an activity:

	(u) أَخَذَ
	(a) أَصْبَحَ
+ IMPERFECT	(u) بَدَأَ
	(u) جَعَلَ
	(u) صارَ

"His behaviour had begun to attract the attention of his colleagues."

أَخَذَ سُلُوكُهُ يَسْتَرْعِي انْتِباهَ زُمَلائِهِ في الكُلِّيَّةِ

"The teacher started to shout when he noticed that none of the students had done their homework."

بَدَأَ المُدَرِّسُ يَصْرُخُ عِنْدَما أَدْرَكَ أَنَّ جَمِيعَ الطُّلابِ لَمْ يُؤَدُّوا واجِبَهُم

جَعَلَ المُدَرِّسُ يَصْرُخُ عِنْدَما أَدْرَكَ أَنَّ لا أَحَدَ مِن الطُّلابِ أَدَّى واجِبَهُ

أَصْبَحَ المُدَرِّسُ يَصْرُخُ عِنْدَما أَدْرَكَ أَنَّ لا أَحَدَ مِن الطُّلابِ أَدَّى واجِبَهُ

"The Arabs will make new concessions."

سَأَجْعَلُ العَرَبَ يُقَدِّمُونَ تَنازُلاتٍ جَديدةٍ

2. Possibility and probability

	يُمْكِنُ ('it is possible')
	يَجُوزُ ('it is permissible, possible')
	يُحْتَمَلُ ('it is probable')
	يُتَوَقَّعُ ('it is to be expected that')
SUBJUNCTIVE + أَنْ +	يُرَجَّحُ (it is held to be probable')
VERBAL NOUN +	
PREF. + أَنْ يَكُونَ قَد +	
(probability of a past event)	مِنَ الجائِزِ
	مِنَ المُمْكِنِ
	مِنَ المُتَوَقَّعِ
	مِنَ المُحْتَمَلِ
	مِنَ المُؤَمَّلِ

e.g.

ما زالَ أَمامَكَ وَقْتٌ طَويلٌ، يُمْكِنُكَ أَنْ تُسافِرَ بِالسَّيّارةِ أَوْ بِالقِطارِ

"You still have a lot of time; you can either go by car or by train."

يُرَجَّحُ أَنَّ الجَبْهةَ الإِسْلاميَّةَ لَنْ يَكُونَ لَها وُجُودٌ كَحِزْبٍ/
يُرَجَّحُ أَنَّ لا يَكُونَ لِلجَبْهةِ الإِسْلاميَّةِ وجودٌ كَحِزْبٍ

"The Islamic Front will probably not exist as a party."

يُحْتَمَلُ أَنْ يُسَافِرَ مُحَمَّدٌ إلى أَمريكا

"It is likely/expected that Muhammad will go to America."

مِنَ الجَائِزِ أَنْ أُسَافِرَ إلى مِصْرَ العَامَ القَادِمَ

"It is possible that I'll go to Egypt next year."

مِنَ الجَائِزِ أَنْ يَكُونَ قَدْ سَافَرَ إلى مِصْرَ العَامَ الماضِي

"It's possible he went to Egypt last year."

لا أَسْتَطِيعُ أَنْ أَجِدَهُ في أَيِّ مَكانٍ ، مِن المُمْكِنِ أَنْ يَكُونَ نَائِماً في غُرفَتِهِ

"I can't find him anywhere; maybe/it is possible that he's asleep in his room."

مِن المُتَوَقَّعِ أَنْ يَقُومَ الرَئِيسُ الأَمريكيُّ بِزيارَةِ الشَرْقِ الأَوْسَطِ مَرَّتَيْنِ كُلَّ سَنَةٍ

"It is expected/anticipated that the American president will pay a visit to the Middle East twice a year."

"It is probable that the crisis will continue."

مِنَ المُحْتَمَلِ أَنْ تَسْتَمِرَّ الأَزْمَةُ

مِنَ المُؤَمَّلِ أَنْ يَكُونُ المُعَلِّمُونَ قَدْ عادُوا إلى صُفُوفِهِم (دروسهم)

"It is to be hoped that the teachers will have returned to their classrooms."

☞ **NOTE**: possibility can also be expressed in the following ways:

قَدْ + imperfect. e.g.

قَدْ يَصِلُ أَخِي اليَوْمَ
"My brother **may** arrive today."

لَعَلَّ, followed by either a nominal or verbal phrase. e.g.

لَعَلَّهُ سَيكُونُ في المَكْتَبِ قَبْلَ الظُّهْرِ
"He **may** be in his office in the morning."

رُبَّمَا, followed by a **perfect** (with present/future meaning). e.g.

رُبَّمَا سَافَرَ إلى باريس
"He **may** travel to Paris./Perhaps, he'll travel to Paris."

3. Imminence

IMPERF. + + أَنْ .SUBJ	كاد/يَكاد
	أَوْشَكَ/يُوشِكُ عَلَى
SUBJ. أَنْ +	عَلَى وَشْكِ
	عَسَى

In addition to verb clauses with '**almost**' or '**nearly**' (**q.v.**), these verbs are translated into English by means of the following:

TO BE	on the brink of	+ ING
	on the verge of	
	on the point of	
	close to	
	about	+ TO INF.

"He was **on the point of** leaving."

يُوشِكُ عَلَى الرَّحِيلِ

"He was **on the verge of** accepting the job offer."

كَانَ عَلَى وَشْكِ أَنْ يَقْبَلَ الوَظِيفَةَ

"The company had been **on the brink of** ratifying the deal."

كَانَت الشَّرِكَةُ قَدْ أَوْشَكَت عَلَى إِبْرامِ الصَّفْقةِ

"He **almost** cried when he heard the news about her death."

كَانَ عَلَى وَشْكِ أَنْ يَبْكِي عِنْدَما سَمِعَ خَبَرَ وَفاتِها

"He can **almost** not believe that the artist left the festival."

يَكادُ لا يُصَدِّقُ أَنَّ الفَنَّانَ غادَرَ المُهْرَجانَ

"Things **nearly** took a turn for the worse when my brother lost his job."

كَادَت أَنْ تَتَدَهْوَرَ الأُمُورُ عِنْدَما فَقَدَ أَخِي وَظِيفَتَهُ

> ☞ **NOTE:** when كادَ is used with a negative particle, it means '**barely, scarcely**' (q.v.). e.g.
>
> "He had barely finished the exam when he fainted ."
>
> ما كادَ/لَمْ يَكَدْ يَنْتَهِي مِنَ الإِمْتِحانَ حَتَّى/عِنْدَما أُغْمَى عَلَيْهِ

Finally, there is the 'dummy' verb قام (يَقُومُ) + بِـ + VN, whose closest equivalent in English is '*to effect, to carry out*' and is a very popular construction in Media Arabic. It may be rendered in a variety of ways in English, including by omission. e.g.

قامَ بِواجِبِهِ
"He **did** his duty."

قامَ بِالتَّمْرين
"He **completed** the exercise."

قامَ بِإِجْراءِ هذا البَحْثِ
"He **carried out/conducted** this research."

قامَ بِتَوْصِيَةٍ لِزَميلِهِ
"He **provided** a reference to his colleague."

قامَ بِتَنْظيمِ مُظاهَرَةٍ
"He **organized** a demonstration."

قامَ الشُّرْطِيُّ بِالقَبْضِ عَلَى اللَّصِّ
"The policeman **proceeded** with the arrest of the thief."

قامَ بِإعادَةِ هَيْكَلِ الشَّرِكَةِ
"He **effected** a restructuring of the company."

قامَ بِإحْرازِ نَجاحٍ مَلْحُوظٍ
"He **achieved** great success."

قامَ بِكِتابَةِ المَقالَةِ

"He **wrote** the article."

☞ Also see 'To Become', 'Keep On ...'; 'Obligation'; 'Hardly ...'

Aw (أَوْ)/am (أَمْ)

Both these conjunctions translate as '**or**', but أَمْ is preferred in **questions**. e.g.

سَنَشْرَبُ عَصِيراً أَوْ قَهْوَةً
"We'll drink juice **or** coffee."

تَكْتُبُ بِالفَحْمِ أَمْ تَرْسُمُ بِهِ ؟
"Do you write **or** draw with charcoal?"

سَنَشْرَبُ عَصِيراً أَوْ قَهْوَةً أَوْ حَلِيباً
"We'll drink juice, coffee **or** milk."

☞ **NOTE:** In English, **or** only occurs before the last element in the series; preceding items are separated by commas.

Though both أَوْ and أَمْ can be used with the negative particle لا to render '**or not**', أَمْ لا is much more common. e.g.

هَلْ شَاهَدْتَهُ أَمْ لا؟
"Did you see him, **or not**?"

☞ **NOTE:** 'or not' is preceded by a comma in English.

☞ Also see 'Correlative Particles'

Beach/shore/coast/seaside

Though closely related in that all four words refer to the edge of the sea, they cannot be used interchangeably. The most general word is **shore**, whereas **coast** is the usual word when talking about the edge of the sea on maps, in relation to the weather, etc.; the **beach** is part of the shore that is smooth and has sand (or shingle) on it. To put it differently, **coast** refers to a wider area of land than **shore**, which denotes a narrow strip, whereas not every area along the sea has a beach! **Seaside** implies both **coast** and **beach**.

In Arabic, ساحِل (.pl سَواحِل) and شاطِئ (.pl شَواطِئ) or (شاطِئُ البَحْرِ) can be used for '**shore**', but only the latter denotes '**beach**', or '**seaside**', though this can also be expressed simply by البَحْرُ ('**sea**').

"This year, we are spending our holidays **at the seaside/coast**."
نَقْضِي إِجازَتَنا هذا العامَّ عَلَى البَحْرِ

"Let's go to the **beach** this afternoon!"
فَلْنَذْهَبْ إلى الشّاطِئِ بَعْدَ ظُهْرَ اليَوْم

"They saw the ship coming into **shore**." (NOT: *beach* or *seaside*)
شاهَدُوا السَّفِينَةَ تَقْتَرِبُ مِن الشّاطِئِ/القادِمَةَ إلَى الشّاطِئِ/قادِمَةً إلى الشّاطِئِ

"At the **coast/seaside**, temperatures are going to rise over the weekend."
سَوْفَ تَرْتَفِعُ دَرَجاتُ الحَرارَةِ في مِنْطَقةِ السّاحِلِ/عَلَى ساحِلِ البَحْرِ في نِهايَةِ الأُسْبُوعِ

"I prefer living near the **coast/seaside**."
أَفَضِّلُ العَيْشَ بِالقُرْبِ مِن السّاحِلِ/البَحْرِ

To become

In Arabic, this copula is usually rendered by صارَ (i) or أَصْبَحَ, with أَمْسَى, أَضْحَى and باتَ (i) being restricted to very formal usage. In general, these verbs are in the **perfect tense**. e.g.

"In the end, he **became** a very traditional artist."
في النِّهايَةِ، صارَ فَنَّاناً تَقْليدِيًّا جِدًّا

"We **became** very close friends after his wife's death."
أَصْبَحْنا أَصْدِقاءَ حَميمِينَ للغايَة بَعْدَ وَفاةِ زَوْجَتِهِ/أَصْبَحْنا بَعْدَ وَفاةِ زَوْجَتِه أَصْدِقاءَ حَميمِينَ جداً

"They **would have become** enemies, if I had not told them how much they needed each other."
لو لَمْ أُخْبِرْهُم كَمْ هُم بِحاجَةٍ إِلى بَعْضِهِم بَعضاً لأَصْبَحُوا أَعْداءً

"I'm sure she will **become** a good painter."
أنا مُتَأَكِّدٌ مِن أَنَّها سَتُصْبِحُ رَسّامةً جَيِّدَةً

☞ **NOTE:**
أَصْبَحَ ('to be in the morning', 'to become clear'), أَضْحَى (to be in the morning', 'to become visible') and باتَ ('to spend the night') can also be used as content verbs. e.g.

تَبيتُ في بَيْتِ جَدِّها
"She'll spend the night/ sleep at her grandfather's house."

أَصْبَحَتْ تَصَرُّفاتُ الْحُكُومَةِ تَكْشِفُ مَوقِفَها المُتَعَصِّبَ ضِدَّ الأَقَلِّيَّاتِ الدِّينِيَّةِ المَوْجُودةِ في البِلادِ
"The government's behaviour reveals its extremist attitude towards religious minorities residing in the country."

أَصْبَحَتِ الْحَقِيقَةُ واضِحَةً بَعْدَ وُصُولِ المُديرِ الْجَدِيدِ

> "The truth came to light when the new director arrived."
>
> صَارَ and أَصْبَحَ can also be used as **auxiliaries of imminence** (q.v.)

In a number of other cases, **to become** is conveyed in Arabic without having recourse to linking verbs. e.g. كَبَرَ (u) ('to become big'; 'to become old'), صَغُرَ (u) ('to become small'), تَعَقَّدَ ('to become complicated'); نَحُفَ (u) ('to become thin'); سَمِنَ (a) ('to become fat'); طَرِشَ (a) ('to become deaf'); سَكَتَ (u) ('to become silent').

Before/in front of/opposite/facing/across

Before is usually used to indicate *earlier than, already*; **in front of** can only be used when talking about a place. **Before** (and not **in front of**) is used for *lists*, to mean *in the presence of*, and in a number of expressions (e.g. 'before my eyes'). In Arabic, **before** is generally rendered as قَبْلَ, which can be used for both time and place, with بَيْنَ يَدَيْهِ occurring with people only.

   In front of is the opposite of *behind* and like **opposite** and **facing** means *directly on the other side of* (e.g. a road, river). When there is a sense of movement, only **in front of** is possible. **Across** also means *on the other/ opposite side of*, but not necessarily directly opposite. In Arabic, '*in front of*' can be rendered by the following: قَبْلَ، أَمَامَ، تُجَاهَ، قُبَالَةَ، قُدَّامَ، حِيَالَ، مُقَابِلَ, all of which have invariable endings. e.g.

"The man ran **towards** (NOT *facing/opposite*!) the bus."

رَكَضَ الرَّجُلُ تُجَاهَ الأُتُوبِيسِ

"The building **across** the street has been broken into twice this week."

أُقْتُحِمَت البِنايَةُ التي تَقَعُ مُقابِلَ الشَّارِعِ مَرَّتَيْنِ هذا الأُسْبُوعَ

إنَّ البِنايَةَ الواقِعَةَ مُقابِلِ الشَّارِعِ أُقْتُحِمَتْ مَرَّتَيْنِ هذا الأُسْبُوعَ

"We came in **before** anyone else."

جِئْنا قَبْلَ أَيِّ شَخْصٍ آخَرَ

"The box **in front of** the cupboard needs to be repaired."

إِنَّ الصُّنْدُوقَ الَّذِي أَمَامَ الدُّولابِ يَحْتاجُ إِلَى تَصْلِيحٍ/يَحْتاجُ الصُّنْدُوقُ الَّذِي أَمَامَ

"**Faced with** continuous attacks, an official source warned that the area would be turned into a living hell."

حَذَّرَ مَصْدَرٌ مَسْؤُولٌ مِنْ أَنَّ الحَياةَ في المِنْطِقةِ سَتَتَحَوَّلُ جَحِيماً/سَتَتَحَوَّلُ إِلَى جَحِيمٍ حِيالَ الاعْتِداءاتِ المُسْتَمِرَّةِ

> ☞ **NOTE**: **across** can also mean '*from one side to the other*', which, depending on the context is rendered in Arabic by نَحْو، فَوْقَ، عَلى، مِنْ جانِبٍ e.g. إِلَى آخَرَ، عَبْرَ.
>
> "He ran **across** the street to see what was going on."
>
> رَكَضَ إِلَى الجانِبِ الآخَرِ مِنَ الشّارِعِ لِمَعْرِفَةِ ما يَجْرِي
>
> "The trousers lay **across** the bed."
>
> إِنَّ السِّرْوالَ مَوْضُوعٌ فَوْقَ السَّرِيرِ
>
> "She is dragging along her stray buffalo across the iron track that cuts through the village."
>
> وَهِيَ تَسْحَبُ جامُوسَتَها الشّارِدةَ عَبْرَ الخَطِّ الحَدِيدِيِّ الَّذِي يَخْتَرِقُ القَرْيةَ

Below/beneath/underneath/under

Below is the opposite of **above** and simply suggests a lower position or level. Both **under** and **beneath** mean '*directly under*', but the latter implies distance; **underneath**, on the other hand, adds to the idea of *touching, covering*. Only the last two can be used in sentence-final positions. In abstract contexts, **under** tends to be preferred to **below**, **under** or **beneath**.

In Arabic, all three are generally rendered by تَحْتَ (or أَسْفَلَ), with دُونَ being used when it involves rank, value, as well as age. e.g.

"If the watch is **below/under** a certain value, then you don't have to return it."

إذا كانَتِ قيمَةُ السّاعَة دُونَ مَبْلغ مُعَيَّن، فَلَنْ يَكُون عَلَيْكَ إعادَتُها

إذا كانَتِ السّاعَةُ دُونَ قيمَةً مُعَيَّنةً، فَلَنْ يَكونَ عَلَيْكَ إعادَتُها

"There are many beautiful things **below/beneath** the surface of the sea."

هُناكَ الكَثيرُ مِنَ الأشياء الجَميلَة تَحْتَ سَطْح البَحْر

يُوجَدُ تَحْتَ سَطح البَحْرِ الكَثيرُ مِنَ الأشياءِ الجَميلَة

"You will find the pen **underneath/under** the papers."

سَتَجِدُ القَلَمَ تَحْتَ الأوْراق

"The city centre came **under** the control of armed gangs."

أصْبَحَ وَسَطُ المَدينة/مَرْكَزُ المَدينة تَحْتَ سَيْطَرَة العِصاباتِ المُسَلَّحة

"The occupying authority refused entry to the mosque to worshippers **below** the age of fifty."

تَمْنَعُ السُّلُطاتُ المُحْتَلَّةُ المُصَلّينَ دُونَ سِنِّ الخَمْسِينَ مِن دُخُولِ المَسجِدِ

Beside/besides

Beside is a preposition meaning *next to*, whereas **besides** is a conjunct (a word linking clauses/sentences) meaning *in addition to*, and is synonymous with *'moreover'* and *'furthermore'*. Both usually found at the beginning of a sentence. **Beside** is usually translated into Arabic by بِجانب; **besides** is rendered as:

أيْضاً

فيما عَدا ذلكَ

بالإضافةِ إلى

وفَوْقَ ذلكَ
وإلى ذلكَ
عَلاوَةً عَلى
إلى جانب
فَضَلاً عَن

"Why don't you want to sit **beside** your brother?"

لِماذا لا تُريدُ أَنْ تَجلِسَ إلى جِوارِ أَخيكَ؟

"I don't enjoy painting. **Besides,** I was never good at it."

لا أَسْتَمْتِعُ بِالرَّسْمِ، وَعَلاوَةً على ذلِكَ ، لَمْ أُحْسِنْهُ عَلى الإِطْلاقِ

"Who **besides** Sarah and Magda attended the party?"

مَنْ حَضَرَ الْحَفْلِ إلى جانِبِ سارةَ وماجِدَة؟
مَنْ الذي حَضَرَ الْحَفْلِ إلى جانِبِ سارةَ وماجِدَةٍ؟

"He gave me a lot of support and many other things **besides**!"

دَعَمَني كثيراً إلى جَانِب أَشْياءَ أُخْرَى كَثيرَة
أعطاني إلى جانب دَعْمِه القَوي لي أشياءَ أُخرى كثيرةً
فَضلاً عَن دَعْمِهِ القَوِيَ لي فَقَدْ أَعْطاني/منحني أَشْياءَ أُخْرَى كَثيرةً

Big/great/large

The main difference between these three words is that **great** is only used in abstract concepts, meaning *'very good', 'magnificent'*. The difference between **big** and **large** is one of register, with the latter being more formal. In terms of meaning, there is no difference between the two.

In Arabic, the adjective كَبير (pl. كِبار or كُبَراءُ) is the usual word for 'big'/'large', with the most common term for '**great**' being عَظيم (pl. عِظام). e.g.

"He came up with a **great** idea to save the company."

طَرَحَ فِكْرَةً عَظيمةً لإِنْقاذِ الشَّرِكَة

"There was a **big/large** fish lying on the table, ready to be cooked."

كانَتْ هُناكَ سَمَكَةٌ كَبِيرَةٌ مَوْضُوعَةٌ عَلَى الطَّاوِلَةِ ، وَجاهِزَةٌ لِلطَّهِي

"The librarian could barely lift the **big/large** volume from the shelf."

بِالكادِ تَمَكَّنَ أَمِينُ المَكْتَبَةِ مِنْ رَفْعِ الكِتابِ الضَّخْمِ مِنْ عَلَى الرَّفِّ

"Harrods is a very **big/large** store in London."

هارودز (هو) مَتَجَرٌ كَبِيرٌ جِدًّا في لَنْدَنَ

"We went out for my birthday and had a **great** meal at the new Indian restaurant."

خَرَجْنا لِلاحْتِفالِ بِعِيدِ مِيلادِي ، وأَكَلْنا وَجْبَةً مُمْتازَةً في المَطْعمِ الهِنديِّ الجَدِيدِ

There are some idiomatic meanings and connotations that may lead to ambiguity:

- the Arabic كَبِير is often short for كَبِيرُ السِّنّ, i.e. 'old', rather than 'big' in the sense of size! In English, on the other hand, 'big' often denotes 'fat', in which case it should be translated by something like سَمِين. e.g.

  "She's a **big** woman."
  هِيَ امْرَأَةٌ سَمِينةٌ/ضَخْمةٌ

  هذا الرجُل كَبِيرٌ ويَسْتَحَقُّ احْتِرامَنا
  "He is an **old** man and therefore deserves our respect."

- **When** كَبِير occurs as the first element in a genitive construction (إضافة), with the second element being in the plural, it is translated into English as 'chief-', 'head-'. e.g.

  كَبِيرُ الأطِبّاء, 'head physician'
  كَبِيرُ القُضاةِ, 'chief justice/magistrate'

Border/frontier/boundary

Both **border** and **frontier** denote the dividing line between two countries. Originally, **frontier** was the term used if there were customs, passport checks etc. Today, however, **border** is used in these contexts as well, **frontier** being restricted to figurative meanings, when it refers to **limits**. **Boundary** is used to delimit smaller areas. In Arabic, the word حُدُود (sg. حَدّ) is used for all, alongside تَخْم (pl. تُخُوم), which cannot, however, apply to a border with customs, etc. Note that the Arabic plural is often translated as a singular in English (a case in point being '**border**'). e.g.

"We crossed the **border** at midnight."

عَبَرْنا الحُدُودَ عِندَ مُنتَصِفِ اللَّيْلِ

"The city **boundaries** are often difficult to define.

إنَّ حُدُودُ المَدينَةِ غالِبا ما يَصْعُبُ تَحْدِيَدها

"The army arrived at the **border** with Israel (/ the Israeli **border**)."

وَصَلَ الجَيْشُ إلى تُخُومِ إسْرائيلَ

"We were close to the city **limits**."

اقْتَرَبْنا من تُخُومَ المَدِينَةِ

"The government announced its willingness to retreat to the June 1967 **border**(s)."

أعْلَنَت الحُكُومةُ اسْتِعْدادَها لِلانْسِحابِ إلى خُطُوطِ حَزيران 1967

"Our University is trying to push back the **frontier**(s) [lit. 'horizons']of science."

تُحاوِلُ جامِعَتُنا أنْ تُوَسِّعَ آفاقَ العِلْمِ

Both

In English, this should only be used when there are two notions or entities. In addition, one should also pay attention to parallelism in the grammar of the construction, especially when prepositions are involved; e.g.

"I was interested **in both** history and French",

OR

"I was interested **both in** history and **in** French" (**NOT** *I was interested both in history and French).

لَقَد كُنْتُ مُهْتَماً بكُلٍّ مِن التَّاريخِ وَاللُّغَةِ الفَرَنْسِيَّةِ

لَقَدْ كُنْتُ مُهْتَمَّاً بالتَّاريخِ وَبِاللُّغَةِ الفَرَنْسِيَّةِ كلَيْهِما

لَقَدْ كُنْتُ مُهْتَمَّاً بالتَّاريخِ وَبِاللُّغَةِ الفَرَنْسِيَّةِ مَعاً

In some cases, Arabic uses كِلا (fem. كِلتا), which is followed by either a **definite dual noun** in the genitive (in an إضافة construction), or with a suffixed **pronoun**. Note that when كِلا is in an إضافة, it agrees in gender with the noun it modifies, but **not** in case. e.g.

"He grabbed the book with **both** hands."

لَقَد أَمْسَكَ الكِتَابَ بكِلتَا يَدَيْهِ

لَقَد أَمْسَكَ الكِتَابَ بِيَدَيْهِ كِلْتَيْهِمَا

"We had a brief talk with **both** of them during the meeting."

كَانَ لَنا حَديثٌ مُقْتَضَبٌ مَعَ كِلَيْهِمَا أَثْنَاءَ الاجْتِمَاعِ

كَانَ لَنا حَديثٌ مُقْتَضَبٌ مَعَ كلٍ مِنهُمَا أَثْنَاءَ الاجْتِمَاعِ

It is important to stress that there is a nuance in the Arabic translations that is missing from the second English sentence. The latter Arabic sentence implies that we had a brief talk with each of them **separately**, whereas the former translation denotes a discussion with both of them **together**!

☞ **NOTE:** in English, *both* is negated by **neither.** e.g.

"Did you see **both** cars? No, I saw **neither!**"
هَل رَأَيْتَ كِلتَا السَّيَّارَتَيْنِ ؟ لا، لَمْ أَرَ أَيًّا مِنْهُما!

Bring/take

These two verbs are often confused; 'to bring' refers to movement *towards* the object, **to take** denotes movement *away* from it. In Arabic, 'to bring' is generally rendered by جاءَ بِ (i), أَتَى بِ، أَحْضَرَ، حَمَلَ لـ/إلى، جَلَبَ (i, u), with 'to take' being translated by أَحْضَرَ إلى، حَمَلَ لـ/إلى. e.g.

"I'll **bring** you some coffee in a minute."
سَوْفَ أُحضِرُ/أَجلِبُ لَكَ القَهْوَةَ خِلال/في دَقِيقَة
سَوْفَ آتِيكَ بِالقَهْوَةِ في دَقِيقَةٍ

"Why don't you **take** her home since it's rather late?"
لِمَ لا تَأْخُذُهَا إلى البَيْتِ فَقَدْ تَأَخَّرَ الوَقْتُ نَوْعًا ما ؟
بِمَا أَنَّ الوَقْتَ قَدْ تَأَخَّرَ فَلِما لا تَأْخُذُهَا إلى البَيْتِ ؟

"We **took** the reports to the sales department."
حَمَلْنا التَّقَارِيرَ إلى قِسْمِ المَبِيعَاتِ

"After I was **brought** before the manager, I was **taken** to the meeting room."
بَعْدَ أَنْ أَحْضَرُونِي إلى المُدِيرِ، أَخَذُونِي إلى قَاعَةِ الإجْتِمَاعَاتِ

☞ **NOTE** that '**to take back**' is rendered by a separate verb, such as
أَعادَ،اِسْتَعادَ،اِسْتَرَدَّ اِسْتَرْجَعَ. e.g.

"Saladdin took Jerusalem back from the Franks."
اِسْتَرْجَعَ صَلاحُ الدِّين الأَيُّوبِيُّ القُدْسَ مِن أَيْدَي الإفْرَنْج

By/with

By is used to indicate the action or method involved in doing something, while
'**with**' refers to a tool. In Arabic the former is rendered by expressions denoting
'*by means of*' : بِطَريقة، بِ (+ gen.), بِواسِطَة (+ gen.), عَنْ طَريق (+ gen.), مِنْ خِلالِ، عَبْرَ (+
gen.). Also Note that '**by**' is used in English when it involves modes of transport.
e.g.

سافَرْنا بالطّائِرَة/بالسَّيّارة/بالباص/بالدَّرّاجة
"We travelled **by** plane/car/bus/bicycle."

"The soldier was killed **with** a knife."
لَقَدْ قُتِلَ الجُنْديُّ بِ/بِواسِطة/عَنْ طَريقِ سِّكينٍ

The use of بِ in this context is more common than عَن طَريق/بِواسِطَة. e.g.

"On arrival, they were taken to the hotel **by** coach."
عِنْدَ وُصولِهِم نُقِلُوا إلى الفُنْدُق بالحَافِلَة

"It was only **with** careful investigation that the crime was solved."
لَقَدْ حُلَّ لُغْزُ الجَريمَة فَقَطْ عَنْ طَريقِ التَّحْقيقِ الدَّقيقِ
لَمْ يُكْشَفْ عَنِ الجَريمَة إلا بِتَحْقيقٍ دَقيقٍ

Can/may/might

These modals are all used to express the notion of possibility or doubt and are part of what is known as 'epistemic modality', which expresses a speaker's judgement regarding the veracity and/or certainty of a statement.

Strictly speaking, however, **can** should be restricted to *ability*, whereas the difference between **may** and **might** is that the latter conveys more doubt than the former. For instance, when one says that one **might** do something, this is more doubtful than when **may** is used; in other words, it is a more remote possibility.

In contemporary English, **can** is used in the same way as **may**, while still retaining its original meaning, which in some cases may lead to confusion. For instance, depending on the context, the sentence "You **can** do it", may mean "You are able to do it" or "You are allowed to do it." In Arabic, the distinction is conveyed as follows:

- ABILITY
  القُدْرَةُ عَلَى
  اِسْتَطَاعَ

- POSSIBILITY
  يُمْكِنُ أَنْ
  لَعَلَّ
  رُبَّمَا

أَنْتَ قادِرٌ عَلَى تَحْقيقِ أَمانيكَ
"You **can** realize your wishes."

تَسْتَطيعُ الشَّرِكَةُ رَفْعَ/أَنْ تَرْفَعَ مُسْتَوَى إِنْتاجِها
"The company **can/is able to** raise its production level."

يُمْكِنُ أَنْ يُؤَدِّيَ الجُوعُ إلى الدِّيمُوقراطِيَّة

"Hunger **may** lead to democracy." (= "It is possible that ...")

لَعَلَّ كُلَّ هذِه الإِرْهاصاتِ تَتَفاعَلُ فيما يُسَمَّى بِالكارِثة العالَمِيَّة

"These signs **may** interact in what is called the global catastrophe."

رُبَّما يُؤَدِّي تَوَسُّعُ الأَزْمةِ إلى بَعْضِ الاخْتِلالاتِ الإِقْتِصادِيَّة المُؤَقَّتة

"The spread of the crisis **may** lead to some temporary economic disturbances."

☞**NOTE**: the noun following لَعَلَّ is in the accusative;

رُبَّما can be used with a perfect verb with present meaning. e.g.

رُبَّما سافَرَ إلى لُبْنانَ

"He **may** travel to Lebanon."

The following sentence illustrates a third meaning of **may**, i.e. *permission*, which may be rendered in a variety of ways. e.g.

يُمْكِنُكَ أَنْ تَسْتَعِيرَ القامُوسَ مَتى شِئْتَ

"You **may** borrow the dictionary whenever you like."

"You **may** (or *can*) sit down now."
يَجوزُ لَكَ/يُمْكِنُكَ أَنْ تَجْلِسَ الآنَ

"**May** (or *can*) I come in?" (= do I have permission to come in)
هَلْ يُمْكِنُنِي الدُّخولَ؟
هَل لِي أَنْ أَدْخُلَ؟
هَلْ أَسْتَطِيعُ الدُّخولَ؟
أَتَأْذَنُ لِي بِالدُّخولِ؟

Though in many cases **can** and **may** are interchangeable when conveying *permission*, they often are not, as in the following sentence, for instance, where **can** and not **may** is the only appropriate modal:

"You **can't** play such loud music in the middle of the night; the neighbours will call the police!"

لا يُمْكِنُكَ/يَصِحُّ/يَجُوزُ لَكَ أَنْ تَعزِفَ مُوسِيقَى صَاخِبَةً في مُنْتَصَفِ اللَّيْلِ إِذْ/وإلا سَيَقُومُ الجِيرانُ بِاسْتِدْعَاءِ الشُّرْطَةِ!

When conveying possibility, **can** and **may** are not always interchangeable. e.g.

"He **can't** have known about her secret." [it was impossible for him to know]

لا يُمْكِنُ أَنْ يَكُونَ قَد عَلِمَ/عَرَفَ بِسِرِّها
مِنْ المُسْتَحِيل أَنْ يَكُونَ عَرَفَ بِسِرِّها

"He **may** not have known about her secret." [it is uncertain that he knew]

رُبَّما لَمْ يَكُنْ يَعْلَمُ/يَعْرِفُ بِسِرِّها

In other cases, it is clear that **can** does *not* reflect ability, as in the following sentence, where the action depends on a third party, not the speaker's ability. e.g.

"You **can** get your money back."

يُمْكِنُكَ/مِنْ حَقِّكَ/يَحِقُّ لَكَ أَنْ تَسْتَرِدَّ نُقُودَكَ
يُمْكِنُكَ/مِنْ حَقِّكَ/يَحِقُّ لَكَ أَسْتِرْدَادُ نُقُودِكَ

English epistemic modality can be rendered in a variety of ways in Arabic:

	Example '*The teacher* may *be in his office*'	Construction	Phrase
(a.)	مِنَ المُمْكِنِ أَنْ يَكُونَ الأُسْتاذ في مَكْتَبِه	+ SUBJUNCTIVE	مِنَ المُمْكِنِ أَنْ
(b.)	يُمْكِن أَنْ يَكُونَ الأُسْتاذ في مَكْتَبِه	+ SUBJUNCTIVE	يُمْكِنِ أَنْ

	Example '*The teacher* may *be in his office*'	Construction	Phrase
(c.)	يَجُوزُ أَنْ يَكُونَ الأُسْتاذُ في مَكْتَبِهِ	+ SUBJUNCTIVE	يَجُوزُ أَنْ
(d.)	مِنَ الجائزِ أَنْ يَكُونَ الأُسْتاذُ في مَكْتَبِهِ	+ SUBJUNCTIVE	مِنَ الجائزِ أَنْ
(e.)	يُرَجَّح أَنْ يَكُونَ الأُسْتاذُ في مَكْتَبِهِ	+ SUBJUNCTIVE	يُرَجَّح أَنْ
(f.)	مِنَ المُرَجَّح أَنَّ الأُسْتاذَ في مَكْتَبِهِ	+ noun/PRON. suffix	مِنَ المُرَجَّح أَنَّ
(g.)	مِنْ/عَلَى الأَرْجَح أَنْ يَكُونُ الأُسْتاذُ في مَكْتَبِهِ	+ SUBJUNCTIVE	مِنْ/عَلَى الأَرْجَح أَنْ
(h.)	مِنَ المُحْتَمَل أَنْ يَكُونَ الأُسْتاذُ في مَكْتَبِهِ	+ SUBJUNCTIVE	مِنَ المُحْتَمَلِ أَنْ
(i.)	يُحْتَمَلُ أَنْ يَكُونَ الأُسْتاذُ في مَكْتَبِهِ	+ SUBJUNCTIVE	يُحْتَمَلُ أَنْ
(j.)	رُبَّما كانَ الأُسْتاذُ في مَكْتَبِهِ	+PERFECT (with present meaning)/ IMPERFECT	رُبَّما
(k.)	رُبَّما أَنَّ الأُسْتاذَ في مَكْتَبِهِ	+ noun/PRON. suffix	رُبَّما أَنَّ
(l.)	عَسَى أَنْ يَكُونَ الأُسْتاذُ في مَكْتَبِهِ	+ SUBJUNCTIVE	عَسَى أَنْ

	Example *'The teacher* may *be in his office'*	Construction	Phrase
(m.)	عَسَى أَنَّ الأُسْتَاذَ فِي مَكْتَبِهِ	+ noun/PRON. suffix	عَسَى أَنَّ

All of the above may convey possibility, with (f), (g), (h), (i) and (k) also denoting *probability*, i.e. an increased degree of possibility ('it is likely that ...').

In English, epistemic modality is unmarked for *present* or *future*. e.g.

"We **may** do it now/tomorrow."
يُمْكِنُنَا فِعْلُ ذَلِكَ الآنَ/فِي الغَدِ (غَداً)

It is important to note that **might** is also the past form of **may**, when it denotes *possibility*. If it refers to *permission*, the past is rendered by 'was/were allowed/permitted'.

"He said she **might** use the laptop whenever she wanted."
قَالَ إِنَّها يُمْكِنُهَا أَنْ تَسْتَخْدِمَ الحَاسُوبَ المَحْمُولَ مَتَى شَاءَت (وَقْتَما تُرِيدُ)

"She **was allowed/permitted** to use my laptop whenever she wanted."
لَقَدْ سُمِحَ لها أَنْ تَسْتَخْدِمَ الحَاسُوبَ المَحْمُولَ مَتَى شَاءَت
لَقَدْ جَازَ لَهَا أَنْ ...
لَقَدْ أُذِنَ لَهَا أَنْ ...

When there is remote possibility, **might** may be replaced by **could**. In other cases, a clear distinction is made, especially if a condition is implicit. e.g.

"She said that he **might** (or *could*) do it if she asked him to."
قَالَتْ إِنَّهُ رُبَّمَا يَفْعَلُ ذَلِكَ إِذَا مَا طَلَبَتْ مِنْهُ
قَالَتْ إِنَّهُ يَسْتَطِيعُ أَنْ يَفْعَلَ ذَلِكَ إِذَا مَا طَلَبَتْهُ مِنْهُ

BUT:

"The teacher **might have** corrected his students' assignments." [= it is possible, but very doubtful]

يُمْكِنُ أَنْ يَكُونَ الأُسْتَاذُ قَدْ صَحَّحَ واجِباتِ طُلّابِهِ

"The teacher **could** have corrected his students' assignments." [= he wouldhave been able to do it (if he hadn't been ill, for instance)]

كانَ يُمْكِنُ لِلأُسْتاذِ أَنْ يُصَحِّحَ وَاجِباتِ طُلّابِهِ

كانَ بِوِسعِ الأُسْتاذِ أَنْ يُصَحِّحَ وَاجِباتِ طُلّابِهِ

In Arabic, **might** is typically rendered by قَدْ + IMPERFECT.

☞ **NOTE**: in reported speech, **may** is replaced by **might**. e.g.

"I **may** be able to do it."

يُمْكِنُ أَنْ أَعْمَلَ هذا

"He said that he **might** be able to do it."

قالَ إِنَّهُ يُمْكِنُ أَنْ يَعْمَلَ هذا

---

e.g.

"The film **may** begin any time."

قَدْ يَبْدَأُ الفِيلْمُ في أَيِّ وَقْتٍ

"I **might** (or *could*) have won the race, if I had trained harder." [*but I didn't*]

لَو تَدَرَّبْتُ أَكْثَرَ فَلَرُبَّما فُزْتُ بِالسِّباقِ

OR

كَانَ مِنَ المُمْكِنِ/كَانَ بِمَقْدُوري الفَوْزُ بِالسِّباقِ، إِنْ كُنْتُ قَدْ تَدَرَّبْتُ أَكْثَرَ

"He **might** not return to Beirut." [OR: 'Maybe he did not return to Beirut.']

رُبَّما لَمْ يَعُدْ إلى بَيْرُوتَ

"You **may** laugh at him."

رُبَّما ضَحِكْتَ مِنْهُ

"They **may/might have** said that; I'm not sure."

يُحْتَمَلُ أَنَّهم قَدْ قالُو ذَلِكَ، فَأَنا لَسْتُ مُتَأَكِّداً

رُبَّما قُالُو ذَلِكَ، فَأَنا لَسْتُ مُتَأَكِّداً

رُبَّما كانُوا يَقُولُونَ ذَلِكَ، فَأَنا لَسْتُ مُتَأَكِّداً

رُبَّما قد قُالُوا ذَلِكَ، فَلَسْتُ مُتَأَكِّداً

"Electricity **may** (or **can**) kill.

يُمْكِنُ لِلكَهرَباءِ أَنْ تَقْتُلَ

قد تَقْتُلُ الكَهرَباءُ

مِنَ المُمْكِنِ لِلْكَهرِباءِ أَنْ تَقْتُلَ

'She **may** (or *could*) have committed the murder, because she was in the village that night."

رُبَّما تَكُونُ قَدْ ارْتَكَبَتْ جَرِيمَةَ القَتْلِ لأَنَّها كَانَتْ مَوْجُودةً في القَريَةِ في تِلْكَ اللَّيَلَةِ

"If they don't receive any help soon, they **may** all get killed."

إِذَا لَمْ يَحْصُلُوا عَلَى أَيِّ مُسَاعَدَةٍ في القَريبِ العَاجِلِ، فقَدْ يَمُوتُونَ جَمِيعاً

"He **may** come over to our house tomorrow evening."

قَدْ يَأْتِي إلى مَنْزِلِنا مَسَاءَ غَدٍ

"He **might have** been killed."

رُبَّما قَدْ قُتِلَ/رُبَّما قُتِلَ

When these modals are negated, the meaning often changes slightly and may pose problems in translation. e.g.

"He **may not** accept the job offer because he doesn't want to move to London."

قَدْ لا يَقْبَلُ العَمَلَ المَعْروض عَلَيْهِ/الوَظِيفَةَ المَعْرُوضَةَ عَلَيْهِ لأَنَّهُ لا يُريدُ أَنْ يَنْتَقِلَ إلى لَنْدَن

"She **may not** have gone to Beirut last year."

رُبَّما لَمْ تَذهَبْ إِلى بَيْرُوتَ في العَامِ الماضي

"It **may not** rain this afternoon."

قَد لا تُمْطِرُ/رُبَّما لَنْ تُمْطِرَ بعدَ ظُهرِ/عَصرِ اليَوْم

"Things **might not** improve after the economic crisis."

قَدْ لا تَتَحَسَّنُ الْحالَةُ بَعْدَ الأَزْمَةِ الاِقْتِصاديَّةِ

"We **might not** have agreed without his assurance to provide the necessary funds."

رُبَّما ما كُنا لِنُوافِقُ عَلَى الأَمْرِ لَوْلا تَأْكيدُه عَلَى تَوْفيرِ الأَمْوالِ اللّازِمَة

لَوْ لَمْ يُؤَكِّدْ عَلَى تَوْفيرِه للأَمْوالِ اللازِمَةِ لَما وَافَقْنا عَلَى الأَمْرِ

"The teacher **can't** be in his office today."

لا يَسْتَطيعُ الْمُعَلِّمُ أَنْ يَكُونَ في مَكْتَبِه الْيَوْمَ

لا يُمْكِنُ أَنْ يَكُونَ الْمُعَلِّمُ في مَكْتَبِه الْيَوْمَ

مِنَ الْمُسْتَحيلِ أَنْ يَكُونَ الْمُعَلِّمُ في مَكْتَبِه الْيَوْمَ

☞ **NOTE:** In the first sentence the teacher for what ever reason, is unable to be in the class, while in the second it negates the possibility that the teacher can be in the class.

"You **can't** have seen her yesterday because she was still in Paris then."

لا يُمْكِنُ أَنْ تَكُونَ قَدْ رَأَيْتَها أَمْسِ لأَنَّها في ذلِكَ الوَقْتِ كانَتْ لا تَزالُ في باريسَ

مِنَ الْمُسْتَحيلِ أَنْ ...

☞ Also see 'May/Maybe' and 'The Conditional'

Canal/channel

The main difference between these two words, both of which refer to stretches of water, is that '**canal**' is man-made, whereas '**channel**' is nature-made. In Arabic, both can be rendered by قَناة (pl. قَنَوات), with تُرْعة (pl. تُرَع) being restricted to a drainage canal or ditch.

When talking about television, only **channel** is used, which in Arabic can be rendered either by قَناة or قَنال. e.g.

'satellite television channel':

قَنَاةٌ (تِليفِزيُونِيَّةٌ) فَضائِيَّةٌ

قَنَاةُ/قَنالُ تِليفِزيُونٍ فَضائِيَّةٌ/فَضائِيٌّ

For radio, **station** is used in English. In Arabic, this is also rendered by قناة (إذاعِيَّة). e.g.

"Each of the three **radio stations** can broadcast to both the Middle East and Europe."

يُمْكِنُ لِكُلِّ قَنَاةٍ مِنَ القَنَوَاتِ الإذاعِيَّةِ الثَّلاثِ أَنْ تَبُثَّ إلى الشَّرْقِ الأَوْسَطِ وَأُورُوبا

☞ **NOTE:** the following geographical proper nouns:

القَنَاةُ الإنْكِليزِيَّةُ: the English Channel

جُزُرُ القَنَاةِ (الإنْكِليزِيَّةِ): the Channel Islands

قَنَاةُ السُّويسِ: the Suez Canal

Classic/classical/classics/classicist/ classicism

The adjective **classic** can refer to one of the following:

(1) *'of the first rank'*. e.g.

"a **classic** film"

فيلْمٌ مُمْتازٌ
فيلْمٌ كلاسيكيٌّ
فيلْمٌ رائِعٌ
فيلْمٌ مِنَ الدَّرَجَةِ الأُولى

(2) *'typical'*. e.g.

"a **classic** mistake'

خَطَأٌ نَمَطِيٌّ/مُتَوَقَّعٌ

(3) *'continuously in fashion'*. e.g.

"a **classic** suit"

بَدْلَةٌ لِكُلِّ المُنَاسَبَاتِ

As a noun, **classic** denotes an author, text etc. of the highest excellence. e.g.

"Hamlet is a **classic**."

هامْلِتْ رِوايةٌ كلاسِيكِيَّةٌ

هَامِلِتْ رِوايَةٌ رائِعَةٌ/مِنَ الدَّرَجة الأُولى

هامْلِتِ مِن رَوائِعِ الأدَبِ الإنْكليزِيِّ القَديم

The plural **Classics** refers to literature which is considered great. e.g.

"He read all the **Classics**."

لَقَدْ قَرَأ جَميعَ الكُتُبِ الكلاسيكِيَّة

لَقَد قَرَأ أُمَّاتِ الكُتُبِ

As a singular **Classics** is an academic subject focusing on Greek and Roman culture. e.g.

"He went on to study **Classics** at London University."

لَقَدْ ذَهَبَ لِدِرَاسَةِ الكِلاسيكِيَّات/الآداب اليونانِيَّة وَاللاتينِيَّة في جَامِعَةِ لَنْدَنَ

Classicism denotes the ideas and principles of ancient Greece and Rome, as well as a style in art and architecture in 18th-century Europe. e.g.

"**Classicism** attempted to combine both the ancient and modern."

حَاوَلَ المَنْهَجُ الكِلاسيكِيُّ أَنْ يَجْمَعَ بَيْنَ القَديمِ وَالحَديثِ

The adjective **classical** refers to:

(4) 'Greek and Roman Antiquity'. e.g.

"Classical sculpture"

النَّحْتِ الكِلاسِيكِيُّ/اليُونَانِيُّ وَالرُّومَانِيُّ

(5) 'serious, traditional' (music), as opposed to 'popular', 'light'. e.g.

'a **classical** composer'

مُلَحِّنُ المُوسِيقِي الكِلاسِيكِيَّة

(6) 'traditional' (science and art). e.g.

"classical economic theory"

نَظَرِيَّةٌ إِقْتِصَادِيَّةٌ تَقْلِيدِيَّةٌ

☞ **NOTE:** Arabic prefers the borrowing كلاسيكي in cultural contexts.

Close/shut

In many cases both can be used; **shut**, however, *cannot* be used attributively. e.g. 'a closed door/eyes' (NOT *'a shut door'), nor to talk about roads, companies, etc. In addition, **shut** is more informal. e.g.

'The door was **shut.**

لَقَدْ أُغْلِقَ البَابُ

كَانَ البَابُ مُغْلَقاً

"Don't forget to **close/shut** the door."

لا تَنْسَ أَنْ تُغْلِقَ البابَ/تَقْفِلَ البابَ

"The factory **closed** (down) last year."

لَقَدْ أَوْقَفَ المَعْمَلُ أَعْمالَهُ العامَ الماضِي

Common/joint

Common means shared (*'in common'*), whereas **joint** denotes combined effort. In Arabic, both tend to be rendered by the passive participle of the verb اِشْتَرَكَ ('to take part'), مُشْتَرَك. e.g.

'Our **common** goal is to become the best in the field.'

هَدَفُنَا المُشْتَرَكُ هُوَ أَنْ نُصبِحَ الأَفْضَلَ في هذا المَجَالِ/المَيْدَانِ

"We'll have to put in a great deal of **joint** effort if we want to complete this task on time.'

إِذَا أَرَدْنَا أَنْ نُكمِلَ هذِهِ المُهِمَّةَ في الوَقْتِ المُنَاسِبِ فَيَجِبُ عَلَيْنا جَميعاً أَنْ نَبْذُلَ أقصى جَهْدٍ مُشترَكٍ لإكمالها

> ☞ **NOTE**: 'to be jointly responsible' = تَضامَنَ

It is important not to confuse this meaning of *common* with 'usual, ordinary', which tends to be rendered in Arabic by عاديّ, as in:

'This is a **common** view which many people would agree with.'

هذِهِ وِجْهَةُ نَظَرٍ عادِيّةٍ/شائِعَةٍ/مَألوفَةٍ يَتَّفِقُ مَعَها الكَثيرُ مِنَ النّاسِ

When *common* is used in the sense of 'ordinary' it can also have a pejorative meaning in that it denotes 'vulgar, unsophisticated'. e.g.

"She really is very **common** in the way that she speaks and behaves."

إِنَّها غَيْرُ مُتَحَضِّرَةٍ في طَريقَةِ كَلامِها وَتَصَرُّفِها

Comparative/superlative

Excluding separate forms such as *'worse/worst'*, the English comparative and superlative essentially come in two forms: the so-called inflectional comparative (e.g. *simpler, fastest*) and the periphrastic construction, which involves the use of *more/most* + adjective.

Traditionally, the latter is reserved for words of more than one syllable, though this 'rule' is commonly broken in the spoken language, where it is quite common to hear *'stupidest'* or *'cleverest'*. However, careful users of English avoid this in formal written language, where examples of this practice are only found for stylistic reasons, for instance, to add intensity.

Equally important to note is that the position of the adjective also plays a part, even if it consists of only one syllable; when the adjective follows the noun, the periphrastic construction is the one that should be used. e.g.

"Have you seen a **kinder** woman than her?"

هَلْ رَأَيْتَ امْرَأَةً أَطْيَبَ/أَحَنَّ مِنْها؟

"I have never seen a woman **more kind**."

لَمْ يَسبِقْ لِي أَنْ رَأَيْتُ امْرَأَةً أَكْثَرَ طِيبَةً/حُنُوناً/حَناناً مِنْها

Although in theory, the periphrastic construction can always replace the inflectional one, idomaticity should be the guiding principle.

In Arabic, the comparative and superlative come in two constructions:

1. The so-called 'elative' pattern أَفْعَل, followed by the preposition مِن, which expresses the English 'than'. The elatives do not show gender, number or definiteness agreement. e.g.

هُوَ/هِيَ أَكْبَرُ مِن أخِيك, 'S/he is **older than** your brother'

الحُبُّ أَكْثَرُ مِن مُجَرَّدِ كَلِمةٍ
"Love is **more than** just a word."

لَنْدَنُ أَكْثَرُ سُكَّاناً مِن مانْشِسْتِرَ

109

لَنْدَنُ (مدينة لندن) أَكْثَر كثافةٍ في السُّكان مِن مانْشِسْتَرَ
"London has more inhabitants than Manchester."

☞ **NOTE:**

▷ Adjectives (usually those referring to colours or defects) that are already in the elative form but that do not have comparative meaning, do inflect for gender and number (with the patterns فَعْلاء and فُعْل for the feminine and plural, respectively), as well as definiteness. e.g.

أَصْلَع ;صُلْع .pl ,صَلْعَاءُ .f, 'bald'
البِنْت الصَّلْعَاء ('the bald girl')
الرِّجال الصُّلْع ('the bald men')

▷ It is possible to use the comparative without its comparator, i.e. without مِن. e.g.

يُفْتَرَضُ أَنْ نَلْعَبَ دَوْراً أَكْبَرَ في الشَّرِكة الجَدِيدة
"It is assumed that we'll play a **greater** role in the new company."

▷ The adjectives خَيْرٌ and شَرٌّ have an additional implicit elative meaning and can thus mean 'good/better' and 'bad/worse', respectively. e.g.

الوِقايةُ خَيْرٌ مِن أَلْفِ عِلاج
"Prevention is **better** than cure." (lit. '... a thousand cures')

العِلاجُ شَرٌّ مِنَ المَرَض
"Treatment is **more** harmful than the disease."

▷ If two qualities of the same referent are compared, a resumptive pronoun must be affixed to the preposition مِن. e.g.

الطَّلَبةُ أَكْثَرُ وُلُوعاً/وَلَعاً بالدَّرَجاتِ/بالعَلامَاتِ العاليَّةِ مِنْهُم بالمَعْرِفة
"Students are **more** eager to get high marks than (they are) knowledge."

2.   a periphrastic construction comprising elatives denoting increasing size or intensity, such as '**greater**' (أَكْبَر), '**stronger**' (أَشَدُّ), followed by the verbal noun derived from the verb of the same root, with the noun being in the indefinite accusative of 'specification' (تَمْيِيز). This is obligatory when the adjective is a participle (except if it is the active participle of a Form I verb); consists of more than three root consonants; or already has the elative form (such as those referring to colours and disabilities). e.g.

هُناكَ جَرِيمَة أَشَدُّ أَلَماً وَحُزْناً
"There is a much **more** painful and sad crime."

تَبْدُو المَسْؤُولِيَّةُ أَكْبَرَ وَأَكْثَرَ تَعْقيداً مِنْ ذِي قَبْل
"The responsibility appears to be **more** important and more complicated than before."

هِيَ أَشَدُّ مِنِّي صَبْراً
"She's **more** patient than I am."

أَصْبَحَ البَيْتُ المَكانَ الأَقَلَّ أَمْناً
"The home has become the **least** secure place."

انْتَشَرَت هذِهِ القِصَّةُ في جَميعِ أنحَاءِ العا لَم لأَنَّ مَقْطَعَ الفيديو كانَ أَحَد أَكْثَر المَقاطِع مُشاهدةً عَلَى مَوْقِع اليوتيوب
"This story spread throughout the world as the video clip on Youtube was one of the **most** watched on the site."

النُّرْويج هِيَ ثَاني أَكْثَرِ دُوَلِ العا لَم تَسامُحاً
"Norway is the **second-most** tolerant country in the world."

الصِّينُ هِيَ أَكْثَر بِلَدان العا لَم كَثافَةً بالسُّكَّان
الصِّينُ هِيَ البَلَدُ الأَكْثَرُ كَثافَةً بالسُّكَّانِ في العا لَم
"China is the **most** populous country in the world."

أنا أَقَلُّ مِنْها اجْتِهاداً
"I am **less** diligent than she is."

إِنَّ الاِكْتِئَابَ أَكْثَرُ أَمْرَاضِ العَصْرِ انْتِشَاراً

"Depression is the **most** widespread illness of the age."

إِنَّ رَئِيسَ الوُزَرَاءِ الجَدِيدَ أَوْسَعُ حِكْمَةً مِنَ الرَّئِيسِ السَّابِقِ

"The new Prime Minister is **more** astute than his predecessor."

- The same elative can also govern several adjectives, as in:

لَيْسَ علماءُ الغَرْبِ أَكْثَرَ ذَكاءً أَوْ قُوَّةً أَوْ خِبْرَةً فِي التَّقْنِيَّةِ مِنَ العُلَمَاءِ فِي الوَطَنِ العَرَبِيِّ

"Western scientists are not **more intelligent**, **stronger** or technically **more advanced** than scholars in the Arab world."

The comparison of equality is conveyed in Arabic by the following particles: e.g. كَـ – مِثْل – عَلَى قَدْر – بِقَدْر

"She is just **as pretty as** her mother (sister)."
هِيَ جَمِيلَةٌ مِثْلَ أُمِّها
هِيَ جَمِيلَةٌ كَأُمِّها
هِيَ مِثْلُ أُمِّها فِي الجَمالِ
هِيَ لا تَقِلُّ جَمالاً عَنْ أُمِّها
هِيَ كَأُمِّها جَمِيلَةٌ

- The Arabic **superlative** still relies on the elative form, but differs in usage in that it is always definite, as a result of:

  ▷ the definite article; e.g.

  البِنْتُ الكُبْرَى: 'the **eldest** daughter'

  ▷ a pronominal suffix; e.g.

  هُوَ أَكْبَرُهُم
  "He's the **oldest** among them."

  ▷ the elative being the first element in a genitive construction (إضافة), with the second noun being

i.   *singular indefinite*; e.g.

الدَّرْفِيلُ (الدُّولْفِين) هوَ أذْكَى حَيَوانٍ بَحْرِيٌّ

"The dolphin is the **most** intelligent marine animal."

في أَسْرَعِ وَقْتٍ مُمْكِنٍ

"As soon as possible."

ii.   *plural definite*; e.g.

أَغْلى الهَدايا في المَحَلِّ

"The **most** expensive gifts in the shop."

The superlative can also occur with the indefinite pronoun ما, followed by a clause introduced by a preposition. e.g.

إنَّ أَسْوَءَ ما في كِتابَةِ المَسْرَحِيّاتِ هُوَ أنَّكَ تَكْتُبُ عَنْ أَشْياءَ شَخْصِيَّةٍ

"The **worst** thing about writing plays is that you write something personal."

The superlative can also occur on its own, with the definite article, in a limited number of expressions. e.g.

كانوا عَلَى الأَقَلِّ نادِمِينَ/مُتَأَسِّفِينَ/آسفين عَلَى تَصْريحاتِهِم

"At **least**, they were sorry about what they had said."

Another difference with the comparative is that the superlative has feminine (فُعْلَى) and plural forms (masc. أَفْعَلُونَ, فُعْل, فَعالِل; fem. فُعْلَيات). However, in Modern Standard Arabic these are rarely employed, except in certain fixed expressions:

بريطانيا العُظْمَى:	'Great Britain'
آسيا الصُّغْرَى:	'Asia Minor'
الحَرْبُ العُظْمَى:	'The Great War'

:الدُّوَلُ الكُبْرَى	'The Great Powers, the Superpowers'
:القُرُونُ الوُسْطَى	'The Middle Ages'
:القُوَى العُظْمى	'The Great Powers, the Superpowers'
:أَمْرِيكا الوُسْطَى	'Central America'

☞ **NOTE**: all of these superlatives are translated into English by ordinary adjectives. Other examples include:

:الشَّرْقُ الأَوْسَط	'the Middle East'
:الشَّرْقُ الأَدْنَى	'the Near East'
:إِسْكَنْدَر الأَكْبِر	'Alexander the Great'

In order to express the English **the+ COMPARATIVE... the + COMPARATIVE**, which denotes 'in the same measure as', Arabic uses كُلَّما, which takes a PERFECT verb, which can have a present or past meaning, depending on the context. e.g.

كُلَّما دَرَسْتَ كُلَّما زادَت فُرَصُ نَجاحِك

"The **more** you study, the **greater** your chances of succeeding."

كُلَّما تَقَدَّمَ في دِراسَتِه ازدادَ احْتِرامُ النَّاسِ له

"The **further** he progresses in his study, the **greater** the respect he earns/ the more respect he earns/gets."

In journalistic writing, the second كُلَّما is often omitted. e.g.

كُلَّما كانَ المُديرُ قاسِياً ازْدادَ كُرْهُ المُوَظَّفينَ لَهُ

"**The more** strict the director was, **the more** his staff hated him."

☞ **NOTE**: كُلَّما should not be confused with كُلُّ ما, which means '**all of**'. e.g.

لَنْ أَنْسَى كُلَّ ما رَأَيْتُهُ في بَيْتِهِ

"I will not forget **all of** the things I saw in his house."

The conditional

The conditional is subject to fixed constructions in both English and Arabic, with constraints being imposed on the tenses in the protasis (the if-clause, containing the condition; شَرْط) and apodosis (the 'consequent', جَوابٌ). Essentially, the choice of constructions and particles (in Arabic) is governed by whether or not there is a real condition, on the one hand, and whether the hypothetical situation is possible or impossible (as in the case of a past hypothesis).

The choice of conditional construction depends on the kinds of conditions involved. Traditionally, these are divided into those that involve possibility that becomes reality when the condition is met (type I) and hypothesis, which is either realizable (type II) or not, if it refers to a past event (type III):

TYPE I (future conditional, i.e. real possibility):

In English, this is rendered by a **PRESENT SIMPLE + FUTURE** or **PRESENT SIMPLE**, whereas in Arabic the construction requires إذا or إنْ with a **PERFECT** or **IMPERFECT** (either with or without the future particle سَـ/سَوْفَ). e.g.

If I DO this, I WILL SUCCEED.
If you DO this, you SUCCEED.
إذا/إنْ عَمِلْتَ ذلِكَ نَجَحْتُ/فَأَنْجَحُ/سَوْفَ أَنْجَحُ/سَأَنْجَحُ
إذا/إنْ عَمِلْتَ ذلِكَ يُمْكِنُ أَنْ أَنْجَحَ
إذا/إنْ عَمِلْتَ ذلِكَ فَرُبَّمَا أَنْجَحُ

TYPE 2 (non-past hypothesis, i.e. possibility):

In English, this type of conditional requires the SIMPLE PAST+ WOULD+ INF. In Arabic, لَوْ + PERFECT is used, with لَ introducing the apodosis, though other constructions are also found. e.g.

If I DID this, I WOULD SUCCEED.
لَوْ عَمِلْتُ ذلِكَ

(1) نَجَحْتُ
(2) لَنَجَحْتُ
(3) فَسَأَنْجَحُ
(4) سَوْفَ أَنْجَحُ
(5) سَأَنْجَحُ

لَوْ عَمَلْتُ ذلك يُمْكِنْ أَن أَنْجَحَ
لَوْ عَمَلْتُ ذلك فَرُبَّما أَنْجَحُ

TYPE 3 (Past hypothesis, i.e. impossibility)

The English construction is PAST PERFECT+ WOULD HAVE+PAST PARTICIPLE usually corresponds to the Arabic لَوْ كان قَدْ followed by a PERFECT, with the apodosis being introduced by لَ, alongside other constructions. e.g.

If I HAD DONE this, I WOULD HAVE SUCCEEDED
لَوْ كُنْتُ قَدْ عَمَلْتُ ذلك لَنَجَحْتُ
لَوْ كُنْتُ قَدْ عَمَلْتُ ذلك لكانَ مِنَ المُمْكِنْ أَن أَنْجَحَ
لَوْ كُنْتُ قَدْ عَمَلْتُ ذلك فَرُبَّما كنت سَأَنْجَحُ
لَوْ كُنْتُ قَدْ عَمَلْتُ ذلك فَرُبَّما كُنْتُ نَجَحْتُ

	English			Arabic	
	Example	Form	Meaning	Form	Translation
TYPE I	*If I DO this, I WILL* SUCCEED...	PRESENT+ FUTURE	Future conditional (= possibility)	إذا/إنْ + / PERFECT INDICATIVE+ /	إذا/إنْ عَمَلْتُ ذَلِكَ نَجَحْتُ فأَنْجَحُ
	If you DO this, you SUCCEED	PRESENT+ PRESENT			
				سَ (سَوْف) INDICATIVE	سَوْفَ أَنْجَحُ سأَنْجَحُ إذا/إنْ عَمَلْتُ ذَلِكَ يُمْكِنْ أَنْ أَنْجَحَ إذا/إنْ عَمَلْتُ ذَلِكَ فَرُبَّمَا أَنْجَحُ
TYPE II	*If I DID this, I WOULD* SUCCEED...	SIMPLE PAST+ WOULD+ INF	Non-past hypothesis (= possibility)	لَوْ + PERFECT لَـ ...	لَوْ عَمَلْتُ ذلك نَجَحْتُ لَنَجَحْتُ فسأَنْجَحُ سَوْفَ أَنْجَحُ سأَنْجَحُ لَوْ عَمَلْتُ ذلك يُمْكِنْ أن أَنْجَحَ لَوْ عَمَلْتُ ذلك فَرُبَّمَا أَنْجَحُ

	English			Arabic	
	Example	Form	Meaning	Form	Translation
TYPE III	*If I HAD DONE this, I WOULD HAVE SUCCEEDED*	PAST PERFECT+ WOULD HAVE+ PAST PARTICPLE	Past hypothesis (= impossibility)	لَوْ كان قَدْ + PERFECT	لَوْ كُنْتُ قَدْ عَمَلْتُ ذلِكَ لَنَجَحْتُ لَـ...
					لَوْ كُنْتُ قَدْ عَمَلْتُ ذلك لكانَ مِنَ المُمْكِنِ أن أَنْجَحَ
					لَوْ كُنْتُ قَدْ عَمَلْتُ ذلِكَ فَرُبَّمَا كنت سَأَنْجَحُ
					لَوْ كُنْتُ قَدْ عَمَلْتُ ذلِكَ فَرُبَّمَا كُنْتُ نَجَحْتُ

☞ **NOTE:** the Arabic **perfect** tense can denote both **present** and **future** possibility.

☞ The English **TYPE I conditional** can also be introduced by *when*, in which case it can be rendered in Arabic by لَّا or عِنْدَما with the protasis and apodosis tenses being in the IMPERFECT. e.g.

"**If** she rejects the decision, she'll be fired, won't she?"

إن هي رفَضَت القَرَارَ، سَوفَ تُفْصَلُ مِنَ العَمَل، أَلَيْسَ كَذَلِكَ؟

☞ in **TYPE III**, the tense in the apodosis can also be **WOULD+INF.** e.g.

'If you **had** not **left** the room to smoke a cigarette, you **would know** that the Paris branch was going to be closed.' (**NOT**: *'... had known')

لَوْ لَمْ تَتْرُكِ الغُرْفَةَ لِتُدَخِّنَ السِّيجَارَةَ/لولا تَرْكُكَ الغُرْفَةَ لِتُدَخِّنَ السِّيجَارَةَ، لَكُنْتَ قَدْ عَرَفْتَ/لَعَرَفْتَ بِأَنَّ فَرْعَ بَارِيسَ سَيَتِمُّ إِغْلاقُهُ

☞ In English, **would** is used with *if* only in very formal requests. e.g.

"The management **would** appreciate it **if** you **would** be so kind as to leave the room in a tidy condition."

سَتَكُونُ الإِدَارَةُ مُمْتَنَّةً لَوْ تَفَضَّلتُم بِتَرْكِ الغُرفَةِ مُرَتَّبَةً

☞ if the apodosis *precedes* the protasis in Arabic, then the لـ and فـ are omitted. e.g.

"I **would have taken** a taxi to the airport **if** she hadn't picked me up."

كُنْتُ سآخُذُ سَيَّارَةَ أُجْرَةٍ/تاكسِي إلى المَطَارِ إذا لَمْ تُقِلنِي/تَأْخُذْنِي
كُنْتُ سآخُذُ سَيَّارَةَ أُجْرَةٍ إلى المَطَارِ لَوْ لَمْ تَكنْ هِي قَدْ أَقَلَّتْنِي

☞ In a number of cases, the Arabic conditional particle is **not** translated into English. e.g.

إنْ شاءَ اللهُ
'God willing.' (**NOT** : *'*If God wills*')

إذا/إنْ شَرِبْتَ هذا فَسَتَمُوتُ
'Drink this, and you'll die.' (**OR**: 'If you drink this, you'll die.')

☞ The protasis with إذا is introduced by فـ if it contains an imperative or particle. e.g.

"If you see the manager, tell him that I shan't be going into the office tomorrow."

إذا رَأَيْتَ المُدِيرَ فَأُخْبِرْهُ بِأَنِّي لَنْ أَذْهَبَ إلى المَكْتَبِ غَداً

☞ The Arabic conditional is **negated** through:

• لَمْ or ما; in the case of لَمْ, the protasis introductory لـ is omitted. e.g.

لَوْ أَنَّها أَنْهَتِ الواجِبَ لَما رَسَبَتْ في الاخْتِبارِ

"If she had finished the assignment, she would not have failed the test."

لَوْ كُنَّا قَدْ أَسْرَعْنا لَما فاتَتْنا الحافِلةُ

"If we had hurried up, we would not have missed our bus."

- (فَ) وَالاَّ (> وَإِنْ لا), meaning **'if not'**, **'or else'**, **'otherwise'**. e.g.

قُومُوا بِعَمَلِكُم وَإِلاَّ فَإِنَّ العَواقِبَ وَخِيمَةٌ

"Do (m. pl.) your work, **or else/if not** there will be dire consequences!"

حَذَّرَتْني :التَّغْييرُ وَإلا الانْفِصالُ

"She warned me to change **or else** there would be a separation."

عَلَينا أَنْ نُعيدَ النَّظَرَ في المَوضُوعِ ، وَإلا فَسَنَخْسَرُ الصَّفْقَةَ

"We must reconsider our position, **if not** (= *otherwise*) we'll lose the deal."

تَشْغَلُ هذهِ القَضِيَّةُ بالَ الرَّأْيِ العامِّ في الشَّرقِ الأَوْسَطِ عَلَى الأَقَلِّ إِنْ لَمْ يَكُنْ في العالَمِ كُلِّه

"This issue is preoccupying public opinion in the Middle East, **if not** the entire world."

☞ **NOTE:** "Were it not for/had it not been for" = لَوْلَا (أَنَّ) + noun/pronoun. e.g.

"The team would have lost **were it not** for the outstanding performance of the goalkeeper."
(= The team would have lost **if it had not been for/had it not been for** ...')

لَوْلَا الأَدَاءُ المُتَمَيِّزُ لِحَارِسِ المَرْمَى لَخَسِرَ الفَرِيقُ

"If I hadn't been ill, I would have come along with you."
"If it wasn't for the fact that I was ill ..."

لَوْلَا المَرَضُ (لَوْ لَمْ أَكُنْ مَرِيضًا) لَسَافَرْتُ مَعَكَ

"**If it wasn't for** the fact that they are rich, they wouldn't be living in this area."

لَوْلَا أَنَّهُم (لَوْ لَمْ يَكُونُوا) أَغْنِيَاء لَمَا سَكَنُوا في هذا الحَيّ

☞ **NOTE:** Arabic tends to prefer the **perfect** in the conditional, even where English uses a present or even future.

The particle لَوْ is also used as a complementizer with the verbs وَدَّ ('to like, wish') and تَمَنَّى ('to hope'), in which case the uncertainty of the action or state is emphasized. e.g.

أَوَدُّ لَوْ تُساعدُني
"I'd like you to help me."

أَتَمَنَّى لَوْ تَكُونُ بِخَيْرٍ
عسى أَنْ تَكُونَ بِخَيْرٍ
"I hope you're fine."

☞ Also see 'Even If'

Confident/confidential/confidant

Confident (adj.) means 'with *confidence, self-assurance*' (عَلَى ثِقَة، واثق); **confidential** (adj.) denotes secrecy and intimacy (سِرِّيّ); and confidant (n.) is a person that one confides in, i.e. tells one's secrets to (نَجِي, pl. أَنْجِية). e.g.

"The Council is **confident** that Iraq is serious about cooperating with the UN."

المَجْلِس/(مجلس الأمن الدولي) واثق مِن أنّ العِراقَ جادةٌ بشأنِ التَّعاوُنِ مَعَ الأُمَم المُتَّحِدةِ

"He is **confident** that hard work will yield the desired results."

إنَّهُ عَلَى ثِقَةٍ مِنْ أَنْ/بِأَنَّ العَمَلَ الشَّاقَ سَوْفَ يُحَقِّقُ النَّتَائِجَ المَرْجُوَّةَ

"This is very **confidential** information that should not leave this company."

هذه المَعْلُوماتُ سِرِّيَّةٌ للغَايةِ وَ يَنْبَغِي أَنْ لا/أَلاّ تتسرَّبَ خارِجَ هذه الشَّرِكَة
هذِه المَعْلُوماتُ سِرِّيَّةٌ للغَايةِ وَلا يَنْبَغِي أَنْ تتسرَّبَ خارِجَ هذِه الشَّرِكَة

"He knows all her secrets since he is her **confidant**."

إنَّه يَعْرِفُ كُلَّ أَسْرارِها لأَنَّه يُحِبُّها

Conscious/consciousness/conscience/ conscientious

Conscious means *awake* (i.e. not unconscious), or *aware*; in the latter case it is followed by the preposition **of**; **consciousness** denotes the state of being alert and awake; **conscience** refers to the sense of right and wrong that determines what a person does; **conscientious** is synonymous with **diligent**. e.g.

122

"As soon as he became **conscious** again/regained consciousness, the police interrogated him."

قَامَت الشُّرطَةُ بِاسْتِجْوابِه، بِمُجَرَّد أَنْ اسْتَرَدَّ وَعْيَهُ

بِمُجَرَّد اسْتَرَداده لِوَعْيِه ، قَامَت الشُّرطَةُ بِاسْتِجْوابِه

"I'm very **conscious of** the fact that we need to adopt a new sales policy."

أَنَا مُدْرِكٌ تَمَاماً/واعٍ جِداً لِحَقِيقَة أَنَّنا في حَاجَةٍ لِتَبَنِّي سِياسةٍ جَديدَةٍ لِلمَبيعَاتِ/سِياسةٍ مَبيعاتٍ جَديدةٍ

"One should always be guided by one's **conscience** when making decisions in life."

يَجِبُ عَلَى المَرْء أَنْ يُراجِعَ ضَميرَهُ دَائماً عِنْدَ اتِّخَاذ القَراراتِ في الحَياة

"I always work very **conscientiously** because mistakes can cost the company a lot of money."

أَنَا دَائِماً أَعمَلُ بِدِقَّةٍ لِأَنَّ الأَخْطَاءَ يُمْكِنُ أَنْ تُكَلِّفَ الشَّرِكَةَ الكَثِيرَ مِنَ المالِ

☞ **NOTE:** the following phrases when **consciousness** refers to '*fainting*':

فَقَدَ الوَعْي: 'to lose consciousness', 'to faint'

عادَ إلى/اسْتَعاد/اسْتَرْجَعَ/ استردَّ وَعْيِه: 'to regain consciousness', 'to come round'

the following expressions:

الوَعْي القَوْمي: 'national consciousness'
ما وَرَاءَ الوَعْي: 'the subconscious'
اللاوَعْي: 'the unconscious'
عَنْ غَيْر وَعْي: 'unconsciously'

Contemptible/contemptuous

Contemptible means *'worthy of contempt'*, while **contemptuous** (which collocates with the preposition **of**) denotes the showing or feeling of contempt, i.e. disdainful. In Arabic, this difference is rendered through active and passive participles of the relevant verbs, respectively. e.g.

"He really is a **contemptible** fellow."

إِنَّهُ حَقّاً شَخْصٌ حَقِيرٌ/مُحْتَقَرٌ/زَرِي

"She was **contemptuous** *of* my actions."

كَانَتْ مُحْتَقِرَةً/مُزْدَرِيَةً لأَفْعَالِي

Continual/continuous/continuation/ continuance/continuity

Continual implies a sequence which is sometimes interrupted (<> **continuous**, which means without interruption); **continuation** refers to the prolongation of an activity. **Continuance** implies duration, perseverance of an action, while in American English it is a legal term for a 'postponement' (or 'adjournment'), especially of a court case. **Continuity** stresses an uninterrupted connection. The translation into Arabic of all generally involves the verbs تَوَاصَلَ or اِسْتَمَرّ. e.g.

"We **continually** tried to call the club chairman."

حاوَلْنا مِراراً أَنْ نَتَّصِلَ بِمُدِيرِ النَّادِي
كُنَّا نُحَاوِلُ بِاسِتمرَار أَن نَتَّصِلَ بِمُدِيرِ النَّادِي

"I was working **continuously**, but I still wasn't able to complete everything on time."

كُنْتُ أَعمَلُ بِاسْتِمرار، وبِالرَّغْم مِن ذلِكَ لَمْ أَتَمَكَّنْ مِن إِكَمالِ كُلِّ شَيْءٍ في الوَقْتِ المُناسِب بِالرَّغْم مِن أَنَّني كُنْتُ أعْمَلُ بِشَكلٍ مُتَواصِل، إلا أَنَّني لَمْ أَتَمَكَنَّ مِن إِتْمام كُلِّ شَيْءٍ في الوَقْتِ المُناسِبْ

"The Judge granted a **continuance** to the defence lawyer so that he could interview more witnesses."

مَنَحَ القَاضِي مُحامِي الدِّفاع مُدَّةً أَطْوَلَ لِيَسْتَمِرَّ في اِسْتِجْواب المَزيد مِن الشُّهُودِ/لِيَتَمَكنَ مِن اِسْتِجْواب شُهُودٍ آخَرِينَ

"It was only thanks to the **continuity** of our efforts that we were able to achieve the desired results."

يَعُودُ الفَضْلُ في تَحْقيق النَّتائِج المَرجُوَّةِ/المَرْغُوب فيها بِالدرجة الأُولى إلى تواصل جُهُودِنَا

"One of the most important things to a bank in determining its loan policy is the **continuity** of management in a firm."

إنَّ اِسْتِمراريةَ الإدارَةِ في شَركَةٍ ما هُوَ المِقْياسُ الَّذي تَعْتَمِدُ عَلَيْه البُنُوكُ في مَنْحِها القُرُوض

"After the war, there was a **continuation** of the peace process."

لَقَدْ اِسْتَمَرَّت عَمَلِيَّةُ السَّلام بَعْدَ الحَرْب

"Broadly speaking, one may say that every child is legitimate which is born during the **continuance** of a marriage or within due time afterwards."

بِشَكلٍ عامٍّ، يُمْكِنُ لِلمَرْءِ أَنْ يَقُولَ بِأَنَّ الطِّفْلَ الشَّرعِيَّ هُوَ الَّذي يُولَدُ خِلال الفَتْرَة التي كانَ فيها الزَّواجُ قائماً أَوْ خِلال فَتْرَةٍ مُناسِبَةٍ/مَعْقُولَة بَعْدَ ذلِكَ

Conversation/conversant

A **conversation** is a noun meaning discussion, while **conversant** (**with**) is an adjective synonymous with **familiar** (with). The former is rendered in Arabic as

حوار, مُكالمة (if it involves talking over the telephone) or حَديث (which is also used for 'interview'), whereas the latter translates as one of the following: مُطّلِع على e.g. ..,واقِف على ,مُلِمّ بـ ,ماهِر بـ ,خَبير في

انْتَقَدَ الصَّحَفِيُّ الوَزيرَ انْتِقاداً لاذِعاً خِلالَ الحَديثِ/ المقابلة/الحَديث الصّحفي/الحديث الإذاعي

"During the **interview**, the journalist severely criticized the minister."

إنَّ المُكالَماتِ مِنَ الهاتِفِ الأرْضِيِّ إلى المَحْمُولِ في مُعْظَمِ الحالاتِ أرْخَصُ بِكَثيرٍ مِنَ المُكالَماتِ مِنَ المَحْمُولِ إلى المَحْمُولِ

"**Calls** from a landline to a mobile are much cheaper in most cases than those between mobiles."

إنّها لا تَحْتاجُ إلى أيِّ تَفْسيرٍ/شَرح إذ أنها مُطّلِعةٌ عَلَى مَبادِئ الهَنْدَسةِ المِكانيكيّةِ

"You don't need to give her any explanation since she is **conversant** with the principles of mechanical engineering."

Correlative particles and conjuncts

In many cases, Arabic particles come in 'discontinuous' or 'split' form, in that there is a second – usually – obligatory element that has to be added later on in the sentence.

This is of particular relevance to Arabic-English-Arabic translation since the same phenomenon is quite rare in English. We have already encountered some of them (see e.g. **ALTHOUGH/...**). The list below lists some other common ones, each with examples of the possible structures.

Translation	Example	Second term	First term
Will you be going to the cinema or the lecture?	أَتَذْهَبُ إلى السِّينما أَمْ إلى المُحاضَرةِ؟	أَم	أ
Would you like to go out or watch television?	هَلْ تُريدُ الخُروجَ أَوْ مُشاهَدةَ التِلفازِ؟	أَوْ	
If you're going to the club, I'll come along.	إذا ذَهَبْتَ إلى النَّادي فَسَأَذْهَبُ مَعَك	فَ	إذا
Besides plays Shakespeare wrote many famous poems.	لَقَدْ كَتَبَ شكسبير مَسْرَحِيَّات وإلى جانِب ذلك فَقَدْ كَتَبَ أشعاراً كَثيرةً مَشْهورةً	(فَ)	[+DEM] إلى جانِب
My father works at a bank, while my mother is a housewife.	والِدي مُوَظَّفٌ في البَنْكِ أمَّا وَالِدَتي فهي رَبَّة بَيْتٍ	فَ	أمَّا
Either you pay the fine, or you'll have to go to jail.	إمَّا أَنْ تَدْفَعَ الغَرامَةَ أَوْ تَدْخُلَ السِّجْنَ	أَوْ	إمَّا
In the coming days there will either be an agreement between the government and the opposition, or a deepening of the crisis.	الأَيَّام المُقْبِلة سَتَشْهَدُ إمَّا اتِّفاقاً بَيْنَ الحُكومة والمُعارَضةِ وإمَّا تَفاقُماً في الأَزَمَةِ	وإمَّا	
Either you agree to the new proposal, or you hand in your resignation.	إمَّا أَنْ تَقْبَلَ المُقْتَرَحَ الجَديدَ وإمَّا أَنْ تَسْتَقيلَ مِن مَنْصِبِكَ	وإمَّا أَنْ	إمَّا أَنْ/أَنَّ
Either the teacher doesn't know, or he pretends not to.	إمَّا أَنَّ الأُسْتاذَ لا يَعْرِفُهُ وإمَّا أَنَّهُ يَتَجاهَلُهُ	وَ إمَّا أَنَّ	
Either he is really ill, or he's faking it.	إمَّا أَنَّهُ مَريضٌ حَقاً أَوْ أَنَّهُ يَتَمارَضُ	أَوْ أَنَّ	

127

Translation	Example	Second term	First term
Either you come to me, or I'll come to you.	إِمَّا أَنْ تَزُورَنَا أَوْ أَنْ أَزُورَكَ أَنَا	أَوْ أَنْ	
If he has enough money, he'll buy a car.	إِنْ كَانَ مَعَهُ مَالٌ فَسَوْفَ يَشْتَرِي سَيَّارة	فَـ	إِنْ
Wherever you go in the world, you see scenes of misery.	أَيْنَما ذَهَبْتَ في العَالَمِ فَسَتَجِدُ مَظاهِرَ البُؤْسِ	(فَـ)	أَيْنَما
Ali is a handsome young man, but he is also very modest.	عَلِي شابٌّ وَسِيمٌ وبِالإضافة إلى ذلكَ فَهُوَ مُتَواضِعٌ جداً	(فَـ)	(وَ) بِالإضافةِ إلى
Despite being ill, he still attended the meeting.	بِالرَّغْمِ مِنْ أَنَّهُ مَرِيضٌ فَقَدْ حَضَرَ الاِجْتِماعَ	(فَـ)	بِالرَّغْمِ مِنْ (أَنَّ)
Despite the lack of options, the labour market has witnessed great development	بِرَغْمِ قِلَّة الإمْكانيات فَقَدْ شَهِدَ سُوقُ العَمَلِ تَطَوُّراً عَظِيماً	(فَـ)	بِرَغْمِ (أَنَّ)
Since/as the weather is nice, we will go for a stroll in the park	بِما أَنَّ الطَّقْسَ جَمِيلٌ فَإنَّا سَنَذْهَبُ إلى النُّزْهَةِ في الحَدِيقَةِ العَامَّة	أَنَّ	بِما أَنَّ
There are many problems between Ali and Omar.	هُناكَ مَشاكِلُ كَثِيرَةٌ بَيْنَ عَلِي وَبَيْنَ عُمَرَ	وَبَيْنَ	بَيْنَ
Wherever you go, you are made to feel welcome.	حَيْثُما ذَهَبْتَ فَسَتَجِدُ التَّرْحِيبَ	(فَـ)	حَيْثُما
Despite announcing its bankruptcy, the company is still paying its staff.	رغْمَ أنَّ الشَّرِكَةَ أَعْلَنَتْ إفْلاسَها فَإنَّها لا تَزالُ تَدْفَعُ رَواتِبَ المُوَظَّفِينَ	(فَـ)	(رَغْمَ أَنَّ)

Translation	Example	Second term	First term
It becomes difficult to remember things, regardless of whether they are happy or painful memories.	يَصْعُبُ تَذَكُّرُ الأُمُورِ سَوَاءَ كَانَتْ سَعِيدَةً أَمْ مُؤْلِمَةً	أَمْ	سَوَاءَ
The message has to be conveyed, either directly or indirectly.	يَجِبُ إِبْلَاغُ الرِّسَالَةِ سَوَاءَ تَصْرِيحاً أَوْ تَلْمِيحاً	أَوْ	سَوَاءَ سَوَاءَ
Everyone was there, both rich and poor.	حَضَرَ كُلُّ النَّاسِ سَوَاءَ أَغْنِيَاءَ وَفُقَرَاءَ	وَ	
In addition to being a talented author, he is also a generous man.	إِنَّهُ كَاتِبٌ بَارِعٌ وَفَوْقَ ذلِكَ فَهُوَ إِنسَانٌ كَرِيمٌ	فَ	فَوْقَ [+DEM]
Neither the first nor the second contestant could finish the race	لا المُتَسابِقُ الأَوَّلُ وَلا الثاني تَمَكَّنَ مِنْ إِنْهَاءِ السِّباق	وَلا	لا
I want nothing except my freedom.	لا أُرِيدُ شيئاً إلا الحُرِّيَّة	إلّا	
It is not that I only like classical literature; I also like detective stories.	لا أُحِبُّ الكُتُبَ الأَدَبِيَّةَ القَدِيمَةَ فَحَسْبُ بَلْ الكُتُبَ البُولِيسِيَّةَ أَيْضاً	فَحَسْبُ/ فَقَط، بَلْ ... أَيْضاً	
I have not been to China or to India.	لَمْ أُسافِرْ إلى الصِّين وَلا إلى الهِنْد	وَلا	لَمْ
If he had studied he would have succeeded	لَوْ دَرَسَ لَنَجَحَ	لَ	لَوْ
If he studies he will succeed.	لَوْ يَدْرُسْ فَيَنْجَحُ	فَ	
	لَوْ يَدْرُسْ سَوفَ يَنْجَحُ	سَوفَ	
	لَوْ يَدْرُسْ سَيَنْجَحُ	سَ	
If he studies he may succeed	لَوْ دَرَسَ لَنَجَحَ	قَدْ	

Translation	Example	Second term	First term
If he had not studied, he would not have succeeded	لَوْ لَمْ يَدْرُسْ ما نَجَحَ	ما	
I do not agree with either solution.	لَنْ أَرْضَى بِهذا الْحَلِّ وَلا بِذاكَ	وَلا	لَنْ
I am not going to seek advice from a solicitor, nor am I going to take any legal action against him.	لَنْ أَسْتَشيرَ الْمُحامِيَ وَلَنْ أَتَّخِذَ أَيَّ إِجْراءٍ قانونِيٍّ ضِدَّهُ	وَلَنْ	
I shall be going to Syria as well as to Lebanon. (I shall be going to both Syria and Lebanon)	لَنْ أُسافِرَ إِلَى سُوريا فَحَسْبُ بَلْ إِلَى لُبْنانَ أَيْضاً	فَحَسْبُ/ فَقَط، بَلْ ... أَيْضاً	
This is merely a temporary situation.	لَيْسَ هذا إِلا حَلاً مُؤَقَّتاً	إِلا	لَيْسَ
Naguib Mahfouz's novels are famous not just in the Middle East, but all over the whole world.	إِنَّ رِوايات نَجيب مَحْفوظ مَشْهورَةٌ لَيْسَ في الشَّرْقِ الأَوْسَطِ فَحَسْبُ بَلْ في جَميعِ أَنْحاءِ العالَمِ أَيْضاً	فَحَسْبُ/ فَقَط، بَلْ ... أَيْضاً	
His proposal is nothing more than a trick to foil the scheme.	لَيْسَ اقْتِراحُهُ سِوَى حِيلةٍ لِإفْشالِ الْمَشْروعِ	سِوَى	
The symptoms you are suffering from are not related to cancer or an ulcer.	الأَعْراضُ الَّتي تَشْكو مِنها لَيْسَ لَها عَلاقَةٌ بِالسَّرَطانِ وَلا بِالْقُرحَةِ	وَلا	
This is nothing but wastage.	ما هذا إِلا مِياهُ الصَّرْفِ	إِلا	ما
I want compensation instead of sympathy.	ما أُريدُ التَّعاطُفَ بَلْ أُريدُ تَعْويضاً	بَلْ	

Translation	Example	Second term	First term
No sooner did he see me, than he greeted me.	ما إِنْ رَآنِي حَتَّى سَلَّمَ عَلَيَّ	حَتَّى	ما إِنْ
As soon as I heard the call to prayer, I stopped working.	ما أَنْ سَمِعْتُ الأَذانَ حَتَّى أَنْهَيْتُ شُغْلِي	حَتَّى	ما أَنْ
It is only a few moments before the herds of buffaloes return to the area.	ما هِيَ إِلاَّ لَحْظاتٌ حَتَّى عادَتْ جُمُوعُ الجَوامِيسَ إلى المِنْطقة	حَتَّى	ما هِيَ إِلاَّ
Even though the method is scientifically sound, it's difficult to apply.	مَهْما كانَ المَنْهَجُ سَلِيماً مِنَ النّاحِيَة العِلْمِيَّة فإِنَّ تَطْبِيقَهُ صَعْبٌ جِدّاً	فَ	مَهْما
Although the questions are difficult, I am certain he will pass.	مَعَ أَنَّ الأَسْئِلَة صَعْبَةٌ فأَنا مُتَأَكِّدٌ مِنْ نَجاحِه	فَ	مَعَ أَنَّ
Although the situation is complicated, I am sure we'll succeed.	مَعَ أَنَّ الظُّرُوفَ مُعَقَّدةٌ إلا أَنَّنِي مُتَأَكِّدٌ مِنْ نَجاحِنا	إلاَ أَنْ	
Given the economic conditions, there is a need for rationalizing expenditure.	نَظَراً للظُّرُوف الاقْتِصادِيَّة فَتَرشِيدُ الإِنَفاقِ مَطْلُوبٌ	فَ	نَظَراً لِ

Credible/creditable

Credible means 'believable' (مُصَدَّق، مَوْثُوق)؛ **creditable** is synonymous with 'praiseworthy, commendable' (مَشْكُور، فاضِل، حَمُود، حَمِيد). e.g.

"These words are neither convincing nor **credible**."

هذا الكَلامُ غَيْرُ مُقْنِعٍ وَغَيْرُ مُصَدَّقٍ

"Everything was satisfactory thanks to the **creditable**/praiseworthy individual efforts."

كُلُّ شَيْءٍ كانَ عَلَى ما يُرامُ بِفَضْلِ الجُهُودِ المَشْكُورةِ لِبَعْضِ الأَفْرادِ

> ☞ **NOTE**: whilst the negative of **credible** is **incredible**, **creditable** can only be negated by 'not', i.e. **not creditable** (NOT *'un-/increditable').

Criticism/critic/critique/critical

Criticism refers to *'disapproval'* (نَقْد); a **critic** is a person whose job it is to evaluate books, plays, etc. (ناقِد, pl. نُقَّاد). A **critique** can be synonymous with a *review* but tends to refer to an academic article or book criticizing something; **critical** is an adjective meaning *'crucial'* (حاسِم, حَرِج, فاصِل) or *'a negative opinion'* (usually followed by the preposition **of**; انْتِقادِي). e.g.

"Al-Sharuni is a major literary **critic**, who reviews novels, plays and short stories."

الشَّارُونِي ناقِدٌ أَدَبِيٌّ مُهِمٌّ في نَقْدِ الرِّواية وَفُنُونِ الدارما وَالقِصَّةِ القَصِيرة
الشَّارُونِي مِن أَهمِّ نُقّادِ الأَدَبِ في مَجالِ الرِّوايةِ والدارما وَالقِصَّةِ القَصِيرة

"The French newspaper *Le Monde* published an article last week **criticizing** the politicization of Egyptian courts. The newspaper was **critical** of the decision made by the previous government."

نَشَرَت جَرِيدة (لوموند) الفَرَنْسِيَّةُ في عَدَدِها الصَّادِرِ الأُسْبُوعَ الماضِي مَقالاً يَنْتَقِدُ
تَسْيِيسَ المَحاكِمِ المِصْرِيَّةِ. كانَتِ الجَرِيدةُ انْتِقادِيَّةً لِقَرارِ الحُكُومةِ السَّابِقة

"The book contains a **critique** on pre-Islamic poetry by the late Taha Hussein."

يَحْتَوِي الكِتَابُ عَلَى مَقالةٍ أَدَبِيَّةٍ بِقَلَمِ المَرْحُومِ طَهَ حُسَيْنْ حَوْلَ الشِّعْرِ في الجَاهِلِيَّةِ

"This is the company that faced formidable chanllenges in a **critical** economic phase."

هذِهِ هِيَ المُؤَسَّسُةُ الَّتِي وَاجَهَت تَحَدِّياتٍ عَظِيمةً في مَرْحَلَةِ اقْتِصادِيَّةٍ حَرِجَةٍ

"The American University in Beirut played a **critical** role for many decades."

لَعِبَت الجامِعةُ الأَمْرِيكِيَّةُ في بَيْرُوتَ دَوْراً حاسِماً في عُقُودٍ مُتَعَدِّدةٍ

"The newspaper was **critical** of the decision made by the previous government."

كانَتِ الجَرِيدةُ انْتِقادِيَّةً/مُنتقِدَةً/ناقِدةً لِقَرارِ الحُكُومة السَّابِقة

Cry/shout/weep/sob

Cry can mean either to shout or to scream (e.g. out of fear, surprise or pain) – in which case it is often followed by the preposition out – or 'to produce tears because of sadness'; '**to weep**' is the formal equivalent of the second meaning of '**to cry**', whereas '**to shout**' simply means to say something in a very loud voice. '**To sob**' means to cry in short bursts.

These are generally rendered into Arabic as follows:

to cry, weep	بَكَى (over sth/s.o., على)

to shout, cry (out)	(i) صاحَ
	(a) زَعَقَ
	صَرَخَ (u) (often for help)
	هَتَفَ i(i) (often for joyous reasons)
to sob	نَهْنَهَ
	(i) شَهَقَ
	(i) نَشَجَ
	(i) نَحَبَ
	اِنْتَحَبَ

e.g.

"He saw his father **sobbing**, the tears rolling down his cheeks."

رَأى أباهُ يَنْشِجُ ودُمُوعُه تَتَساقَطُ عَلَى وَجْنَتَيْهِ

"Nobody is **crying** over our children that are being killed on a daily basis."

لا أَحَد يَبْكِي عَلَى أوْلادِنا الَّذينَ يُقْتَلُون يَوْمِيًّا

"They were surprised when one of the occupants of the car **shouted**: 'The elections are rigged!'"

فُوجِئوا بِأَحَدِ رُكَّابِ السَّيَّارةِ يَصيحُ مِن داخِلِها قائِلاً:«الاِنْتِخاباتُ مُزَوَّرةٌ!»

Note the figurative meanings of **cry** and **shout** in the following phrases:

- **cry out + to+ infinitive/for + noun** ('*to be in great need of*'). e.g.

☞**NOTE** the following expressions:

'to break into tears', أَشْهَقَ/اِنْفَطَرَ بِالبُكاءِ
'to break into sobs' /'be on the verge of tears': أَجْهَشَ بِالبُكاءِ
'to cry bitterly', بَكَى بُكاءً مُرّاً
'to cry crocodile tears', بَكَى بِدُمُوعِ التِّمْساحِ

"This car is **crying out** to be cleaned!"

إِنَّ السَّيّارَةَ فِي أَمَسِّ الحاجةِ إِلى التَّنْظيفِ

* **cry off** ('*to cancel*'). e.g.

"When the manager suffered a heart attack, they **cried off** holding the meeting."

أَلْغَوا الاِجْتِماعَ لَمّا أُصِيبَ المُدِيرُ بِأَزْمةٍ قَلْبِيّةٍ

* **shout down** ('*to silence someone by shouting at them*'). e.g.

"The president of the council **shouted down** members of the opposition and threatened them with expulsion from the hall."

أَسْكَتَ رَئِيسُ المَجْلِسِ المُعارِضِينَ وَهَدَّدَهُم بِطَرْدِهِم/بِإِخْراجِهِم مِن القاعةِ

* **shout out** ('to announce in a loud voice'). e.g.

"The minister **shouted out** the results of the ballot."

أَعْلَنَ الوَزِيرُ نَتائِجَ القُرْعةِ بِصَوْتٍ عالٍ

Dare/dare say

Dare denotes having the courage to do something or to take a risk, and is translated into Arabic by جَسَرَ عَلَى (u), جَرُؤَ على (u), تَجَرَّأ عَلَى, تَجَاسَرَ عَلى.

"When you come back, no-one will **dare** to behave in this way."

حِينَ تَعُودُ لا يَجْرُأُ أَحَدٌ عَلَى التَّصَرُّفِ بِهذِه الطَّرِيقة

"Will there be anyone who **dares** to skive or feign illness?"

وهَلْ سَيَكُونُ أَحَداً يَجْرُأُ عَلَى التَّهَرُّبِ مِن العَمَل والتَّظاهُرِ بِالمَرَض

"He doesn't dare to commit the same crime again."

لا يَتَجَرَّأُ عَلَى ارْتِكابِ جُرْمِهِ مَرَّةً أُخْرَى

"Will they, unlike their fathers, **dare** to change this corrupt system?"

هَلْ سَيَتَجرَأُونَ عَلَى عَكْسِ آبائِهِم عَلَى تَغْيِيرِ هذا النِّظامِ الْفَاسِدِ؟

From a grammatical point of view, 'dare' (like '**need**') can also be used as a modal, in which case it has only one form, and tends to occur only in negative contexts and in questions. e.g.

"He **daren't** visit his friend."

لا يَجْسُرُ عَلَى زِيارةِ صَدِيقِه

The expression 'I **dare** say (or **daresay**) ', which is only used in the first person singular, means '*I suppose*' or '*it is (quite) possible that*'. e.g.

"I **dare say** the main issue that gave rise to controversy and lengthy debate is that related to the nomination."

أَحْسَبُ أَنَّ أَهَمَّ الأُمُورِ التي دارَ حَوْلَها جَدَلٌ وَحِوارٌ طَوِيلٌ هِيَ الَّتِي تَتَعَلَّقُ بِالتَّرْشِيح

أَظُنَّ أَنَّ أَهَمَّ الأُمُور التي أَدَّت إلى جِدَالٍ وَحِوارٍ طَويل هِوَ الأَمرُ المُتَعَلِّقُ بالتَّرْشيحاتِ

Definite/definitive

Definite denotes certainty and/or clarity; **definitive** is synonymous with **final**. In Arabic, قاطع or قَطْعي can be used to render both, with مُحَدَّد also being possible for 'definite'. e.g.

"It is necessary for the judge to render a **definitive** judgement in this matter."

إِنَّهُ مِنَ الضَّروريِّ أَنْ يُصْدِرَ القاضِي حُكْمَهُ النِّهائيّ/القاطعَ/القَطْعيّ في هذِه القَضِيَّةِ

"He couldn't get a **definite** reply, either negative or affirmative, before the meeting of the committee."

لَمْ يَحصُل عَلَى أَجوبةٍ قاطعةٍ سَواءَ بالنَّفي أَوْ بالإيجابِ قَبْلَ اجْتِماعِ اللَجْنةِ

"The government has a **definite** responsibility."

هُناكَ مَسْوُوليَّةٌ مُحَدَّدَةٌ أمامَ الحُكومةِ

Depend/dependent/dependant

The adjective derived from the verb to **depend** (= 'to rely on') is **dependent** (**on**), whereas **dependant** is a noun denoting somebody who relies on somebody else for food, money, etc. In Arabic, the usual verbs in this context are(عَلى) عَوَّلَ when it involves 'relying on someone for sustenance' (cf. عالة and عِيال, **dependants**). This is also the root of the word for 'family', عائلة, as this means 'those

137

who are dependent on someone for sustenance', whereas in some dialects (e.g. Egyptian) عَيِّل is a word for 'child'. In general contexts, اِعْتَمَدَ عَلَى is used. e.g.

"The country's citizens were **dependent (up) on** cooperative societies."

كانَ المُواطِنُونَ مُعَوِّلِينَ عَلَى الجَمْعِيَّاتِ التَّعاوُنِيَّة

"The factory **relies on** ethylene oxide and ammonia for its production."

يَعْتَمِدُ المَصْنَعُ في إِنْتاجِهِ عَلَى أُوكْسِيدِ الايِثِيلِين والأَمُونِيا

The negatives **independence** and **independent** pose some potential pitfalls for the translator who may be tempted to render then as اِسْتِقْلال and مُسْتَقِلّ; in fact, this translation is only possible in a political context. In the sense of not needing sustenance or support, they should be more appropriately rendered as غَير مُعَوِّل or عَلَى, اِكْتَفَى ذاتِياً (مُكْتَفٍ ذاتِياً). e.g.

"The scholar created the theory **independent of**/without relying on philosophy."

كانَ الباحِثُ يُبْدِعُ غَيْرَ مُعَوِّلٍ عَلَى الفَلْسَفة

☞ **NOTE: dependence** is followed by **on**, while **independent(ly)** and **independence** take the prepositions **of** and **from**, respectively.

Disinterested/uninterested

Disinterested refers to impartiality (نَزاهة), whereas **uninterested** denotes a lack of interest or indifference (لا مُبالاة، عَدَمُ الاِهْتِمام). e.g.

"A **disinterested** judiciary is the only guarantee for freedom in public life."

نَزاهةُ القُضاةِ هِيَ الضَّمانَةُ الوَحيدَةُ للحُرِّيَّةِ في الحَياةِ العامَّة

"It is clear he is completely **uninterested** in this initiative."

يَبْدُو لِي أَنَّهُ غَيْرُ مُهْتَمٍّ بَتاتاً بِهذِهِ المُبَادَرةِ
وَاضِحٌ أَنَّهُ غَيْرُ مُهْتَمٍّ بَتاتاً بِهذِهِ المُبَادَرةِ

"This was the result of negligence and **indifference** to the difficult conditions in which the people were living."

كانَتْ هذِهِ نَتِيجةَ الإهْمالِ وَاللامُبالاةِ بالظُّرُوفِ الصَّعْبةِ الَّتِي يَعِيشُها الشَّعْبُ

Distinct/distinctive

Distinct means 'clear' or 'separate from'; **distinctive** means 'serving to distinguish'. In Arabic, these may be rendered by مُبِين، مُمَيَّز and مُتَمَيِّز. e.g.

"This perfume doesn't have a **distinct** odour."

لَيْسَ لِهذا العِطْرِ رِيحةٌ مُمَيَّزةٌ

"Does she have any **distinctive** features?"

هَلْ تَتَمَتَّعُ هي بِصِفاتٍ مُمَيَّزةٍ؟

Disused/misuse/abuse

Disused means 'no longer used', **misused** denotes 'not used in the way it is supposed to be used', whereas **abuse** refers to 'maltreat'. 'injure' or 'insult'. e.g.

"**Misuse** of the equipment constitutes a health hazard."

إنَّ سُوءَ اسْتِعْمالِ/اسْتِخْدامِ الجِهازِ يُضرُّ بالصَّحّةِ

"EU Ministers are set to impose sanctions over human rights **abuses**."

بدأ وُزَراءُ الاِتِّحادِ الأُوروبِيِّ العَمَلَ لِفَرْضِ عُقُوباتٍ بِشَأْنِ اِنْتِهاكاتِ حُقُوقِ الإِنْسانِ

"The osteoporosis was the result of **disuse** of the bones."

قَدْ أَسْفَرَ عَدَمُ اِسْتِعْمالِ العِظامِ عَنْ تَرَقُّقِ العِظامِ

"He was summoned before the magistrates for sexual **abuse**."

أُسْتُدْعِيَ إِلَى المَحْكِمةِ بِتُهْمةِ التَّحَرُّشِ الجِنْسِيِّ

☞**NOTE** the expression **to fall into disuse** (not 'misuse'!), which is rendered in Arabic as: عَطَّلَ تَعَطَّلَ or (u) بَطَلَ.

During/for/in/since

Both **during** and **in** can be used to refer to periods of time; **in** is used to indicate exactly when something happened, while **during** is used to stress the idea of duration and when referring to an activity, rather than a period. **For** refers to how long something lasts. **Since** denotes the starting point of a period and tends to be translated into Arabic by مُنْذُ.

However, Arabic has a number of adverbs and adverbial phrases to render the same meaning of **during**, **in** and **for**:

إِبّانَ	في غُضُونٍ
في (أَثْناء)	في مُدَّةٍ
خِلالَ	في
طَوالَ	على مَدارِ
طِيلَةَ	مَدَى

e.g.

"he has worked here **for** five years."

يَعمَلُ هُنا مُنْذُ خَمْسِ سَنَواتٍ

[Note the use of the imperfect tense in Arabic!]

"The city will become pollution-free **for** (a period of) three months."

سَتُصْبِحُ المَدينةُ خاليةً مِن التَّلَوُّثِ في غُضُونِ ثلاثةِ شُهُورٍ

"**during** the whole of Tuesday"

طيلة/طوالَ يَوْمِ الثُّلاثاء

"**during** the test"

إبّانَ/(في)/أثناء/في الامْتِحانِ

"The students were talking **during/throughout** the lesson."

كَانَ الطّلابُ يَتَكلَّمُونَ خِلالَ/طيلةَ/إبّانَ/طوالَ الدَّرْسِ

"We do not accept a presidency **for** life!"

لا نَقْبَلُ الرِّئاسةَ مَدَى الحَياةِ!

Note that sometimes there are semantic differences, which means that, for instance, **throughout** and **during** are not always interchangeable; indeed, **throughout** carries a more intensive meaning. For instance, in the above example, the sentence with 'throughout' would imply that they talked incessantly, while the one with 'during' simply denotes that there was talking during the lesson.

Similarly, the Arabic طَوال, طيلة are used to stress a continuous aspect, as opposed to خِلال or أَثناء. There are also restrictions in terms of the referent: في, إبّانَ and أثناء are generally not used with specific numbers. e.g.

في/إبّانَ حَرْبِ التَّحْريرِ للكُوَيْتِ

"**during** the war for the liberation of Kuwait"

خِلالَ أرْبَعةِ أيّامٍ (NOT* في/إبان أربعة أيّامٍ)

"**for** four days."

141

أَثْناءَمؤْتَمَرِ الحِزْبِ الشُّيوعِيِّ الصِّينِيِّ الَّذي عُقِدَ سابِقاً في بِكِين

"**during** the Chinese Communist Party Congress which was previously held in Beijing"

Conversely, مُدّة في is mostly used with numbers, and less with events. e.g.

في مُدّةٍ لا تَتَجاوَزُ شَهْرَيْن

"**for** a period of no more than two months"

The translation of the particle مُنْذُ constitutes a particular pitfall for Arabic-speakers as it is rendered into English as **since** (marking the beginning of a period) or **for** (if it refers to the period). The second problem is that of tense in both cases; as the effects of the activity or event are still present today, they require a **present perfect** in English. e.g.

"She has been in Cairo **since** the beginning of the week."

كانَت في القاهِرة مُنْذُ بِداية الأُسْبُوع

"I have lived here **for** (**NOT** *since!*) three years."

عِشْتُ هُنا مُنْذُ ثَلاثَةِ أَعْوام

Negative interference from Arabic often results in errors of the following type:

* "He is a teacher since 1999." (cf. يَعمَلُ أُسْتَاذاً مُنْذُ عام 1999)
* "He **has been** a teacher **since** 1999."

* "He's a teacher for twenty years." (cf. يَعمَلُ أُستَاذاً مُنْذُ عِشْرينَ سَنَةً.)
* "He **has been** a teacher **for** twenty years."

142

Each/every

Each is used when referring to the individual members of a group, **every** when considering a whole group, or when making general statements. Only **each** can be used before **of**, or after a subject. In Arabic, both are rendered by كُلّ, often followed by the preposition مَنْ. e.g.

"**Every** six months."

كُلُّ سِتَّةِ أَشْهُرٍ

"**Each** of them went out."

كُلُّ مِنْهُم خَرَجَ

"**Each** of them is totally different from the other."

كُلُّ مِنْهُما يَخْتَلِفُ تَماماً عَن الآخَرِ

"The students **each** handed in their assignments."

سَلَّمَ كُلُّ طالِبٍ وَظِيفَتَهُ/واجِبَهُ

Each other/one another

Contrary to popular belief, these two phrases, which express reciprocity, can be used interchangeably in English, despite the myth that **each other** can only apply to two people and **one another** to more than two. In Arabic, this is expressed in one of two ways, i.e. by a Form VI verb (e.g. تَحارَبَ, 'to fight each other') or by means of بَعْض, which is a definite noun and therefore does not take the definite article (cf. كُلّ). It occurs either by itself (with or pronoun), with a second بَعْض which then requires a pronoun, or is put in the accusative case (بَعْضاً). e.g.

They wrote to **each other** every day."

كانُوا يَتَراسَلُونَ كُلَّ يَوْمٍ

"We understand **each other** /one another."

نَفْهَمُ بَعْضُنا بَعْضاً

"And because of this, the inhabitants of the building do not know **each other**/one another."

ولِذَلِكَ فَسُكّانُ العِمارَةِ لا يَعْرِفُونَ بَعْضُهُم بَعْضا

"The balconies are arranged on top of **each other**/one another."

الشُّرَفاتُ مَبْنِيةٌ بَعْضُها فَوْقَ بَعْضِها
الشُّرَفاتُ مَبْنِيةٌ بَعْضُها فَوْقَ بَعْضٍ

☞ **NOTE:**

i.   بَعْضاً can only be used with بَعْض when there is no preposition after the verb as in this case بعضا is treated like an object of the verb.

ii. if a verb requires a preposition, the latter must come immediately after the verb. In addition, it is NOT possible to use بَعْضاً in these contexts. e.g.

أنضَمَّ بَعْضُهم إلى بَعْضٍ
(NOT* أنضموا إلى بعضهم)
"They joined forces with each other."

iii. In Media Arabic, it is, however, not uncommon to find بَعْض with البَعْض. e.g.

"He prohibited them from using their forces against **each other**/ one another."

مَنَعَهُمْ مِن اِسْتِخْدامِ قُوَّاتِهِمْ ضِدَّ بَعْضِها البَعْضِ

"To be sure, the two injuries were related to **each other**/one another."

بِالتَّأْكِيدِ الإِصابَتانِ مُرْتَبِطَتانِ بِبَعْضِهِما بَعْضاً

In Modern Arabic, it has become customary to add the pronoun, even with Form VI verbs. e.g.

"The government agencies are competing with **each other**/one another."

إِنَّ الوكالاتِ الحُكومِيَّةَ تَتَنافَسُ بَعْضُها مَعَ بَعْضٍ

إِنَّ الوكالاتِ الحُكومِيَّةَ يُنافِسُ بَعْضُها بَعْضاً

"These words contradict **each other**."

هذِهِ الكَلِماتُ تَتَناقَضُ بَعْضُها بَعْضاً

In some cases the English verb already has an inherent quality of reciprocity and it is possible, therefore, to omit 'each other/one another' in translation. e.g.

"This is a very important and busy road, which links several villages (with one another/each other)."

هذا الطَّريقُ هامٌّ جِدّاً وَحَيَوِيٌّ وَيَرْبُطُ عِدَّة قُرَى مَعَ بَعْضِها

هذا الطَّريقُ هامٌّ جِدّاً وَحَيَوِيٌّ وَيَرْبُطُ عِدَّة قُرَى بَعْضَها بِبَعْضٍ

"All of them were mixed together (with **each other**)."

كانُوا جَميعاً مُخْتَلِطِينَ بَعْضُهم بِبَعْضٍ/بَعْضِهِم بَعْضاً

☞ Also see 'Self'

Eatable/edible

Strictly speaking, **eatable** refers to food which is in a fit condition to be eaten, whereas **edible** (<> inedible) refers to food which is fit for human consumption. In practice, however, the distinction has blurred and both are increasingly used as synonyms. Note that only the latter can take a plural, **edibles.**

In Arabic, there is a similar difference with **eatable** being rendered by قابِلٌ للأَكْلِ and **edible** by صالِحٌ للأَكْلِ. e.g.

"There is a type of alfa that is **edible.**"

هُناكَ نَوْعٌ مِنَ الحَلْفاءِ قابِلٌ للأَكْلِ

"He said that the lamb (meat) was sound and **eatable.**"

قالَ إنَّ لَحْمَ الأَغْنامِ سَلِيمٌ وصالِحٌ للأَكْلِ

Economic/economical

Economic refers to the economy, whereas **economical** means using time or money without waste. In Arabic, the most usual translation for both is اقْتِصادِيّ. e.g.

"He made it clear that the **economic** situation had an impact on may fields."

أَوْضَحَ أنَّ الحالَةَ الاقْتِصادِيَّةَ تُؤْثِّرُ كَثيراً عَلى مَجالاتٍ عَديدةٍ

"The reader will find a list of the ten most **economical** cars on the next page."

يَجِدُ القارِئُ في الصفحة التالية قائمةً بأَفْضَلِ 10 سَيَّاراتٍ اقْتِصادِيَّة

Sometimes, **economical** can be translated, simply, as رَخِيصٌ ('cheap'). e.g.

"What is the most **economical** way of travel?"

ما أَرْخَصُ طَرِيقَةٍ لِلسَّفَرِ؟ (lit.: 'what is the cheapest way of travelling?")

Effective/efficient/efficacious

Effective refers to the producing of an effect; **efficient** denotes action aimed at minimizing loss and waste of energy; **efficacious** is a formal equivalent of **effective**. The translation. The usual translations for **effective** are فاعل and فَعَّال (فَعالِيَّة, 'effectiveness'), which are also sometimes used to render **efficient**, though this is more properly translated by مُقْتَدِر or كُفْء. e.g.

"The government has carried out **effective** measures in order to deal with bribery."

تَقُومُ الحُكومةُ بِإجْراءاتٍ فاعِلةٍ في مُواجَهةِ الرَّشْوةِ

"Aspirin is an **effective** drug against headaches."

الأَسْبِرينُ دَواءٌ فَعَّالٌ ضِدَّ الصُّداعِ

"The foreign trading policy of the countries in the Union has proven its great **effectiveness**."

إنَّ السِّياسةَ التِّجاريَّةَ الخارِجيَّةَ لِدُوَلِ الاتِّحادِ الأُوروبي قَدْ أَثْبَتَتْ فعاليَّةً كَبيرَةً

"He was trained by **efficient** (or capable!) teachers."

كانَ يَأْخُذُ عِلْمَهُ عَنْ مُعَلِّمينَ مُقْتَدِرينَ

"This is the most fuel **efficient** car."

هذِهِ السَّيَّارةُ الأَكْثَرُ كَفاءةً في اِسْتِهْلاكِ الوُقُودِ

147

Either/neither

Just like **both** (q.v.), **either** should only be used when two elements are involved. e.g. "either John or Sarah' (NOT *'either John or Sarah or David'). In formal English writing, **either** is followed by a singular verb. In Arabic **either … or** is translated as: إمّا … أو/وَإمّا, though in some cases a simple أوْ is also possible. e.g.

"**Either** you are with us **or** against us."

إمّا أَنْ تَكُونَ مَعَنا أوْ ضِدّنا

"**Either** victory **or** death!"

إمّا النَّصْرُ وَإمّا المَوْتُ

"We are faced with two choices: **either** to accept these threats **or** to sign the document."

كُنَّا أَمامَ أَمْرَيْنِ، إمّا القُبُولُ بهذا التَّهْدِيدِ، وَإمّا أَنْ نُوَقِّعَ الوَثِيقَةَ

"It was **either** John **or** Sarah who attended the conference."

لَقَدْ حَضَرَ المُؤْتَمَرَ إمّا جون أو سارا

In the case of an exclusive choice of more than two elements, English uses commas, with 'or' preceding the last element; in Arabic, each element is preceded by أ. وَ e.g:

"He saw James, John, Sarah, Elisabeth or Peter – I'm not sure."

رَأَى جيمس أَوْ جون أَمْ سارا أَوْ إلزابِث أَوْ بُطْرُس، لَسْتُ مُتَأَكِّداً

In order to render **either of**, أَحَدُ مِن or أَيٌّ مِن is used. e.g.

أَيٌّ مِن المُوَظَّفَيْنِ

"**Either of** the employees." (OR: "One of the [2] employees']

"**Either of** them has to clean up the mess."

يَجِبُ على أَحَدٍ مِنْهُما أَنْ يُنَظِّفَ القاذُوراتِ

يَجِبُ عَلَى أَحَدِهِما أَنْ يُنَظِّفَ/تَنْظِيفِ القاذُوراتِ

Neither is the negative of **either** and is subject to the same restrictions and rules in terms of number (only two) and agreement (singular verb). In Arabic, there are a number of possible constructions, the most usual of which is by repeating the negative particle لا with the coordinator و. e.g.

"**Neither** in London **nor** in Paris."

لا في لَنْدَنَ ولا في باريسَ

Neither the Hebron nor the Oslo agreement has been implemented.

لَمْ تُنَفَّذْ اِتِّفاقِيَّةُ الخَليلِ وَلا اِتِّفاقُ أُوسْلُو

Neither one is translated into Arabic by أَحَدٌ. e.g.

"**Neither (one)** of us can ride the horse."

لَيْسَ في اِسْتِطاعةِ/مُستَطاعِ أَحَدِنا أَنْ يَرْكَبَ الخَيْلَ

"**Neither (one)** of them is in the house."

لا يُوجَدُ أَحَدٌ مِنهُما في البَيْتِ

Whilst in English **neither...nor** offer an exclusive choice of only two elements, the Arabic construction can be extended to include an unlimited choice, which requires rephrasing in translation. e.g.

"The Egyptians didn't take part, nor did the Algerians, Tunisians and Moroccans."

لَمْ يُشارِك المِصْرِيُّونَ وَلا الجَزائرِيُّونَ وَلا التُّونِسِيُّونَ وَلا المَغارِبةُ

Note the difference in verb form in the two languages – affirmative vs negative – when **either/neither** and **or/nor** do not appear together. e.g.

"Have you done the homework? **Neither/Nor** have I."

هَل عَمِلْتَ الواجِبَ ؟ لَمْ أَعْمَلْهُ أَنا أَيْضاً

Remember that **either** is used for **also** in negative sentences. e.g.

"I have **also** met him."

قابَلْتُهُ أَيْضاً

"I haven't met him **either**."

لَمْ أُقابِلْهُ أَيْضاً

Emigrate/immigrate/migrate

All imply movement of people from their native area to settle (usually) in a foreign place. The most general is **migrate** (> migrant); **emigrate** (> emigrant, emigré) means to migrate **out of** (a place), **immigrate** (> immigrant) denotes an **inward** movement. In other words, the distinction is one of perspective in the sense that one country's emigrant is another's immigrant!

In Arabic, the general verb to denote migration is نَزَحَ مِن/إلى (i, a) (> نازِحٌ), while هاجَرَ (> مُهاجِرٌ), strictly speaking, refers to emigration only, even if in modern Arabic it is also commonly used for immigration. e.g.

"He was born in Poland and **emigrated** as a child to France."

وُلِدَ في بُولَنْدا وهاجَرَ صَغيراً إلى فَرَنْسا

"He studied at the college of Ayn Tura in Lebanon before he left his (native) village and **emigrated** to Cairo."

دَرَسَ في كُلِّيَّةِ عَيْنْطُورةِ اللُّبنانِيَّةِ قَبْلَ أَنْ يَنْزَحَ عَنْ قَرْيَتِهِ/يُغادِرَ قَرْيَتُهُ مُهاجِراً إلى القاهرةِ

"She was born in the United States and **immigrated** here with her mother who was of Egyptian origin."

هِيَ مِنْ مَواليدِ الوِلاياتِ المُتَّحِدةِ فهاجَرَت إلى هُنا مَعَ أُمِّها الّتي كانَت مِصرِيَّةَ الأَصْلِ

"The island asked the European Union for help, especially in light of the increased number of **migrants** there." (Immigrants people who have immigrated.)

اِسْتَغاثَت الجَزيرةُ الاتِّحادَ الأُوروبِيَّ، خاصَّةً في ضَوْءِ تَزَايُدِ أَعْدادِ النّازِحينَ إلى هُناكَ

Note that مُهاجِرُون often denotes **immigrants** or **migrants**. e.g.

"We are second- and third-generation **immigrants**."

نَحْنُ أَبْنَاءُ المُهاجِرِينَ مِن الجِيلِ الثَّاني والثَّالِثِ

"The company's workforce includes many **migrant workers**."

تَشْتَمِلُ الشَّرِكةُ على عَدَدٍ كَبِيرٍ مِن العُمَّالِ المُهاجِرِينَ

Other nouns related to هاجَرَ are هِجْرَة ('*emigration*) and مَهْجَر ('*place of emigration*') both of which have a connotation of 'exile', and هِجْرَة can often be rendered as '*flight*'. In addition, مَهْجَر is a technical term to denote diaspora (esp. the Arab one). e.g.

"The poet decided to visit his homeland Syria for the first time after his **emigration** (after he had emigrated) thirty-eight years earlier."

قَرَّرَ الشَّاعِرُ زِيَارَةَ وَطَنِهِ سُوريا للمَرَّةِ الأُولَى بَعْدَ هِجْرَتِهِ الَّتِي امْتَدَّت ثَمانيةً وَثَلاثِينَ عاماً

"The injustice is that of our sons' **flight** (fleeing) from war in the capital, from one district to another."

الإِجْحافُ هُوَ هُروبُ أَبْنائِنا مِن الحَرْبِ في العاصِمَة مِن حَيٍّ إلى آخَرَ

"Some Coptic **émigrés** (or: members of the Coptic diaspora) are calling for foreign intervention to protect their community."

يَدْعُو بَعْضُ أَقْباطِ المَهْجَرِ إلى التَّدَخُّلِ الأَجْنَبِيِّ لِحِمايةِ مِلَّتِهِم

"The Romantic movement was a revolution and its leaders were authors in the (Arab) **diaspora**."

الحَرَكةُ الرُّومانْتِيكِيَّةُ ثَوْرَةٌ وَرُوَّادُها أَدَباءُ المَهْجَرِ

☞**NOTE** the expression **brain drain**, هِجْرَةُ العُقُول

151

Ensure/insure/assure

To ensure (US: **insure**) is close to guarantee and takes a clause as object; **to insure** means to protect against risk or loss. In an insurance context, **to assure** is the traditional verb used in British English for protection against the loss of something inevitable, which in practice means **life assurance**. However, the American English **life insurance** is increasingly being used.

In Arabic, all can be rendered by أَمَّنَ/تَأْمِين ('insurance'). e.g.

"Our **insurance** company prides itself on the fact that it is the oldest in the Arab world."

تَفْخَرُ شَرِكَتُنا للتَّأْمِينِ بِأَنَّها أَقْدَمُ شَرِكَة تَأْمِينٍ في العالَمِ العَرَبِيِّ

"Every individual is entitled to treatment under the national health **insurance** scheme."

لِكُلِّ فَرْدٍ الحَقُّ في العِلاجِ طِبْقاً لِنِظامٍ/حَسَبَ نِظامِ التَّأْمِينِ الصِّحِّيِّ الوَطَنِيِّ

"The Egyptian electricity network association entered into an agreement with networks from other Arab countries in order to **ensure/guarantee** the supply of electricity for all uses."

قامَت جمعيَّةُ الشَّبَكَةِ المِصْرِيَّةِ للكَهْرَباء بِاتِّفاقِيَّةٍ مَعَ شَبَكاتِ الدُّوَلِ العَرَبِيَّةِ بِهَدَفِ تَأْمِينِ/ تَزْوِيدِ/إمداد الطَاقةِ الكَهْرَبائِيَّةِ لِكافَّةِ الاسْتِخْداماتِ

"I have taken out life **assurance**/insurance since I do try, as much as I possibly can, to **ensure** my sons' future."

عَنْدي تَأْمِينٌ (على) الحَياةِ لأنِّي أُحاوِلُ بِقَدْرِ المُسْتَطاعِ أَنْ أُؤَمِّنَ مُسْتَقْبَلَ أَبْنائى

"I'm one of those people who is no good at planning and life **assurance**/insurance, but I do try, as much as I possibly can, to **ensure** my sons' future."

أنا وَاحِدَةٌ مِن النَّاسِ الَّذِينَ لا يُجِيدُونَ التَّخْطِيطَ وَالتَّأْمِينَ (على) الحَياةِ لَكِنِّى أُحاوِلُ بِقَدْرِ المُسْتَطاعِ أَنْ أُؤَمِّنَ مُسْتَقْبَلَ أَبْنائى

Even/even if/even though/even so

In Arabic, 'even' is usually rendered by the particle حَتَّى, whereas the following noun appears in the same case as the one preceding حَتَّى. Note that حَتَّى can never take a suffix. e.g.

"She took everything, **even** the car."

أَخَذَتْ كُلَّ شَيْءٍ حَتَّى السَّيَّارَةِ

"**Even** he rejected the initiative."

رَفَضَ (الجَّمِيعُ) المُبادَرَةَ، حَتَّى هُوَ

The difference between **even if** and **even though** is that the former denotes hypothesis, whereas the latter refers to an action that has actually taken place. Consider the following examples:

"**Even if** I agree to lend you the money, you still won't have enough for a new car."

حَتَّى لَوْ وافَقْتُ عَلَى إِقْرَاضِكَ المَالَ، فَلَنْ يَكُونَ مَعَكَ مَا يَكْفِي لِشِرَاءِ سَيَّارَةٍ جَدِيدَةٍ

"**Even though** you were there, you didn't say anything when they were criticizing my performance."

بِالرَّغْمِ مِن أَنَّكَ كُنْتَ هُنَاكَ، فَأَنْتَ لَمْ تَقُلْ شَيْئًا عِندَمَا كَانُوا يَنْتَقِدُونَ أَدَائِي

In Arabic, both **even if** and **even though** can be rendered by the following:

حَتَّى وَإِنْ – حَتَّى إِذا – حَتَّى لَوْ – وَإِنْ – وَلَوْ – وَإِنْ كانَ

☞ **NOTE:** Arabic tends to use in the **perfect tense.**

"I shall not say anything, **even if** they torture me."

لَنْ أَقُولَ أَيَّ شَيْءٍ وَلَوْ عَذَّبُوني

سَيُصَدِّقُونَكَ حَتَّى لَوْ لَمْ تُسَلِّمِ الأَدِلَّةَ

"They will believe you, **even if** you don't provide the evidence."

> ☞ These constructions can often also be translated as **if only**. e.g.
>
> "I want to visit my mother in hospital, **if only** for an hour."
> أُرِيدُ أَنْ أَزُورَ أُمِّي فِي المُسْتَشْفَى حَتَّى وَلَوْ لِساعةٍ واحِدةٍ

'Even so' is a conjunct, meaning 'yet' or 'nevertheless' and is rendered in Arabic by لَكِنَّ/لَكِنْ. e.g. مَعَ أَنْ ,رَغْمَ ,بِالرَّغْمِ مِن ذلِكَ ,بِرَغْمِ or even, simply, as

"He refused to lend me any money. **Even so**, he did agree to give me an advance on my salary."
لَقَدْ رَفَضَ أَنْ يُقْرِضَنِي أَيَّةَ أَمْوالٍ وَبِالرَّغْمِ مِنْ ذَلِكَ فَقَدْ وَافَقَ عَلَى أَنْ يُعطِيَنِي دُفْعَةً مُقَدَّمةً مِن رَاتِبِي
لَقَدْ رَفَضَ أَنْ يُقْرِضَنِي أَيَّةَ أَمْوالٍ وَلَكِنْ وَافَقَ عَلَى أَنْ يُعطِيَنِي دُفْعَةً مُقَدَّمةً مِن رَاتِبِي

> ☞ also see 'In Case/ In Spite'

Ever/never

Ever means '*at any time*', whereas **never** signifies '*at no time*'. However, in many cases they are used to denote the same, except that **never** occurs with affirmative verbs and **ever** usually (but not exclusively) in negative and interrogative sentences. Both generally occur with a (present) perfect tense, though in American English the simple past is commonly used. Both are rendered in Arabic by the adverbs أَبَداً, قَطُّ, كَلاَّ, عَلَى الإِطْلاق or مُطْلَقاً with negative verbs. The last two can also translate as '(**not**) **at all, in any way** ...'. e.g.

"Women can **never** seduce men with their looks alone."

لا تَسْتَطِيعُ النِّساءُ أَبَداً مِن إِغْراءِ الرِّجالِ بِمَظْهَرِهِنَّ فَحَسْبُ

"He has **never** been outside his village in South Lebanon."

لَمْ يَخْرُجْ مِن قَرْيَتِهِ في جَنُوبِ لُبْنانَ قَطَّ

"We will **never** open the file, except after the negotiations have ended."

لَنْ نَفْتَحَ هذا المِلَفَّ عَلَى الإِطْلاقِ إِلاَّ بَعْدَ انْتِهاءِ المُفاوَضاتِ

"I have **never** interfered in their affairs."
(OR: "I have not interfered in their affairs in any way.")

لَمْ أَتَدَخَّلْ مُطْلَقاً في أُمُورِهِم

"The government's austerity programme **never** succeeded in reducing the budget deficit."

لَمْ يَنْجَحْ بَرْنامِجُ التَّقَشُّفِ الحُكُومِيِّ أَبَداً في تَخْفِيضِ نَقْصِ المِيزانِيّةِ

"This is the first time I have **ever** seen behaviour like this."

لَمْ أَرَ تَصَرُّفاً مِثْل هذا أَبَداً قَبْلَ الآنَ
(or: هذِهِ أَوَّلَ مَرَّةٍ أَرَى تَصَرُّفاً مِثْلَ هذا)

☞ **NOTE: never** and **ever** can even occur together to stress the intensive aspect. e.g.

"I will **never ever** forget this."

لَنْ أَنْسَى ذلِكَ أَبَداً

The use of **ever** (NOT *never) in superlative constructions. e.g.

"This is the most terrible thing I have **ever** seen."

هذا أَفْظَعُ ما شاهَدْتُهُ عَلَى الإِطْلاقِ

قَطُّ is used with past tenses, and أَبَداً with present and, especially, future tenses.

☞ also See 'Already/Yet/Still'

Everyone/every one

In English, **everyone, no one, everybody, someone, somebody, nobody** are all followed by a singular verb. **Every one** stresses each individual person or thing in a group and is equivalent to *'every single one ...'*. In Arabic, all are rendered by كُلٌّ مِنْ ,كُلّ واحِدٍ or جَميعاً. e.g.

جاءَ كُلُّ مِنْهُم بِهَدايا
"**Every one** of them came with presents."

"**Every one** of them took his share."
أَخَذَ كُلُّ واحِدٍ نَصيبَهُ

"**Every one** of them is working towards achieving their goal."
كُلُّ واحِدٍ مِنْهُم يَعْمَلُ لِتَحْقيقِ هَدَفِه

"**Every one** of them is happy."
كَانُوا مَسْرُورِينَ جَميعاً
كانَ كُلُّهُم مَسْرُورِينَ/سُعَداءَ

"**Every one** of the workers went on strike."
قامَ جَميعُ/كُلُّ العُمَّالِ بِإِضْرابٍ

Exception (الإِسْتِثناءُ)

In English, the common exceptive expressions are **except (for)**, **but**, **with the**

exception of, bar, all of which can be used with both affirmative and negative clauses. Their main Arabic counterparts are غَيْرٌ ,ماعَدا ,باسْتِثْناء, إلاَّ and سِوَى. The following grammatical points merit attention:

  i.   When إلاَّ follows an affirmative, the exceptive noun is in the *accusative*, regardless of the case its position requires. Conversely, if إلاَّ is used with a negative clause, the following noun has the inflection related to its position in the sentence;

 ii.   The noun after ماعَدا is always in the *accusative*;

iii.   غَيْرٌ as the first element in a genitive (إضافة) construction;

 iv.   The noun after باسْتِثْناء is in the genitive;

  v.   سِوَى as the first element in a genitive (إضافة) construction.

> ☞ **NOTE:**
>
> in English, a negative construction with exception is often translated by means of an affirmative and the adverb **only**.
>
> ماعَدا and سِوَى always follow a negative clause.

e.g.

"Everyone came, **except (for)/but** a secretary." [= "Only the secretary came."]

جاءَ كُلُّهُم إلاَّ/ما عَدا السِّكِرْتيرة

ما جاءَ أَحَدٌ إلاَّ السِّكِرْتيرة

"He doesn't do anything **except/but** complain." [= "He only complains."]

لا يَفْعَلُ شَيئًا إلاَّ/باسْتِثْناء الشَّكْوَى

"I haven't seen anyone **with the exception of/except** Sarah." [= "I saw only Sarah."]

لَم أرَ أَحَداً باسْتِثْناءِ سارَةٍ/إلاَّ سارةً

"I haven't met him anywhere **except** in Tunis." [= "I (have) only met him in Tunis."]

لَمْ أُقابِلْهُ إلاَّ في تُونُسَ

"No-one remained in the hall **except** Hind." [= "Only Hind remained in the hall."]

ما لَبِثَ أَحَدٌ بِالقاعةِ إلاَّ هِنْدٌ

"This is the best-selling product, **bar** none [= without exception]."

إنَّ هذا المُنْتَجَ أَكْثَرُ مُبِيعاً بِدُونِ اسْتِثْناء

"I didn't eat anything **except** the cheese." [="I only ate the cheese."]

ما أَكَلْتُ غَيْرَ جِبن
ما أَكَلْتُ شَيْئًا إلاَّ جِبْناً

"He didn't continue his primary education **except** for a few years." [="He only continued his primary education for a few few years."]

لَمْ يَسْتَمِرَّ دِراسَتَهُ الابْتِدائِيَّةَ سِوَى بِضْعِ سنواتٍ

"He didn't oppose anyone **except** a tyrannical government."

لَمْ يُعَارِضْ/لَمْ يَتَصَدَّرْ عَلَى أَحَدٍ إلاَّ عَلَى حُكومَةٍ ظالِمَةٍ

Exclamations (التَّعَجُّبُ)

The usual constructions in English are:

- *What a* ... e.g. "What a nice man!'"

- *PRON + TO BE + such* ... e.g. "He is such a nice man!"

Arabic has a number of constructions to convey exclamation:

- ما أَفْعَلَ, followed by a noun. e.g.

ما أَجْمَلَ الكِتَابَ

'What a wonderful book!'

- حَبَّذا, followed by a (nominative) noun. e.g.

حَبَّذا مُحَمَّدٌ

"What a nice man Muhammad is!"

When used with لَوْ and a (PERFECT) verb, it means '**how nice it would be if ...**'. e.g.

حَبَّذا (الحالُ) لَوْ عَمِلَهُ

"How nice it would be if he did it!"

- بِ + أَفْعِلْ followed by a noun. e.g.

أَحْسِنْ بِزَيْدٍ

"How good is Zayd!" [= 'Zayd is such a good man!']

- بِ + كَفَى. e.g.

كَفَى بِزَيْدٍ مُدَرِّساً

"Zayd is such a good teacher!"

Two dummy verbs, which appear in a frozen (3rd person masculine singular) form, i.e. بِئْسَ ('how bad it is!') and نِعْمَ ('how good it is!'), both of which can only be followed by a noun in the nominative case, whereas they are generally not inflected for gender. e.g.

بِئْسَ الرَّجُلُ

"What a terrible man!"

بِئْسَ المَرْأَةُ

"What a terrible woman!"

بِئْسَ المَرْأَةُ زَيْنَبُ

"What a terrible woman Zeinab is!"

159

بِئْسَ صاحِباً هو عَمْروٌ

"Amr is a terrible companion."

بِئْسَ الصَّاحِبُ إبراهِيمُ

"Ibrahim is the worst of companions."

Fairly/quite/rather/pretty

All these adverbs of degree mean '*not entirely*'. **Fairly**, however, is less strong than **quite** (which in US English means 'very') and **rather** (which comes very close to *very*). **Pretty** is the most informal and often means 'very'. **Quite** (not to be confused with the adjective **quiet**, which means 'not loud'!) can give rise to some confusion since, depending on the context, it means either 'not entirely' (and is then similar in meaning to '*fairly*' or '*fully*'). In Arabic, the translation of these four adverbs tends to involve إلى حَدٍّ ما/بِنَوْع ما or تَماماً, depending on whether it means *fully* or '*fairly*', respectively. e.g.

"The results were **fairly** predictable."

كانَتِ النَّتائِجُ مُتَوَقَّعَة إلى حَدٍّ ما

"It is well-known that they **rather** feared the new technology."

مِنْ المَعْلُومِ أَنَّهُمْ خافُوا مِنَ التَّقنِيةِ الجَدِيدَةِ إلى حَدٍّ ما

"The conversation was **pretty** interesting."

كانَ الحِوارُ شائِقاً جِدًّا

"The composition of bee venom is **quite** [= fairly] complicated as it contains more than 80 components."

التَّرْكِيبُ الكِيماوِيُّ لِسُمِّ النَّحْلِ مُعَقَّدٌ إلى حَدٍّ ما فَهُو يَحْتَوِي على أَكْثَر مِن 80 مادَّةً

"I am **quite** [= very] sure he is incompetent."

أَنَا مُتَأَكِّدٌ تَماماً أَنَّهُ غَيْرُ كُفءٍ

"The play was **quite** good."

كَانَت المَسْرَحِيَّةُ جَيِّدَةً بِنَوْع ما

"He's **quite** [= fairly] fond of Maryam." (US)

تُعْجِبُهُ مَرْيَمُ جِدّاً

Few/little/fewer/less/(lesser)

Few and **little** sometimes pose problems for a number of reasons.

Firstly, **few** is used for countables only and little with uncountables. e.g.

"This faction was formed very quickly, in the space of a **few** days."

تَمَّ تَشْكِيلُ التَّكَتُّلِ بِسُرْعَةٍ، في غُضُونِ أَيَّامٍ قَلائِلَ

"He is one of the **few** Arab thinkers who has a clearly defined philosophy."

هُوَ واحِدٌ مِن المُفَكِّرِينَ العَرَبِ القَلائِل الَّذِينَ كانَتْ لَهُمْ فَلْسَفةٌ مُحَدَّدةٌ

"He left Egypt with a cultural landscape that was a **little**/slightly better than what it had been before his arrival."

لَقَدْ تَرَكَ لَنا المَشْهَدُ الثَّقافِيّ المِصْرِيّ أَفْضَلَ قَلِيلاً مِمَّا كانَ عَلَيْهِ قَبْلَ مَجِيئِه

There are very **few** films that convey real human feelings."

هُناكَ أَفْلامٌ قَلِيلةٌ جِدّاً تَنْقُلُ الأَحاسِيسَ الإِنْسانِيَّةَ الحَقِيقِيَّةَ

"There are **few** sanctions left after the improvement in relations between the two countries."

هُناكَ بعضُ العُقُوباتِ القَلِيلةِ التي بقيت بَعْدَ تَحْسِينِ العَلاقاتِ بَيْنَ الدَّوْلَتَيْنِ
بَقِيَتْ عُقُوباتٌ قَلِيلةٌ بَعْدَ تَحْسِينِ العَلاقاتِ بَيْنَ الدَّوْلَتَيْنِ

"He left us a cultural landscape that was **a little** /slightly better than what it had been before his arrival."

لَقَدْ تَرَكَ لَنا مَشْهَداً ثَقافِيًّا أَفْضَلَ قَلِيلاً مِمَّا كانَ عَلَيْهِ قَبْلَ مَجِيئِه

Secondly, whereas **a few** and **a little** have the positive meaning of 'some', **few** and

little without the indefinite article have a negative connotation as they denote *'not enough'*. e.g.

"There was only **little** money left."

ما بَقِيَ مِن المالِ قليلٌ

ما بَقِيَ مِن المالِ إلاّ قليلٌ

بَقِيَ هُناكَ قليلٌ مِن المالِ فَقَطْ

"He spends what/the **little** money he makes on alcohol and drugs."

يُنْفِقُ ما يَكْسَبُ مِن مالٍ قَليلٍ عَلَى الخَمْرِ والمُخَدِّراتِ

"There were **few** cars on the roads."

كانَ هُناكَ عَدَدٌ قَليلٌ مِنَ السَّيّاراتِ عَلَى الطَّريقِ

The difference in usage in terms of countable/uncountable also applies to the comparatives **less** (uncountables) and **fewer** (countables). **Lesser** tends to be restricted to formal usage and occurs only in a small number of idiomatic phrases like *"the lesser of two evils"*. In Arabic, (a) **few** and (a) **little** are rendered by قَليلٌ (pl. قَلائِلُ), less/fewer by أَقَلُّ. e.g.

"The Finance Minister pointed out that foreign loans represented **less** than 1 per cent."

أَشارَ وَزيرُ المالِيَّةِ إلى أنَّ القُرُوضَ الخارِجِيَّةَ لا تُمَثِّلُ إلاّ أَقَلَّ مِن 1%

"There were **fewer** seats up for election than there were in the House of Representatives."

كانَتْ المَقاعِدُ المَطْرُوحَةُ للإنْتِخاباتِ أَقَلَّ عَدَداً مِن إجمالي المَقاعِدِ في مَجْلِسِ النُّوّابِ

"As one of the political analysts said: 'He is the **lesser** of two evils'!"

كَما قالَ أَحَدُ المُحَلِّلينَ السِّياسِيِّينَ هُوَ أَقَلُّ الشَّرَّيْنِ (/ أَخَفُّ الضَّرَرَيْنِ/أَحْلَى المُرَّيْنِ)

"They are **lesser-known** members of the British royal family."

هُمْ أَعْضاءُ الأُسْرةِ المَلَكِيَّةِ البريطانِيَّةِ الأَقَلُّ شُهْرَةً

☞**NOTE:** عَلَى الأَقَلّ, 'at least'. e.g.

حَاوَلَ عَلَى الأَقَلّ, '**At least** he tried!"

قَلِيل as the equivalent of English 'low' (especially in adjectival compounds). e.g.

ما هِيَ فَوائِدُ الحَلِيبِ القَلِيل الدَّسَمِ؟
"What are the benefits of **low**-fat milk?"

Flammable, inflammable

In general English both terms denote that something may catch fire. However, in technical usage, only **flammable** is used in order to avoid confusion as **inflammable** may also be interpreted as 'not flammable'. For the same reason, the negative of **flammable** is **non-flammable**. In Arabic, the usual translation is قابِلٌ للاشْتِعال or قابِلُ الالْتِهاب, قابِلٌ للاحْتِراق, rather than قابِلٌ للاحْتِراق as this is the translation of 'combustible', with **non-flammable** being rendered by غَيْرُ قابِل للاشْتِعال. The noun (**in**) **flammability** is either قابِلِيَّة عَلَى الاحْتِراق, قابِلِيَّةُ الاحْتِراق (قابِلِيَّةٌ للاحْتِراق) or القُدْرَةُ عَلَى الاشْتِعال. e.g.

"Methyl chloride is flammable when it comes into contact with air."
كلُوريد المِيثِيل قابِلٌ للالْتِهابِ عِنْدَ خَلْطِهِ بِالهَواءِ

"Helium is **non-flammable**, as opposed to the dangerous hydrogen."
إنَّ غازَ «الهِلْيُوم» غَيْرُ قابِلٍ للاشْتِعالِ خِلافاً عَن الغازِ الهِيدْرُوجِين الخَطِيرِ

"In addition, they used fuel which increased the **flammability**."
بِالإضافَة إلى ذلِكَ اسْتَخْدمُوا الوُقُود الَّذي يَزِيدُ مِن القُدْرة عَلَى الاشْتِعال

Note that the noun **inflammation** (الالْتِهاب) is only used in medicine and refers to an infection, whereas **inflammatory** in non-medical contexts means 'inciting violence'. e.g.

"Lebanese circles have strongly condemned the **inflammatory** media campaigns organized by militants from abroad."

شَجَّبَت الأَوْساطُ اللُّبْنانِيَّةُ الحَمْلات الإِعْلامِيَّة التّحْرِيضِيَّة التي يُنَظّمُها ناشطونَ مِن الخارِج

"There are plenty of medicines to treat an **inflammation** of the intestines."

هُناكَ أدوية عَديدةٌ لِعِلاجِ الْتِهابِ الأَمْعاءِ

The future (المُسْتَقْبَلُ)

In the Arabic tense system, the imperfect (المُضارِع) is used for both the present and the future; e.g. يَدْرُسُ الطّالِبُ may mean either 'the student **studies/is studying**' or 'the student **will study/will be studying.**'

However, in MSA the particle سَوْفَ or its abbreviation سَـ added to the imperfect is used to denote the future. Although they are often used interchangeably, careful users make a distinction between near (سَـ) and distant (سَوْفَ) future, whereas سَوْفَ is often imbued with a higher degree of certainty. In the absence of the particle, the context and/or the use of an adverbial is sufficient for the imperfect to be translated as a future tense in English. e.g.

"The vice-President will arrive tomorrow."
يَصِلُ نائبُ الرَّئيسِ غَداً

سَوْفَ يَزْدَهِرُ الشَّجَرُ والنّباتُ في الرَّبيع
"The trees and flowers will bloom in spring."

سَنَقُومُ بِرِحْلةٍ بَعْدَ أُسْبُوعَيْنِ
"We'll go on a trip in two weeks' time."

In addition to 'WILL + INF.', the construction 'TO BE+ GOING + TO.' is also used to denote the future in English, particularly when it involves a planned action: e.g.

"I'm going to visit the museum next week."

سَأَزُورُ المُتْحَفَ الأُسْبُوعُ القادِمُ

The Arabic imperfect is also used to denote a 'future in the past' and the 'past in the future', the so-called **future perfect** (for events that take place before others in the future), which are expressed, respectively, by سَـ/سَوْفَ + IMPERFECT and (قَدْ) + سَـ/سَوْفَ يَكُونُ + **PERFECT**. e.g.

"He **will have been waiting** for an hour before she arrives."

سَيَكُونُ قَد انْتَظَرَ ساعةً قَبْلَ وُصُولِها

"He **will have had** the necessary rest on Saturday."

سَيَكُونُ قَد حَصَلَ عَلَى الرَّاحَةِ اللازِمَةِ يَوْمَ السَّبْتِ

"The character of Jerusalem **will have** completely **changed** so that negotiations will become sterile and pointless."

قَد يَكُونُ طابَعُ مَدِينَةِ القُدْسِ قد تغيَّر تَماماً بِحَيْثُ تُصْبِحُ المُفاوَضاتُ إجراءً عَقيماً لا فائدةَ مِنْهُ

"He **would** go on to win the nomination of the Republican party."

كان سَيَفُوزُ بِتَرْشِيحِ الحِزْبِ الجُمْهُورِيِّ

In English, the future progressive (will + be + PART.) stresses the ongoing nature of an activity in the future and is translated into Arabic like a future simple or, more usually by سَـ/سَوْفَ يَكُونُ + PART. e.g.

"The Constitution **will be sitting** at the negotiation table and **watching** what is going on."

المَنْدُوبُ سَيَكُونُ جالِساً عَلَى طاوِلةِ المُفاوَضاتِ وَشاهِداً عَلَى ما يَحْدُثُ

Genial/genius/genuine/ingenious/ingenuous

Genial means 'cheerful' (بَشُوش، باشّ، لطيف)؛ a **genius** denotes an extremely talented person (عَبْقَرِيَّة) or 'an exceptional talent'; **ingenious** denotes 'inventiveness' (مُبْدِع, ماهِر, عَبْقَرِيّ) and **ingenuous** is synonymous with 'innocent' or 'naive' (ساذَج). e.g.

"Every time she entered the office, she saw the **genial** face of the doorman."

كُلَّما دَخَلَت المَكْتَبَ وَجَدَت وَجْهَ البَوَّابِ بَاشّاً

"In spite of this, he is a very **genial**/amiable/pleasant fellow."

بِرَغْمِ ذَلِكَ فَهُوَ رَجُلٌ لَطيفٌ جِدّاً

"His literary **genius** stood out in his first novel."

بَرَزَت عَبْقَرِيَّتُهُ الأَدَبِيَّةُ في رِوايَتِهِ الأولى

"This device is an **ingenious** and simple invention for the dispensing of soap."

هَذا الجِهازُ اختراعٌ عبقريٌّ وَبَسيطٌ لِلاسْتَغْناءِ عَن الصَّابُونِ

"Either she is **ingenuous**/naïve or acting in collusion with him."

هِيَ إمّا ساذَجَةٌ أَوْ مُتَواطِئَةٌ مَعَهُ

Hal (هَلْ)/a (أ)

In order to render Yes/No questions, Arabic requires the use of the question particles (أَحْرُفُ الاِسْتِفْهام) هَلْ or أ for this purpose. Whereas both can be used interchangeably in a number of cases, أ is more restricted inasmuch as it cannot occur before a definite article or any word that begins with أ. English, on the other hand, uses inversion of verb and subject for the same purpose and so neither of the Arabic particles appears in translation. e.g.

"Will you approve the proposal?"
هَلْ تَوافِقُ على المُقتَرَح/العرض؟

"This is the truth, **isn't it?**"
هذِهِ هِيَ الحَقيقَةُ أَلَيْسَ كَذلِكَ؟

☞**NOTE:**

- the particle أ is **prefixed** to the first word of the sentence;

- in spoken – or even formal – discourse, these particles are often omitted as intonation marks the interrogative nature of the utterance. As a result, translators should be wary of 'classicizing' literary dialogue, for instance: e.g.

  "Did he really do it?"
  (هَلْ) عَمَلَهُ فِعْلاً؟

Happen/occur/take place

Even if these three verbs are often used interchangeably, in careful usage **take place** is reserved for events that are planned, whereas **happen** and **occur** are used to denote unexpected events. As a result, it is unidiomatic to say 'The meeting happened yesterday', since meetings are usually planned and thus require the verb **take place** (or '**to hold**'). A similar difference exists in Arabic, with حَصَلَ being the common verb for **happen**, while **take place** is rendered by verbs like عَقَدَ(i), قامَ (i), أَجْرَى (u). e.g. جَرَى ,انْعَقَدَ ,عَقَدَ(i)

"I don't understand what **happened** there."

لا أَفْهَمُ ماذا حَصَلَ هُناكَ

"Yesterday, the draw in the Arabic football championships **took place/were held**."

أُجْرَيْت مساءَ أَمْسِ قُرْعَةُ البُطُولَةِ العَرَبِيَّةِ في كُرةِ القَدَم

"Last month the sessions of the sixty-fifth conference of the Cairo Academy of the Arabic Language **took place/were held**.

انْعَقَدَت الشَّهْرَ الماضيَ جَلْساتُ مُؤْتَمَرِ الدَّوْرَة الخامِسَةِ والسِّتِّينَ لِمَجْمَعِ اللُّغة العَرَبِيَّة في القاهِرَة

Also note the translations of '**it occurred to ...**', in the sense of 'the idea suggested itself to ...'

- 'I/you... came to think...'
- 'it appeared to ...'
- 'it seemed to ...'
- 'the thought/idea came/occurred to...'.

In Arabic the following expressions are used:

تَبادَرَ إلى ذِهْنِه
طَرَأَ عَلى ذِهْنِه
تَبادَرَ إلى + أَنَّ
خَطَرَ (يَخْطُرُ) لِـ /في /بِبالِه
أوحِيَ إلَيه
خُيِّلَ إلَيْه/أنَّه
هَجَسَ (يَهْجِسُ) في نَفْسِه

e.g.

خُيِّلَ إلَيَّ أَنَّ مِن الضَّرُورِي أنْ أُجيبَ عَلَى اتِّهاماتِه
"It occurred to me that I should respond to his accusations."

السُّؤالُ الَّذِي تَبادَرَ إلى ذِهْنِي هُوَ هَلْ كانوا يَعرِفُونَهُ؟
"The question that came to mind is whether they knew him."

خُيِّلَ إلَيَّ أنَّكَ رَضَخْتَ لِمَطالِبَهُ
"It seemed to me that you gave in to his demands."

Hardly/barely/scarcely/no sooner

Hardly and **scarcely** (like **barely**) mean '*almost not*', '*with difficulty*', and may be translated into Arabic by ما كادَ, لا يَكاد, لَمْ يَمْض, قَلَّما. e.g.

"The visitor had **barely/scarcely** left their house."
لَمْ يَكَدْ يَخْرُجُ الزّائِرُ مِنْ بَيْتِهِم

"**Barely** a day went by without insults and humiliations."
ما كادَ يَمُرُّ يَوْمٌ واحِدٌ دُونَ شَتائِمَ وإهاناتٍ

"**Scarcely** a month went by without demonstrations and protests."

170

لَمْ يَمْضِ شهرٌ بِدُونِ تَظاهُراتٍ وَاحْتِجاجاتٍ

"One of the results of this inquiry, which **hardly** came to light, was that the party had become bankrupt."

إِنَّ أَحَدَ نَتائِجَ هذا التَّحْقِيقِ وَالَّتِي قَلَّما تَظْهَرُ لِلْعِيانِ، هُوَ أَنَّ الْحِزْبَ أَصْبَحَ مُفْلِساً

Note that, as these adverbs are already inherently negative, there is no need for another negative in the same clause in English. e.g.

"There was **scarcely/hardly** any (NOT *'scarcely/hardly no') bread left."

"The African newspapers **barely/scarcely/hardly** print more than thirty thousand copies."

الصُّحُفُ الإِفْرِيقِيَّةُ قَلَّما تَطْبَعُ ما يَفُوقُ الثَّلاثِينَ أَلْفَ نُسْخَةٍ

When they mean '*immediately after*', they are followed by **when. No sooner** is a synonymous expression, but is followed by **than**. In Arabic, these adverbs are expressed as follows:

			ما كاد
		IMPERF.+	لا يَكادُ
PERF. + (IMPERF.)	حَتَّى		لَمْ يَكَدْ
		SUBJ.+	ما إِنْ
		JUSSIVE +	
PERF. +		على + VN	لَمْ يَمْضِ

e.g.

"**No sooner** had the man sat down **than** he jumped up (again) and made a dash for the room."

(OR: "The man had scarcely sat down, when he jumped up and made a dash for the room.")

ما كادَ الرَّجُلُ يَجْلِسُ حَتَّى هَبَّ واقِفاً وانْدَفَعَ نَحْوَ الغُرْفة

"The ink was **barely** dry on one of the spying scandals, **when** another one appeared on the American scene."

لم يَكَدْ يَجِفُّ حِبْرُ إِحْدَى فَضائِح التَّجَسُّسِ حَتَّى ظَهَرَ غَيْرُها عَلَى السّاحة الأَمِيرِكِيَّة

"The ink was **barely** dry on one of the spying scandals, **when** another one appeared on the American scene."

لَمْ يَكَدْ يَجِفُّ حِبْرُ إِحْدَى فَضائِحَ التَّجَسُّسِ حَتَّى يَظْهَرَ غَيْرُها عَلَى السّاحة الأَمِيرِكِيَّة

"**No sooner** did the president read this report **than** he ordered that the situation be improved."

ما إِنْ قَرَأَ الرَّئِيسُ هذا التَّقْرِيرَ حَتَّى أَمَرَ بِتَصْحِيحِ الوَضْع

"The night was **barely** over **when** the press caravans started to move towards the capital."

لَمْ يَمْضِ اللَيْلُ حَتَّى انْطَلَقَت القَوافِلُ الإِعْلامِيَّةُ بِاتِّجاه العاصِمة

"**Barely** two days passed after his speech **when** the book became a bestseller."

لَمْ يَمْضِ على خِطابِه يَوْمانِ حَتَّى أَصْبَحَ هذا الكِتابُ الأَكْثَرَ مَبِيعاً

High/tall

High is the opposite of **low** and refers to the distance from ground level; **tall** is the opposite of **short** and actually means *'higher than average'*. The former is used only for things, the latter for people and for things which are high and narrow. e.g.

"We climbed a **high** mountain."

قَدْ تَسَلَّقْنا جَبَلاً عَالِياً

"Can you see that **tall** building over there?"

هَلْ تُشاهِدُ ذلكَ المَبْنَى العالي؟

Arabic-speakers have to pay particular attention to not confusing **tall** with **long**, due to the fact that in Arabic both are rendered by طويل in some contexts. e.g. شُعُور طَويلة, '**long** hair', رَجُلٌ طَويلٌ, '**tall** man'. In other cases, Arabic uses عالٍ to denote highness or tallness. e.g. 'a tall/high mountain', جَبَلٌ عالٍ.

Hire/rent/let/lease/charter

All of these refer to 'selling/buying the right to use something'. In British English, the distinction between **hire** and **rent** is based on the length of time (e.g. a couple of hours or a day); **hire** is used when it involves a short period of time, with **rent** denoting longer time spans. In American English, **rent** is used in both contexts.

Note that both verbs can be used by the person who owns the property and the one who borrows it. If you want to stress the fact of *selling* the use, it is possible to add the preposition **out**.

To let is used only for buildings in British English (AE: **rent**), whereas **charter** is restricted to ships or airplanes. **Lease** is similar to **let** or **rent** but is used only for buildings or vehicles. The noun **lease** refers to the rental contract.

Arabic does not make a distinction in terms of period of lease and uses the same verbs for all contexts: أَجَّرَ, اِسْتَأْجَرَ, كارى, اِكْرى, أَكْرى, اِكْتَرَى, اِسْتَكْرَى. The noun **rent** translates as كِراء, إيجار or أُجْرة. e.g.

"He **rented** a flat (AE: apartment) with only two rooms."

اِسْتَأْجَرَ شَقَّةً صَغِيرَةً تتكوَّن مِن غرَفتَيْنِ فَقَطْ

"They **rented out** their land to the farmers."

أَجَّرُوا أَراضِيَهُمْ لِلمُزارِعِينَ

"My colleague **rented out** his spare room to me."

زَمِيلِي اِكْتَرَى لِي غُرْفَتَهُ الإِضافِيَّة في بَيْتِهِ

"He **hired/rented** a car and went on a family trip to the mountains of Colorado."

اِسْتَأْجَرَ سَيَّارَةً وَذَهَبَ في زِيارَةٍ عَائِلِيَّةٍ إلى جِبالِ كولورادو

"The government delegation **chartered** a private plane for their European tour."

اِسْتَأْجَرَ الوَفْدُ الحُكُومِيُّ طائِرَةً خاصَّةً لِجَوْلَتِه الأُورُوبِّيَّة

"During the economic crisis he was forced to decrease the **rent** on the house substantially."

اضطرَّ أثناء الأزمَةِ الاقتِصادِية إلى تَخفيضٍ إيجارِ البَيتِ كَثيراً

"He has not once paid **rent** on the flat he has been living in for the past three (consecutive) months."

لَمْ يَدْفَعْ ولَو مَرَّة/قَط إيجارَ الشَّقَّةِ الَّتِي يَسْكُنُها الآنَ مُنذُ ثَلاثَةِ أشهُرٍ عَلَى التَّوالي

"The owners of the institutions are complaining about the high costs of **renting** to shops."

يَشْتَكِي أرْبابُ المُؤَسَّساتِ مِن كَثْرَةِ المَصاريف مِن كِراءٍ لِلمَحَلاتِ

> ☞ NOTE: for rent/hire, to let: للإيجار

Historic/historical

Historic means *'of great significance'* or important from the point of view of history, whereas **historical** refers to) the science of) history. In Arabic, both tend to be translated as تاريخيّ. e.g.

"This theory generally leads to the concealment of the **historical** dimension of the text."

تُفْضِي هذِهِ النَّظَرِيَّةُ غالِباً إلى إخْفاءِ البُعْدِ التّارِيخِيِّ للنَّصِّ

"They were inflicted a **historic** defeat during the world championships."

تَكَبَّدُوا هَزِيمةً تاريخيّةً في بُطولةِ العالَم

Holiday/holidays/vacation/leave

'**Holiday**' is the general word for 'a period of rest from work'. Some days are granted by law; these are known as '**public holidays**' (some of which are known in British English as **Bank Holidays**). Note also that you go '**on holiday**' (NOT *holidays). Also, a single day's holiday is referred to as a day off, which should not be confused with an '**off day**' as this means a day when one is not feeling on top form! e.g.

"Christmas is a **public holiday** in all government institutions."

عِيدُ المِيلادِ عُطْلَةٌ رَسْمِيَّةٌ في جَمِيعِ مُؤَسَّساتِ الدَّوْلَةِ وأَجْهِزَتِها

"In our country, employees get thirty days official annual **holidays**."

أَيّامُ العُطْلاتِ الرَّسْمِيَّةِ السَّنَوِيَّةِ للمُوَظَّفِينَ في بلادِنا ثلاثونَ يَوْماً

"His Highness the Emir attended the celebrations on the occasion of the Kuwaiti **National Day**.

حَضَرَ صاحِبُ السُّمُوِ الأمِيرُ الاحْتِفالاتِ بِمُناسَبَةِ العُطْلَةِ الوَطَنِيَّةِ لِدَوْلَةِ الكُوَيْتِ

'**Vacation**' refers to the long periods during which universities are closed. Note, however, that in American English it is also often used instead of the British English '**holiday**' (e.g. 'on vacation'). e.g.

"Students are feeling frustrated during the summer **vacation** because of the paucity of recreational areas."

يَشْعُرُ الطُّلَّابُ بِالإِحْبَاطِ فِي العُطْلَةِ الصَّيْفِيَّةِ نَظَراً لِعدمِ تَوَّفر/وجود المَواقِعِ التَّرْفِيهِيَّةِ

Soldiers tend to go 'on leave'. However, **leave** can also apply to other people in expressions like '**maternity leave**' or '**sick leave**'. e.g.

"The soldier is not allowed to travel abroad during his **leave**."

يُمْنَعُ الجُنْدِي مِنَ السَّفَرِ إِلى الخَارِج أَثْناء عُطْلَتِه

"As long as the **maternity leave** is justified by a medical certificate, the employer cannot dismiss the woman."

ما دامَتْ عُطْلَةُ الأُمومَةِ مُوَثَّقَةً بِالشَّهاداتِ الطِّبِّيَّةِ فَإِنَّهُ لا يُمْكِنُ لِصاحِبِ العَمَلِ أَنْ يَفْصِلَ المَرأَةَ مِنْ عَمَلِها

For the period during which parliament and the courts are not working, the word '**recess**' is used, rather than 'vacation' or 'holiday'. e.g.

"The court **recess** runs every year from the first of July until the end of September."

تَبْدَأُ العُطْلَةُ القَضائِيَّةُ كُلَّ عَامٍ مِنْ أَوَّلِ يُولِيُو وَتَنْتَهِي آخِرَ سِبْتِمْبِر

> ☞**NOTE:** In Arabic, the same words tend to be used for all contexts: عُطْلَة or إِجازة, though the latter is avoided by careful users since it is perceived to be a regionalism (Egypt) and as it is also the word used to denote an academic degree (cf. شهادة) or 'official approval', 'authorization', etc.

> ☞ **NOTE:** do not confuse **vacation** with **vacant**, an adjective meaning *'empty, available'* (e.g. a seat, position) and **vacancy**, a noun denoting an *'unfilled place* (e.g. room in a hotel) *or job'*. Both are rendered in Arabic by شاغر (pl. شَواغِرُ) or خالٍ: e.g.
>
> "Are there are any **vacancies/vacant** positions in the company now ?"
> هَلْ هُناكَ وَظائِفُ شاغِرةٌ/خاليةٌ في الشَّرِكةِ الآنَ؟
>
> "People in the city are not used to seeing **vacancies** in the hotels."
> النَّاسُ في المَدينةِ غَيرُ مُعتّادينَ عَلَى وُجودِ غُرَفٍ شاغِرةٍ/خاليةٍ في الفَنادِقِ

Human/humane

Human refers to *'human beings, mankind'*, whereas **humane** is synonymous with *'compassionate'*, and is related to **humanitarian**. In Arabic, both are rendered by إنْسانيٌّ.

"Political disputes do not mean that there are arguments at the level of **human** relations."
إنَّ الْخُصُومَةَ السِّياسيَّةَ لا تَعْني خُصومَةً عَلَى صَعيدِ العلاقاتِ الإِنْسانيَّةِ

"Islamic slaughter is not considered **humane** under French law."
يَعْتَبِرُ القانُونُ الفَرَنْسيُّ الذَّبْحَ على الطَّريقةِ الإسْلاميّةِ غَيْرَ إنْسانيٌّ

"The **humanitarian** aid arrived in the stricken region, despite efforts by the terrorists to prevent it."
وَصَلَتِ المُساعَدَةُ الإنْسانيّةُ إلى المِنْطَقَةِ المُصابَةِ بالرَّغْمِ مِن جُهودِ الإرْهابيّينَ لِعَرْقَلَةِ وُصُولِها

"Last month, there were calls for international measures to prosecute him for crimes against **humanity**."

شَهَدَ الشَّهْرُ الماضِي بَوادِرَ إِجْراءاتٍ دُوَلِيَّةٍ لِمُلاحَقَتِهِ بِتُهْمَةِ جَرائِمَ ضِدَّ الإِنْسانِيَّةِ

Hyphens

As a general principle, hyphens are used in English in adjectival compounds pre-modifying (= appearing before) nouns to indicate a close relationship between items, often underscoring the fact that they act as one unit. e.g.

- **'well-known** author' (a 'well known author' could be one who is well – not ill – and who is known). Note the absence of the hyphen in 'an author is **well known**', since there is no such ambiguity;
- **'blue-green** eyes' (rather than eyes that are blue *and* green, they are a mixture of blue and green);
- **'physician-patient** confidentiality issues';
- **'high-frequency** sound waves';
- **'first-floor** flat';
- **'kind-natured** child';

Note that hyphenated adjectival compounds are generally not marked for plural. e.g.

- **'four-week** holiday' (NOT *four-weeks holiday);
- **'six-kilogram** box' (NOT *six-kilograms box);
- **'twenty-pound** shirt' (NOT *twenty-pounds shirt);

Most hyphenated compounds consist of two elements, but it is by no means uncommon to have more than two. e.g.

- 'a **well-thought-out** theory'
- 'don't give me this **little-Miss-touch-me-not** attitude!'

In some cases the hyphen indicates other types of relationship between the elements. e.g.

178

- '**Arabic-English** translation' ('translation **from** Arabic **to** English')
- 'The **Cairo-Alexandria** train' (the train **from** Cairo **to** Alexandria')

Hyphens are not traditionally used in Arabic and to this day occur only very rarely. Most of the above examples are translated in a more explicit manner, which often may mean by a single word. e.g.

أَمْواجٌ صَوْتِيَّةٌ عالِيَةُ التَّرَدُّد, 'high-frequency sound waves'

عُطْلَةٌ لأَرْبَعَة أَسابِيعَ, 'four-week holiday'

صُنْدُوقٌ وَزْنُهُ سِتَّةَ كيلوغرامات, 'six-kilogram box'

عُيُونٌ خُضْرٌ زُرْقٌ, 'blue-green eyes'

كاتِبٌ مَعْرُوفٌ, 'well-known author'

One of the few exceptions, where Arabic follows English practice is:

التَّرْجَمةُ إِنْكليزيّ-عَرَبيّ, 'English-Arabic translation'.

One should hasten to add, however, that this is considered non-normative usage by many and the preferred translation here would be:

التَّرْجَمةُ مِن الإِنْكليزِيِّ-إِلَى العَرَبِيِّ

If/whether

In addition to introducing conditions (**q.v.**), **if** is also used in reported speech with Yes/No questions, in which case it is often interchangeable with **whether**. In Arabic, they are often translated by أَمْ ... أَ, إِذا/إِنْ (if there is more than one element) or, simply, by a prepositional phrase. e.g.

"I don't know **if/whether** he'll be there."

لا أَعْرَفُ إِذا كانَ هُناكَ

"Do you know **if/whether** he'll be at home or at work?"

هَلْ تَعْرِفُ إِنْ/إِذا كانَ في البَيْتِ أَمْ في المَكْتَبِ؟

In some cases, however, **if** is excluded and ONLY **whether** is allowed:

- Before '**to + infinitive**'. e.g.

"I don't know **whether** to replace the computer."

لا أَعْرِفُ إِنْ كانَ يَنْبَغي عَلَيَّ تَغْييرُ الحاسُوبِ

- After a preposition: e.g.

"Everything depends on **whether** they will be able to sell the house."

كُلُّ شَيءٍ يَعْتَمِدُ عَلَى تَمَكُّنِهم مِنْ بَيْعِ البَيْتِ

- in sentence-initial positions: e.g.

"**Whether** we agree (or not) is not important at this stage."

إِنِ اتَّفَقْنا أَمْ لا فَهَذا غَيْرُ مُهِمٍّ في هذهِ المَرْحَلةِ

180

- with '**... or not**'. e.g.

"It doesn't matter **whether or not** he chooses to resign."

لا يُهِمُّ إذا/إنْ قَرَّرَ أَنْ يَسْتَقيلَ (أَمْ لا)

In case/in spite of

In case means '*to allow for the possibility that*'; **in case of** is synonymous with 'in the event of'; **in no case** means '*under no circumstances*'. **In spite of** (= **despite**) is a preposition meaning '*irrespective/regardless of*'. The first three are translated into Arabic by means of a circumstantial clause (حال), whereas **in spite of** is rendered by a construction involving رَغْم. e.g.

"We have to issue austerity measures **in case** the government refuses the new proposal submitted by the opposition."

يَجِبُ أَنْ نُصْدِرَ إِجْراءاتِ التَّقَشُّفِ في حالةِ رَفْضِ الحُكُومةِ لِلاقْتِراحِ الجَديدِ الَّذي قَدَّمَتْهُ المُعارَضةُ

"The detention can **in no case** be more than three days."

لا يُمْكِنُ أَنْ يَزيدَ التَّوْقيفُ في أَيِّ حالٍ عَلَى ثَلاثةِ أَيّامٍ

"**In case of** rain, you can collect water."

تستطيعُ أن تَجْمَعَ المِياهَ في حالةِ سُقُوطِ المَطَرِ

"I don't understand the reasons for Britain's lack of sympathy with the Arab cause, **in spite of** the fact that their interests lie with the Arabs."

لا أَفْهَمُ أَسْبابَ عَدَمِ تَعاطُفِ بريطانيا مَعَ القَضايا العَرَبِيَّةِ عَلَى الرَغْمِ أَنَّ مَصالِحَها مَعَ العَرَبِ

"**In spite of** the fact that the National Party won the elections, Scotland will remain part of the United Kingdom, with the Queen as its monarch."

بِالرَّغْمِ مِن فَوْزِ الحِزْبِ الوَطَنيّ في الانْتِخابات فَسَتَظَلُّ اسْكُتْلَنْدا جُزْءًا مِن المَمْلَكَة المُتَّحِدَة وَعَلَى رَأْسِها المَلِكَةُ

"The population made preparations for Ramadan **despite** the blockade."
بِرَغْمَ الحِصارِ اسْتَعدَّ الشَّعْبُ لِشَهْرِ رَمَضانٍ

"We find that the majority of Iraqi politicians remain optimistic, **in spite of** all the violence."
بِالرّغْمِ من كُلِّ العُنْفِ (الذَّي يَحدُثُ في العِراق) فإننا نُلاحِظُ أنَّ أكْثَرِيَةَ السِّياسِيِّينَ العِراقِيِّين مُتَفائلُونَ

Incredible/incredulous

Despite obvious similarities in form, these two words have quite different mean-
ings: **incredible** (لا يُصَدَّق) means *hard to believe*; **incredulous** (مُرْتاب) *showing disbelief*.
e.g.

"He told me an **incredible** story about how he was attacked by sharks."
لَقَدْ حَكَى لي قِصَّةً لا تُصَدَّقُ عَنْ كَيْفِيَّة مُهَاجَمةِ أَسمَاكِ القِرْشِ لَهُ

"They looked at her with an **incredulous** expression on their faces."
لَقَد نَظَروا إلَيْهَا وَعلى وَجوهِهِم نَظْرَةٌ مُرتَابَةٌ

> ☞ **NOTE:** the opposite of 'incredulous', **credulous** is synonymous with
> '*naive*', '*gullible*'. e.g.
>
> "Only someone as **credulous** as his mother would believe his
> inventions."
> لا يُمكِنُ إلا لِشَخصٍ في سَذَاجَةِ والدَتَهُ أَنْ يُصَدِّق اخترَاعَاتِه

Industrial/industrious

Industrial is related to **industry**, whereas **industrious** is synonymous with *'hard-working, diligent'*, which are rendered in Arabic by, respectively, صِناعيّ and مُجْتَهِدٌ. e.g.

"The report refers to the need to set up **industrial** unions and to increase cooperation with the Ministry."

يُشيرُ التَّقْريرُ إلى ضَرُورةِ/الحاجةِ إلى تَأْسيسِ الاتِّحاداتِ الصِّناعيّةِ وَزيادَةِ تَعاوُنِها مَعَ الوِزارَةِ

"If a pupil is **industrious**, he will get the secondary school certificate."

وَإذا كانَ التِّلْميذُ مُجْتَهِداً فَسَيَحْصُلُ عَلى شَهادةِ الثَّانَويَّةِ العامَّةِ

Information

The main issue in the use and translation of **information** is that in English it is an **uncountable**, so it is incorrect to talk about 'informations', whereas in Arabic it tends to be rendered by a **plural**, i.e. أخْبار, مَعْلُومات, اسْتِعْلامات. e.g.

"The **information** desk is on the second floor."

يَقَعُ مَكْتَبُ الاسْتِعلاماتِ في الطَّابِقِ الثَّاني

"We have no **information** regarding foreign fighters on the outstkirts of the city."

لَيْسَت لَدَيْنا أَيُّ مُعْلوماتٍ عَن وُجُودِ مُقاتِلينَ أَجانِبَ عَلَى مَشارِفِ المَدينةِ

"We have **information** (news) on the violent attack in the market place."

لَدَيْنا أَخْبارُ عَنْ الهُجُومِ العَنيفِ في السُّوقِ

Interfere/interrupt/intervene

Interrupt (قَطَعَ [a], اِنْقَطَعَ) means to stop someone doing something for a short while; to **intervene** (داخَلَ, تَوَسَّطَ) means to enter into something (e.g. a dispute) in order to find a solution, and to mediate; **interfere** (تَدَخَّلَ) refers to an unsolicited intervention which is considered irritating. e.g.

"Troublemakers **interrupted** the lecturer, who made as if he was going to be quiet and then resumed his talk."

قَطَعَ مُشاغِبُونَ كَلامَ المُحاضِرِ فَبَدا كَأَنَّهُ سَكَتَ ثُمَّ اِسْتَأْنَفَ

"The National Security Council has to **intervene** in the dispute between the parties and the Intelligence Agency."

يَجِبُ أَنْ يَتدخَّلَ مَجْلِسُ الأَمْنِ القَوْمِيِّ في الخِلافِ بَيْنَ الأَحْزابِ ووَكالَةِ الاِسْتِخْبارات

"The Organization of the Islamic Conference (OIC) will **intervene** between the two parties."

سَتَتَوَسَّطُ مُنَظَّمَةُ المُؤْتَمَرِ الإسْلامِيِّ بَيْنَ الطَّرَفَيْنِ

"The main thing is that the state should not **interfere** in economic activity."

أَهَمُّ شيءٍ/الشيءُ الأَساسي هو أَلاَّ تَتَدَخَّلَ الدَّوْلَةُ في النَّشاطِ الاِقْتِصادِيِّ

184

Intolerable/intolerant

Intolerable is used for something which cannot be tolerated, although in informal English it means *'irritating'*. **Intolerant** denotes a lack of respect for others, their beliefs, etc. In Arabic, they may be translated as غَير مُحْتَمَل/لا يُطاقُ and مُتَسامِح, respectively. e.g.

"They responded to the **intolerable** provocation in an appropriate and lawful manner."

رَدُّوا عَلَى الاسْتِفْزاز الذي لا يُطاقُ بِطَريقةٍ مُناسِبَةٍ ومشْروعةٍ

"He is a Muslim and an Arab and he will respond to **intolerable** provocation in an appropriate and lawful manner."

إنه عَرَبيٌّ ومُسْلِمٌّ يَرُدُّ عَلَى اسْتِفْزاز لا يُطاقُ بِطَريقةٍ مُناسِبَةٍ ومشْروعةٍ

"During his university days he learned that the authorities are unjust and **intolerant**."

يَعْلَمُ مُنْذُ دِراسَاتِه الجامِعيَّةِ أَنَّ السُّلْطاتِ غَيْرُ عادلةٍ وغَيْرُ مُتَسامِحةٍ

Note that in some contexts, غَيْرُ مُتَسامِح can also be rendered by مُتَعَصِّبٌ, 'fanatical'. e.g.

"This view is part of an **intolerant** colonialist mindset."

تندمج/تندرج هذِه الرُّؤْيَةُ في إطارِ عَقْلِيَّةٍ اسْتِعْماريَّةٍ مُتَعَصِّبةٍ

Invaluable/valueless

In spite of the prefix –*in*, which generally has a privative function (like *un*-, or *non*-), **invaluable** does not mean 'without value', but rather the opposite, i.e. *'too precious to put a value on'* (لا يُقَدَّر بِثَمَنٍ، لايُثَمَّنُ). The absence of value is conveyed through the adjective **valueless** (بلا/بِدُونَ قيمَةٍ). e.g.

"This painting is **invaluable**."

لا تُقَدَّرُ هَذِهِ اللَوحَةُ بِثَمَنٍ

"Counterfeit money is **valueless**."

الأَموَالُ الْمُزَيَّفةُ بِلا قِيمَةٍ

Judicial/judicious/judiciary/judicature

Judicial (قَضائِيّ) is an adjective that refers to the courts, lawyers etc.; **judicious** (حَكِيمٌ, حَصِيفٌ) means 'prudent'; both the **judiciary** and **judicature** can be used to denote the body of judges in the courts of law (جَماعةُ القُضاة).

"They were getting closer to a solution after settling the disputes and the publication of the **judicial** rulings regarding the grievances submitted by the people."

أَوْشَكوا عَلَى الوُصولِ إلى حَلٍّ بَعْدَ فَضِّ المُنازَعاتِ وَصُدُورِ الأَحْكام القضائِيّة بِشَأْنِ الاعْتِراضاتِ التي قَدَّمَها المُواطِنونَ

"The same **judicious** equilibrium in his views was observed in his words on the Cold War that was raging."

كانَ نَفْسُ التَّوازُنِ الحَكِيمِ في فِكْرِهِ وَراءَ قَوْلِهِ في الحَرْبِ الباردَةِ المُتَأَجِّجَة

"The Central Bank imposed a **judicious** loans policy."

فَرَضَ البَنْكُ المَرْكَزِيّ سِياسَةَ إِقْرَاضٍ حَصيفَةً

"The union expressed the view of the **judiciary** on the ongoing struggle between the legal profession and the District Attorney."

أَفْصَحَت النِّقابَةُ عَن رَأْي (جَماعةِ) القُضاةِ في مِصْر فيما يَتَعَلَّقُ بالنِّزاع الدَّائِر بَيْنَ المُحامِين وَوَكِيلِ النِّيابَةِ العامّ

Just/just now

As a time adverb, **just** is always used with a perfect tense. **Just now** can mean '*a very short time ago*' or '*at this moment*', and can be followed by a present progressive, simple past or present perfect. In Arabic, this is generally rendered by the use of the adverbial تَوّ [+ PRON] and the PERFECT. e.g.

"We have **just** finished eating."

لَقَدِ انْتَهَيْنا لِتَوِّنَا مِن تَنَاولِ الطَّعامِ

"He has **just now** driven onto the car park."

لَقَدْ دَخَلَ لِتَوِّهِ الآنَ إلى مَوْقَفِ السَّيَّاراتِ

"I'm leaving the flat **just now**, so I'll be at your place in fifteen minutes."

سَأُغَادِرُ الشُّقَّةَ الآنَ تَوًّا، لِذا سَأَصِلُ لِمَنْزِلِكَ خِلالَ خَمْسَ عَشْرَةَ دَقِيقَةٍ

> ☞ **NOTE**: the use of '**just**' in the sense of '**only**'. e.g.
>
> "I'm **just** saying that you shouldn't shout at her like that."
> أَنَا أَقُولُ فَقَط أَنَّهُ لا يَنْبَغِي أَن تَصرُخِي في وَجْهِهَا هَكَذَا

Keep on ...

This progressive construction is translated into Arabic by some of the so-called
'sisters of كانَ: ظَلَّ (a), ما زالَ/لا يَزالُ and the **imperfect.** e.g.

"He **keeps on** writing and his pen does not stop (/ continues) detailing
stories and novels on paper."

يَظَلُّ يَكْتُبُ وَلا يَتَوَقَّفُ قَلَمُهُ عَن سَرْدِ الحِكاياتِ وَالرِّواياتِ عَلَى الوَرَقِ

"We **keep on** considering participating in Parliament."

ما زِلْنا نَتَباحَثُ مَسَألةَ المُشارَكَةِ في البَرْلَمانِ

"He will **keep on** thinking like that until he arrives at the airport."

سَيَظَلُّ يُفَكِّرُ هَكَذا حَتَّى يَصِلَ إلى المَطارِ

"She **keeps on** talking about the party's desire to win the local elections."

لا تَزَالُ تَتَحَدَّثُ عَنْ رَغْبَةِ الحِزْبِ في الفَوْزِ في الانْتِخاباتِ المَحَلِّيَّةِ

> ☞ **NOTE:** despite the past tense form of ما زال it has to be translated
> by a present in English.

Lawyer/solicitor/barrister

All these terms refer to someone who acts on someone's behalf to protect their interests in a legal context. In American English, the words **lawyer**, **attorney** (**-at-law**), **counselor** (**-at-law**) are used interchangeably. In England, however, the general term is **lawyer**, whereas **solicitor** and **barrister** refer to specific types of lawyers. **Advocate** is a term used in certain legal systems (e.g. Scotland) for lawyer.

Arabic has only one word for all of them, مُحامٍ. In practice, it is generally appropriate to translate this by the most generic term, i.e. **lawyer**.

> "The two **lawyers** brought a case before the Administrative Tribunal of Mansoura."
>
> أقامَ المُحامِيانِ دَعْوَى أَمامَ مَحْكَمَةِ القَضاءِ الإِدارِيِّ بِالمَنْصُورَةِ

Let's ...

This so-called hortative imperative (a contracted form of '**let us**'), is followed in English by an INFINITIVE; in Arabic, the usual construction is with the so-called لَامُ الأَمْرِ ('the imperative lām') followed by the JUSSIVE, or by the interjection هَيَّا, often followed by the preposition بِ before pronouns. e.g.

لِنَذْهَبْ
"Let's go."

"**Let's** study French!"

هيَّا بِنا نَتَعلَّمُ الفَرَنْسِية

With the imperative *lām*, it is possible to add ﻓ, in which case the ل loses its vowel: e.g.

فَلْنَذْهَبْ
"Let's go."

Another possible construction is with the (invariable) imperative دَ عْ (< وَدَعَ), which often occurs with a pronoun suffix: e.g.

دَعْنا نَذْهَبْ
"Let's go."

Make/do

The distinction between *make* and *do* in translation is often confusing as in many cases both verbs are translated by the same words in Arabic, i.e. فَعَلَ (a) or عَمَلَ (i). e.g.

"I **did** my homework."
عَمِلْتُ/فَعَلْتُ وَظائِفِي/واجِباتِي

"She **made** the cake."
عَمَلَت/فَعَلَت الكَعْكَ

In both cases, the Arabic verbs are interchangeable.

However, when **make** expresses causality – the fact of making someone do something – the usual translation involves جَعَلَ (a) as an auxiliary, which may occur with either perfect or imperfect verbs. e.g.

"These jokes will **make** you laugh."
تَجْعَلَكَ هذِه النُّكَتُ تَضْحَكُ/هذِه النُّكَتُ سَتَجْعَلَكَ تَضْحَكُ

"He **made** me the laughing-stock of the entire university."
جَعَلَني أُضْحُوكةً أمامَ كُلِّ الجامعة
جَعَلَني أُضْحُوكةَ الجامِعةِ كُلِّها

Marine/maritime/nautical/naval

All these adjectives denote a connection with the sea, but tend to have their own collocates; 'maritime' is usually used when it involves shipping and navigation. e.g.

"The Phoenicians were a trading/mercantile and **maritime**/seafaring nation."

كانَ الفِينِيقِيُّونَ شَعْباً تِجارِيًّا وَمِلاحِيًّا

"The new **maritime** trade law will come into force next month."

يَدْخُلُ القانُونُ الجَدِيدُ لِلتِّجارَةِ البَحْرِيَّةِ في السَّرَيانِ/حَيِّزِ التَّنْفِيذِ الشَّهْرَ القادِمَ

Close to maritime in meaning, '**Nautical**' collocates with, for instance, maps and speeds (e.g. 'nautical mile'). e.g.

"The **maritime/nautical** museum owns a large collection of old nautical maps."

يَمْتَلِكُ المَتْحَفُ البَحْرِيُّ مَجْمُوعةً كَبِيرَةً مِنْ خَرائطَ بَحْرِيَّةٍ/مِلاحِيَّةٍ قَدِيمةٍ

'**Naval**' occurs in connection with the Navy (a country's warships, البَحْرِيَّة العَسْكَرِيَّة) and **marine** with the biology of the sea. e.g.

"The government announced the projects aimed at strengthening the country's **naval** defence capability."

أَعْلَنَتِ الحُكُومةُ بِأَنَّ الهَدَفَ مِن مَشارِيعِها هُوَ تَعْزِيزُ القُدْراتِ الدِّفاعِيَّةِ البَحْرِيَّةِ لِلدَّوْلةِ

"These measures are intended to protect the **marine** environment."

تَسْتَهْدِفُ هذِهِ الإِجْراءاتُ حِمَايةَ البِيئةِ البَحْرِيَّةِ

"Fishermen are afraid of the depletion of **marine** wildlife."

يَتَخَوَّفُ الصَّيادُونَ مِن اِسْتِنْزافِ الثَّرْوةِ الحَيَوانِيَّةِ البَحْرِيَّةِ

"The **marine/maritime** shipyard was set up during the reign of Muhammad Ali Pasha."

أُنْشِئَتْ دارُ الصِّناعةِ البَحْرِيَّةِ في عَصْرِ مُحَمَّد عَلِي باشا

BUT:

"The **naval** shipyard built the aircraft carrier for the French Navy."

اِنْتَجَتْ دارُ الصِّناعَةُ البَحريَّةُ حامِلةَ الطَّائِراتِ لِلبَحريَّةِ الفَرَنْسِيَّةِ

The above shows that these adjectives are more likely to pose a problem in Arabic>English translation rather than the other way around since in Arabic all three can be rendered by بَحْرِيٌّ, with مَلاحِيُّ also being possible when it involves transport(ation), though it primarily denotes navigation.

> ☞ **NOTE**: the use of the capital in '**Navy**' when it refers to the military. In some expressions, it can refer to a non-military fleet of ships, in which case there is no capital. e.g. 'merchant **navy**', أُسْطُول تِجارِيّ.

Maybe/may be

Although they are near-identical in form, their usage varies considerably inasmuch as **maybe** is an adverb meaning *'perhaps'* (رُبَّما, لَعَلَّ, يُمْكِن/مُمْكِنْ أَنْ), whereas **may be** is a verb phrase denoting *'it is possible that'*. e.g.

"**Maybe** most of the articles in the new law are controversial."

لَعَلَّ أَكْثَرَ مَوَادِّ القانُونِ الجديد مُثيرةٌ لِلجَدَلِ

"**Maybe** we have to wait until 27 May in order to find out the truth about the political identity of the country."

رُبَّما يَنْبَغي الاِنْتِظارُ إلى 27 أَيَّارِ/مايُو لِمَعْرِفةِ حَقيقةِ الهُويَّةِ السِّياسِيَّةِ لِلبِلادِ

"**Maybe** she's hidden all the bags."

رُبَّما قَد أَخْفَتْ كُلَّ الحَقائِبَ

"It **may be** difficult to forgive him, but he is your father." (= Maybe it's difficult...)

يُمْكِنُ أَنْ يَكُونَ غُفْرانُ مُعامَلَتِه صَعْباً عَلَيْكَ ولكِنَّهُ أَبُوكَ

Moral/morale

Moral can be both a **noun** and an **adjective**: as a noun, it refers to an ethical rule, with the adjective meaning that one acts in compliance with such rules (= **ethical**). **Morale** is a noun only and denotes '*mental confidence/strength*'. In Arabic, the former is rendered by خُلْق (plural أَخْلاق, adj. أَخْلاقِيّ, خُلُقِيّ), the latter by رُوحّ مَعْنَوِيّةّ. e.g.

"This principle has no **moral**/ethical basis."

إنَّ هذا المَبْدَأَ مَبْنِيٌّ عَلَى أُسُس غَيْر أَخْلاقِيّة
ليسَ لِهذا المَبْدَأ أَسُسٌّ أَخلاقِيّةّ
لا أَساسَ أَخْلاقِيَّ لِهذا المَبْدَأ

"He refused to invest in the project or take any part in it since it violates **moral**/ethical principles."

رَفَضَ تَمويلَ المَشْرُوع أَوْ المُساهَمَةَ فِيه لأَنَّ المَشْرُوعَ يَنْتَهِكُ القَواعِدَ الأَخْلاقِيّةَ

"In their reflections and experiments, scholars have to take account of **moral**/ethical considerations."

وَعَلَى العُلَماءِ أَنْ يَأْخُذُوا في حِساباتِهِم وتَجارِبِهِم هذِهِ الاعْتِبارات الخُلُقِيّةَ

"The victory will urge the players to enter the championships with heightened **morale**."

الفَوْزُ يَدْفَعُ اللاعِبِينَ إلى دُخُولِ البُطُولاتِ بِرُوحٍ مَعْنَوِيّةٍ عالِيَّةٍ

More/most/mostly

These three words are often confused. Furthermore, **most**, in particular, can have different meanings. e.g.

"I was **most** (= very) impressed by his performance."

أَعْجَبَني أَداوُهُ إِعْجاباً عَظيماً

أَعْجَبَني أَداوُهُ جِدّاً

"I was **mostly** (= particularly) impressed by his performance." [less by his clothes, for instance]

أَعْجَبَني أَداوُهُ بِصِفةٍ خاصّةٍ

In comparisons, **more** and **most** should be distinguished in that **more** applies to two elements, **most** to three or more. Arabic makes no such distinction and renders both by means of a superlative construction. e.g.

"This is the **more** complex solution of the two"

هذا هو أَكْثَرُ الحَلَّيْن تَعْقيداً

"She is the **most** beautiful of the family."

هِيَ الأَجْمَلُ في عائلَتِها

☞ for **the more ... the more**, see the 'Comparative'

Much/many

The difference between these two words is one of grammatical usage: **many** is used with countables, **much** with uncountables and is often interchangeable with *a great deal*. In Arabic, both are rendered by the same adjective, i.e. كَثير. e.g.

"It received interest and **much** (/ a great deal of) appreciation from world leaders and economists."

لَقَدْ حَظِيَ بِاهْتِمامٍ وَتَقْديرٍ كَثيرٍ مِن زُعَماء العالَمِ وَالخُبَراء الاقْتِصاديِّين

"**Many** cars will be put up for auction."

سَتُعْرَضُ سَيَّاراتٌ كَثيرَةٌ في المَزادِ

Also note the use of **much** as an adverb, meaning 'a great deal', 'a lot', which is also usually translated as كَثيرٌ: e.g.

"The government did not achieve much."

لَمْ تُحَقِّق الحُكومةُ كَثيراً

The expression '**many + a + sing. noun**' is a formal equivalent to 'many + plural noun'. e.g.

"**Many a** time, the public servants demanded a raise in salary."

طالَبَ المَوَظَّفُونَ بِرَفْعِ رَواتِبِهِم مَرَّاتٍ كَثيرةٍ

"**Many a** student fell into this trap."

وَقَعُ كَثيرٌ مِنَ الطُّلَّابِ في هذِهِ المِصْيدةِ

Nevertheless/notwithstanding

Nevertheless means *'in spite of that'* and is synonymous with **nonetheless**. As we have seen (q.v. 'even so'), it is rendered in Arabic by: مَعَ أن، عَلَى الرَّغْمِ مِنْ ذَلِكَ، بِالرَّغْمِ مِن ذَلِكَ، رَغْمَ، بِرَغْمِ. Note that **nonetheless** should not be confused with **none the less**, which simply means *'not less'*. **Notwithstanding** means *'in spite of (this)'* and often follows its object. It tends to be restricted to very formal and/or legal contexts. e.g.

"**Nevertheless**, we shall be forced to go ahead with the plans."

بِالرَّغْمِ مِن ذلِكَ فَإِنَّنا سَنُضْطَرُّ إِلى تَنْفيذِ الخُطَطِ

"I'm **none the less** happier for having lost my job."

بِرَغْمِ إِقالَتِي فَأَنا ما زِلْتُ سَعيداً

"She travelled to Egypt, doctor's orders **notwithstanding**."

سافَرَت إِلى مِصْرَ بِرَغْمِ نَصيحةِ طَبيبِها

Northeast/southeast/...

Whilst in English the combinations of the cardinal points come in a particular order, i.e. **north/south** preceding **east/west**, Arabic allows for either order, with the two elements appearing either in an إضافة, or as a **noun phrase** in which the second item is a *nisba* adjective modifying the first. e.g.

لَقِيَ 18 شَخْصاً حَتَفَهُم بِانْفِجارٍ في مَخْبَزٍ بِمَدينَةِ شَمالِ شرق/شَمال شرقي باكِسْتان

"Eighteen people were killed by an explosion at a bakery in a city in the **northeast** of/northeastern Pakistan."

زَحَفَ الجَيْشُ إلى جَنُوب شَرق البِلاد

"The troops moved towards the **southeast** (NOT *eastsouth) of the country."

☞ **NOTE:**
- these compounds can also be spelled with a hyphen. e.g. *north-east, south-west*;
- when they refer to a specified geopolitical entity, rather than a general geographical area, the cardinal points are spelled with a capital in English. e.g. '*North-South* dialogue' (حِوارٌ شَمال جَنُوب) where 'North' and 'South' represent industrialized countries and developing countries, respectively. Similarly, *North Africa* (إفْريقيا الشَّماليَّة) refers to a clearly defined entity, i.e. Tunisia, Morocco and Algeria, but not Egypt, even though it is in the north of the African continent.
- The forms **northeast<u>ern</u> /–west<u>ern</u>** and **south-east<u>ern</u>/–west<u>ern</u>** always refer to an undefined area and are thus not capitalized. In Arabic, both defined and undefined uses are translated identically. e.g.

'**South Africa**' (country): إفْريقيا الجَنُوبيَّة
'**southern** Africa' (area in the south of the African continent): مِنْطَقةٌ في شَمالِ إفْريقيا or جَنُوب إفْريقيا
'**Southeast** Asia' (geopolitical concept)/'**southeastern** Asia' (area in the southeast of the continent'): جَنُوبُ شَرقِ آسيا
'**northern** Africa' (area in the north of the continent): شِمال إفْريقيا

☞ **NOTE:** The English '**north /... OF...**' is rendered in Arabic by the respective noun in a genitive construction: e.g.

"The region **east of** the capital was hit by the storm."
كانَت المِنْطَقةُ شَرقُ العاصِمةِ مُصابةً بالعاصِفة

Not long before ...

The English constructions 'it was **not long before**', 'it does/did not take + **PRON long before**', 'it was/will not be long before' are rendered into Arabic by the verbs لَبِثَ and مَضَى:

PERFECT	أَنْ + حَتَّى	ما لَبِثَ
		لَمْ يَلْبَثْ
SUBJUNCTIVE	حَتَّى + أَنْ	لا يَلْبَثُ
		لَنْ يَلْبَثَ
PERFECT	حَتَّى +	لَمْ يَمْضِ
SUBJUNCTIVE	حَتَّى +	لَنْ يَمْضِيَ

e.g.

"**It wasn't long before** the militia responded to the attack on its headquarters."

ما لَبِثَتْ أَنْ رَدَّت الكَتائِبُ عَلَى اِقْتِحامِ مَقَرِّها

"**It wasn't long before** she discovered that he had not warned them of the danger."

لَمْ تَلْبَثْ أَنْ اِكْتَشَفَت أَنَّهُ لَمْ يُحَذِّرْهُم مِن الخَطَرِ

"**It wasn't long before** the dollar fell back once again."

ما لَبِثَ حَتَّى عادَ الدُّولارُ الأَميرِكِيُّ إلى التَّراجُعِ مِن جَديدٍ

"**It wasn't long before** he joined the intelligence services."

لَمْ يَمْضِ وَقْتٌ طَويلٌ حَتَّى اِنْتَمَى/اِنْضَمَّ إلى الاِسْتِخْباراتِ

"It doesn't take long before there is firing from all directions."

لا يَلْبَثُ أَنْ تَنْطَلِقَ النَّارُ مِن كُلِّ الاِتِّجَاهَاتِ

"She doesn't leave him unless she is forced to and **it does not take long before** she returns to him."

لا تُغادِرُهُ إلا مُضطَّرةً وَلا تَلْبَثُ حَتَّى تَعُودَ إلَيْهِ

"It won't be long before he gets a grip on himself and realizes his responsibilities towards his wife and children."

لَنْ يَلْبَثَ أَنْ يَسْتَعِيدَ نَفْسَهُ وَيُدْرِكَ مَسْؤُولِيَّاتَهُ تِجَاهَ زَوْجِتِهِ وأَبْنائِهِ

"It wasn't (/ was only) two centuries before oil changed the face of the world."

لَمْ يَمْضِ أَكْثَرُ مِن قَرْنَيْنِ حَتَّى غَيَّرَ النَّفْطُ وَجْهَ العالَمِ

"It will not be long before we're going to be forced to cooperate with that company."

لَنْ يَمْضِيَ وَقْتٌ طَويلٌ حَتَّى نَجِدَ أَنْفُسَنا مُجْبَرِينَ عَلَى التَّعامُلِ مَعَ تِلْكَ الشَّرِكَةِ

Not only/just ... but also

This construction can be rendered in a variety of ways in Arabic:

(أَيْضاً) (كَذَلِكَ)			JUSSIVE+	لَمْ
أَيْضاً	... بَلْ ...	فَحَسْبُ / + فَقَطْ	IMPERF. +	لا
			SUBJ. +	لَنْ
كَذَلِكَ			NOM. SENTENCE	لَيْسَ

e.g.

"He was **not only** a university teacher and educationalist **but also** a critic and a writer."

لَمْ يَكُنْ أُسْتاذاً جامِعيًّا وَمُرَبِّيًا فَقَطْ بَلْ ناقِداً وَكاتِباً كذلكَ

"This will **not only** be a failure of our policy **but** it will **also** dash our hopes of an independent country."

لَنْ يَكُونَ هذا سَبَباً في فَشَلِ سِياسَتِنا فَحَسْب بَلْ أَيْضاً سَيُخِيبُ آمالَنا في بلدٍ مُسْتَقِلٍّ

"It is **not just** a mistake ethically, **but also** – and above all else – unproductive."

لَيْسَت خاطِئَةً اِخْلاقِياً فَحَسْبُ بَلْ هِيَ، قَبْلَ كُلِّ شَيْءٍ، غَيْرُ مُثْمِرَةٍ

Not to mention …

This construction which is synonymous with *'let alone'* or *'to say nothing of'* is translated in Arabic by: ناهِيكَ عَنْ/مِن or بِغَضِّ النَّظَرِ عَن ,فَضْلاً عَن. e.g.

"The Ministry cannot pay the pensioners, **not to mention**/let alone the unemployed."

لا تَسْتَطيعُ الوِزارةُ أَنْ تَدْفَعَ للمُتَقاعِدينَ ناهيكَ/فَضْلاً عَن العاطِلينَ

"Five basic documents were submitted during the session, **not to mention** the interventions by the members of the Conference."

قُدِّمَتْ في الجَلْسَةِ خَمَس أَوْراقٍ أَساسِيَّةٍ بِغَضِّ النَّظَرِ عَنِ المُداخَلاتِ مِن قِبَلِ أَعْضاءِ المُؤْتَمَرِ

In Media Arabic, فَضْلاً عَن can be followed by the complementizer أن. e.g.

فَضْلاً عَنْ أَنَّ الوَضْعَ الحالِيَّ في العِراقِ هُوَ وَضْعٌ مَرْحَلِيٌّ ومَعْزُولٌ
'**Not to mention** that the current situation in Iraq is transitory and isolated.'

> **NOTE:** فَضْلاً عَن, especially when followed by ذلك can also denote 'besides, furthermore'. e.g.
>
> فَضْلاً عَنْ ذَلِكَ فإنَّهُ اكْتَسَبَ خِبْرَةً واسِعةً وعَميقةً في هذا المَجالِ
> '**Besides,** he acquired significant in-depth expertise in this field.'

Number/figure/digit/numeral

Number refers to a quantity, as well as the symbol used to represent it, whereas **digit** and **figure** tend to denote only the latter, for which **numeral** is also used. In Arabic, عَدَدٌ (p. أَعْداد) is used for quantities, series, etc. with رَقْم (pl. أَرْقامٌ) for the **figure**. e.g.

"The book didn't arrive because it was sent to the wrong PO Box **number**."

لَمْ يَصِلِ الكِتابُ لأَنَّهُ أُرْسِلَ إلى رَقْمِ صُنْدُوقِ بَريدٍ خَطَأً

"She called him on the new (telephone) **number**."

اِتَّصَلَتْ بِهِ عَلَى الرَّقْمِ الجَدِيدِ

"After the collision, the supervisor called all boats in, except for **number** five."

بَعْدَ الصَّدَمةِ اِسْتَدْعا المُشْرِفُ كُلَّ المَراكِبِ بِاسْتِثْناءِ الرَّقْمِ خَمْسةِ

"You have to write the **numbers** in **digits**."

يَجِبُ أَنْ تَكْتُبَ الأَعْدادَ بِأَرْقامٍ

"Arabic **numerals/digits** go back to Indian **numerals/digits**."

تَتَحَدَّرُ الأَرْقامُ العَرَبِيَّةُ مِنَ الأَرْقامِ الهِنْدِيَّةِ

"The swimming pool is in the shape of the **figure** nine."

إِنَّ المَسْبَحَ بِشَكْلِ رَقْمِ تِسَعةٍ

> ☞ **NOTE:** when it involves a series of a newspaper, magazine, etc., Arabic uses عَدَدٌ, which should be translated as **issue** in English. e.g.
>
> "The article on the French expedition in Egypt was published in the eighth **issue** of the journal."
>
> نُشِرَتِ المَقالةُ الَّتِي تُعالِجُ/تَتَناوَلُ الحَمْلَةَ الفَرَنْسِيَّةَ في مِصْرَ في العَدَدِ الثامِنِ لِلْمَجَلَّةِ

When used to denote an unspecified quantity, in the meaning of '*several*', **a number of** is rendered in Arabic by عَدَدٌ مِن (never with the definite article!) or عِدَّةٌ, which is used in apposition. e.g.

"The police arrested **a number of/several** thieves."

قَبَضَتِ الشُّرْطَةُ عَلَى لُصُوصٍ عِدَّةٍ
قَبَضَتِ الشُّرْطَةُ عَدَداً مِنَ اللُّصُوصِ

Note that the verb is in the plural in English:

"**A number of** workers are demonstrating in front of the company."

يَعْتَصِمُ عَدَدٌ مِنَ العُمَّالِ أَمامَ الشَّرِكةِ

When there is reference to a specified group of items, the English construction involves the use of the definite article – **the number(s) of –**, whereas in Arabic the noun عَدَدٌ is used, in a genitive construction (إضافة). e.g.

"This Act is aimed at reducing **the number(s) of** youngsters not in employment."

يَهْدُفُ هَذا القانُونُ إلى تَخْفِيضِ عَدَدِ الشَّبابِ العاطِلِينَ

Obligation

In English, this is expressed through a variety of verbs: **must, have to, ought to, should.** These can be classified according to degree and type of obligation. In terms of the former, the hierarchy is, in descending order of intensity, i.e. from strong (**must – have to**) to medium (**should**) and weak (**ought to**).

In addition, **must** and **have to** express different types of obligation, with the latter being used when it is imposed from without (external), and the former if it is by the speaker him/herself (internal): e.g. 'You have to lock the car doors' (because it's not a safe neighbourhood) vs 'I must remember to buy my mother a card for her birthday' (nobody is telling me to do this).

In Arabic, there is a similar set of distinctions, expressed through verbs, prepositions and adverbial constructions expressing necessity.

In order to express a strong obligaton (**must, have to**) the following can be used:

يَجِبُ			SUBJ. + أَنْ
يَتَحَتَّمُ			
يَتَعَيَّنُ ('it is incumbent upon someone to ...')	عَلَيْهِ		
يَتَوَجَّبُ ('it is necessary to...')			
مِنَ الواجِبِ ('it is a duty to ...')			VN/أَنْ
مِنَ اللازِمِ			
لا مَنْدُوحَةَ ('it is imperative')	لَهُ	عَنْ	
لا بُدَّ ('it is inescapable')		مِنْ	VN/أَنْ
لا مَفَرَّ ('it is inescapable')			
لا مَناصَ ('it is unavoidable')		مِنْهُ	

e.g.

"The curricula **have to** be designed with the children' ages in mind."
يَجِبُ أَنْ تُوضَعَ المَناهِجُ الدِّراسِيَّةُ مع مُراعاةِ عُمْرِ الأَطْفالِ

"The state which ratifies the agreement **has to/must** enforce it."
يَتَحَتَّمُ عَلَى الدَّوْلَةِ الَّتي تُصَدِّقُ عَلَى الاتِّفاقِيَّةِ أَنْ تُنَفِّذَها

"Turkey **will have to/must achieve** more tangible progress in order to accede to the European Union."

سَيَتَعَيَّنُ عَلَى تُرْكِيا أَنْ تُحَقِّقَ مَزِيداً مِنَ التَّطَوُّرِ المَلْمُوسِ حَتَّى تَنْضَمَّ إِلى الاتِّحادِ الأُورُوبِيِّ

"What are the measures that **have to** be taken to avoid the crisis from spilling over into Lebanon?"

ما هِيَ الإِجْراءاتُ الَّتِي يَتَعَيَّنُ اتِّخاذُها لِتَفادِي انْتِقالِ الأَزْمةِ إِلى لُبْنانَ؟

"Every journalist **has to/must** follow his conscience."

يَتَوَجَّبُ عَلَى كُلِّ صُحُفِيٍّ أَنْ يُتْبِعَ ضَمِيرَهُ

"Workers in this field **have to/must** broaden the concept of critical experiment."

مِنَ الواجِبِ عَلَى العامِلِينَ فِي هذا المَجالِ تَوْسِيعُ مَفْهُومِ التَّجْرِبَةِ التَّقْدِيَّةِ

"At the same time we **have to/must** realize that progress lies in creativity and technology."

فِي الوَقْتِ نَفْسِهِ يَجِبُ عَلَيْنا أَنْ نُدْرِكَ أَنَّ التَّقَدُّمَ فِي الابْداعِ وَالتِّكْنُولُوجِيا

"There **must** be a proper reading of the charter in order to reveal the real aims of the parties concerned."

لا مَنْدُوحةَ عَنْ قِراءَةٍ صَحِيحةٍ لِهذِهِ المِيثاقِ كَيْ يَرْفَعَ الحِجابِ عَنِ الهَدَفِ الحَقِيقِيِّ لِلأَطْرافِ

"We also **have to/must** recognize that this development is dangerous for our defensive capability."

لا مَفَرَّ لَنا مِنَ الاعْتِرافِ بِأَنَّ هذا النَّمُو ضارٌّ بِقُدْرَتِنا الدِّفاعِيَّة

"Sometimes, we **have to/must** take decisions like these which are difficult for all of us."

فِي بَعْضِ الأَحْيانِ يَجِبُ أَنْ نَتَّخِذَ مِثْلَ هذِهِ القَراراتِ الصَّعْبَةِ عَلَيْنا جَمِيعاً

In English, advisability is generally expressed by should and ought to, which may be rendered by (in descending order of obligation):

مِنَ الضَّرُوريّ أَنْ ('it is necessary that ...')

يَنْبَغي أَنْ ('it is desirable ...')

يُسْتَحْسَنُ أَنْ ('it is advisable ...')

يَجْدُرُ (بِهِ) + مصدر ('it is proper, appropriate ...')

e.g.

"There **should/ought to** be a truly effective monitoring system."

مِنَ الضَّرُوريّ أَنْ يَكُونَ نِظامُ المُراقَبَة فَاعِلاً تَماماً

"The committee **should** widen its scope."

يُسْتَحْسَنُ أَنْ تُوَسِّعَ اللَجْنةُ عَمَلَها

"If these symptoms recur frequently, even after resting, you **should** seek the advice of your physician."

إذا تَكَرَّرَت نَوْباتُ هذِهِ الأَعْراضِ حَتَّى بَعْدُ الاسْتِراحةِ يُسْتَحْسَنُ الأَخْذُ بِرَأْيِ طَبيبِكَ

"People **should** take a good look at this historic period and ask themselves: 'Is this our future?'"

يَنْبَغي أَنْ يَتَمَعَّنَ النَّاسُ جَيِّداً في هذِهِ الفَتْرةِ التَّاريخِيَّةِ وَيَتَساءَلَ: هَلْ هذا هُوَ مُسْتَقْبِلُنا؟

"Perhaps, that question **should** be put to him."

رُبَّما يَجْدُرُ طَرْحُ ذلِكَ السُّؤالِ عَلَيْهِ

Occasionally, weak obligation can also be translated by مِنَ الأَحْسَنِ: e.g.

"I **ought** to think of this."

مِنَ الأَحْسَن أَنْ أُفَكِّرَ في هذا

In addition to should and ought to, advisability is also rendered by had better, which, however, often has threatening undertones. In Arabic, this is often translated by يَتَعَيَّنُ. e.g.

"The government had better approve the budget in order to avoid another crisis."

يَتَعَيَّنُ عَلَى الحُكُومةِ أَنْ يُوافِقَ عَلَى المِيزانِيةِ حَتى تَتَمَكَّنَ تَجَنُّبِ أَزمةٍ جَدِيدةً

When **should** and **ought to** denote **expectation**, they can be used interchangeably with '**be supposed to + INF**', which is best rendered in Arabic by مِن المُفْتَرَضِ or أَنْ يُفْتَرَضُ + though يَتَعَيَّنُ can also be used in cases where the expectation is close to an obligation: e.g.

"An army of occupation is supposed to protect the lives of the people it has occupied."

يُفْتَرَضُ أَنْ تُؤَمِّنَ قُوّاتُ الِاحْتِلال حَياةَ الشَّعْبِ الّذِي اِحْتَلَّتْها

"The Supreme Court **is supposed to** hand down its decision in mid-June."

مِن المُفْتَرَضِ أَنْ تُصْدِرَ المَحْكَمةُ العُلْيا قَرارَها في مُنْتَصِفِ حَزِيران (يونيو)

"We don't know what we're **supposed to** do."

لا نَعْرَفُ ماذا يَتَعَيَّنُ عَلَيْنا أَنْ نَفْعَلَ

Should/ought to have + PART. is translated as كانَ يَنْبَغِي أَنْ when it involves past **expectation** and as كانَ مِن الواجِب عَلَيهِ أَنْ in the case of past **obligation**. e.g.

"The exam **should have** started at 8 am."

كانَ يَنْبَغِي أَنْ/مِنَ المُفْتَرَضِ أَنْ يَبْدَأَ الِامْتِحانُ في السَّاعةِ الثَّامِنةِ صَباحاً

"The UN stressed that the government **should** not **have** accepted this situation."

شَدَّدَتِ الأُمَمُ المُتَّحِدةُ عَلَى أَنْ كانَ يَنْبَغِي أَلا تَقْبَلَ الحُكُومةُ هذا الوَضْعَ

"She **should have** asked herself: 'How are we going to work together in order to achieve our common goals.'"

كانَ مِنَ الواجِبِ عَلَيْها أَنْ تَسْأَلَ نَفْسَها: كَيْفَ نَتعاوَنَ مِن أَجْلِ تَحْقِيقِ أَهْدافِنا المُشْتَرَكةِ

Negative prohibition is rendered by **mustn't**, which is expressed in Arabic by يَجِبُ أَلا.

"You **mustn't** (/shouldn't) forget to move the furniture." [= You must remember to move the furniture.]

يَجِبُ ألا تَنْسَى أَنْ نَنْقُلَ الأثاثَ

☞ **NOTE**

- The use of **needn't** to express **lack of necessity**, which can be translated into Arabic by the following:

  لا يَجِبُ أَنْ
  لَيْسَ لِزاماً
  لَيْسَ مُلْزِماً
  لا حَاجَةَ أَنْ

  e.g.

  "We **needn't** (/don't have to) attend the next meeting."
  لا يَجِبُ/لَيْسَ لِزاماً/لَيْسَ مُلْزِماً/لا حَاجَةَ أَنْ نَحْضُرَ الاِجْتِماعَ المُقْبِلَ

- The use of **must be** (**have been** in the past) to denote a degree of certainty:

  لا بُدَّ أَنَّ in the past). (كانَ + (قَدْ) + لا بُدَّ أَنَّ) لا بُدَّ أَنَّ

  e.g.

  "The teacher **must be** in his office by this time."
  لا بُدَّ أَنَّ الأُسْتاذَ في مَكْتَبِهِ في هذا الوَقْتِ

  "The teacher **must have been** in his office." [= It is very likely that he was in his office.]
  لا بُدَّ أَنَّ الأُسْتاذَ قَدْ كانَ في مَكْتَبِهِ في هذا الوَقْتِ

☞ **NOTE** the following correspondences:

mustn't: يَجِبُ ألا

needn't: لا يَجِبُ أنْ

e.g.

"We **mustn't** (/shouldn't) forget to move the furniture."

يَجِبُ ألا نَنْسَى أنْ نَنْقُلَ الأثاثَ

"We **needn't** (/don't have to) stop feeling sorry for the victims of the attack."

لا حاجَةَ أنْ يَتَوَقَّفَ تَعاطُفُنا مَعَ ضَحايا الهُجومِ

The passive (صِيغَةُ المَجْهُول)

In terms of form, the Arabic passive distinguishes itself from its English counterpart by the number of possible constructions. The English passive voice is expressed by an auxiliary verb added to the past participle of a transitive verb. e.g. 'is eaten', 'will have been done'. Arabic, on the other hand, can render the passive by means of:

1. **Inflection**: most verb forms have a passive voice, but some do not (VII and IX), whereas others (V, VI) are extremely rare. e.g.

"Several guards **were killed** near the presidential palace."

قُتِلَ بَعْضُ الحُرّاسِ قُرْبَ قَصْرِ الرِّئاسة

"They **were goaded** to accept the agreement before the arrival of the delegation."

حُرّضُوا عَلَى قَبُولِ الاتِّفاقِيَّةِ قَبْلَ وُصولِ الوَفْد

"Experts **were surprised** that the percentage of people living in the countryside in Egypt amounted to 75 per cent."

فُوجِئَ الخُبَراءُ بِأَنَّ نِسْبَةَ سُكَّانِ مِصْرَ المُقيمينَ في الرِّيفِ بَلَغَت 75 بِالمِئة

"The teacher **was invited** to give private classes to the children."

أُسْتُدعِيَ المُدَرِّسُ لِإعْطاءِ الأَوْلادِ دُرُوساً خُصُوصِيَّةً

2. **Form I** verbs that have inherent passive meaning. e.g.

"The report will be published to commemorate the liberation of the country."

سيَصْدُرُ التَّقْريرُ بِمُناسَبةِ ذِكْرى تَحْريرِ البِلادِ

3. **derived verb forms** that have inherent passive meaning (V, VII, VIII, IX). e.g.

"The remainder of the seats **was distributed** among the small parties."

تَفَرَّقَتْ بَقِيَّةُ الَمقَاعِدَ عَلَى الأَحْزاب الصَّغِيرَة

"The student **got upset** when he saw the principal at the club."

اِنْفَعَلَ الطَّالِبُ عِنْدَما رَأَى مُدِيرَ الَمدْرَسة فِي النَّادِي

"The agreement **was concluded** in Tunis."

أُبْرِمَتْ الاتِّفَاقِيَّةُ فِي تُونُس

"Multinational forces **are spread** all over the province."

إِنَّ القُوَّاتِ الَمتَعَدِّدَةِ الجِنْسِيَّات تَنْتَشِرُ فِي الوِلاية

"Faces **were turned** red, and heads bowed in shame."

اِحْمَرَّت الوُجُوهُ وطَأْطَأَتِ الرُّؤُوسُ بِخَجَلٍ

4. an **auxiliary** (تَمَّ, جَرَى), the so-called 'periphrastic' passive, which is a popular device in some types of Media Arabic. e.g.

"The goals of this strategy **are being investigated**."

يَتِمُّ تَحْقِيقُ أَهْدافِ هذِهِ الاسْتِراتِيجِيَّاتِ

"The final touches **are being put** to the 15,000 housing units."

يَجْرِي حالِيّاً تَنْفِيذُ الأَعْمالِ النِّهائِيَّةِ فِي 15 أَلْفَ وَحْدَةٍ سَكَنِيَّةٍ

Unlike the English passive voice, in which the agent or doer (the one performing the action) may be mentioned, the rules of Arabic grammar preclude this, though an exception is made for instruments, which are then introduced by the preposition بِـ. e.g.

"The letter **was written** with invisible ink."

كُتِبَتِ الرِّسالةُ بِحِبْرٍ لا مَرْئِيٍّ

In modern Media Arabic, it is not uncommon to find the agent expressed, in which case it is introduced by preposition مِنْ or adverbials such as مِنْ طَرَف ('on the part of'), عَلَى يَد ('at the hands of') or مِنْ قِبَل ('on behalf/the part of'). Despite its common occurrence, it is not considered normative usage and is frowned upon by careful users of Arabic. e.g.

"The debts **were cancelled** by the central banks."

أُلْغِيَت الدَّيُونُ مِنْ طَرَفِ الْبُنُوكِ الْمَرْكَزِيَّةِ

"The truce **was broken** by the government."

تَمَّ اخْتِرَاقِ الْهُدْنةِ مِن جانِبِ الْحُكومةِ

"The three rebels **were killed** at the airport by the special anti-terrorist unit."

قُتِلَ الْمُتَمَرِّدُونَ الثَّلاثَةُ عَلَى يَدِ القوَّاتِ الخاصَّةِ بِمكافَحَةِ الإِرْهابِ في الْمَطارِ

"He visited the American embassy there, and **was received** by one of the officials who welcomed the delegations."

قامَ بِزِيارَةِ السّفارَةِ الأَمْريكيَّةِ هُناكَ حَيْثُ اسْتُقْبِلَ مِنْ قِبَلِ أَحَدِ الْمَسْؤُولِينَ الَّذي رَحَّبَ بِالوُفُودِ

> ☞ **NOTE** that the object of action is the SUBJECT of the verb and is thus takes the **nominative** case.

▶ With **ditransitive** verbs, i.e. those that take two objects (as opposed to a verb and a preposition), the passive construction turns one of them into the (dummy) subject, whereas the other becomes the object and is thus marked in the accusative case. e.g.

"This kind of talk **is considered** an abominable insult in the Arab world."

هذا الكَلامُ يُعَدُّ شَتيمةً فَظيعَةً في الوَطَنِ العَرَبِيِّ

"The general **was given** a present."

أُعْطِيَ الجَنرالُ هَديةً
أُعْطِيَتْ هَديَّةٌ للجَنرالِ

"The child **was named** Hind."

سُمِّيَت الْبِنْتُ هِنداً

▸ With **indirect transitive** verbs, the indirect object is maintained and no subject is expressed; as a result, the verb always remains in the third person masculine form. e.g.

"The criminals were convicted."

حُكِمَ عَلَى الْمُجْرِمِينَ

This peculiar feature also extends to the participle. e.g.

"the convicted criminals."

الْمُجْرِمُونَ الْمَحْكُومُ عَلَيْهِم

▸ In some instances, an Arabic passive must be translated by an **active** verb in English. e.g.

"He died two days ago."

تُوُفِّيَ قَبْلَ يَوْمَيْنِ

▸ In many cases the Arabic passive has **potential** meaning and is therefore often translated into English by an adjective ending '–able/ible'. This applies to both passive participles and finite verbs (most notably with a negative). e.g.

مَسْمُوع, 'audible'
مَشْرُوبات ('drinkables'), 'beverages'
لَا يُصْبَرُ عَلَيْه, 'unbearable'
لَا يُعاشَرُ, 'unsociable'
لَا يُسْتَغْنَى عَنْهُ, 'indispensable'
لَا يُحْصَى, 'innumerable'

مُحْتَرَم, 'respectable'
مَنْقُول, 'movable'
لَا يُشْرَبُ, 'undrinkable'
لَا يُنْسَى, 'unforgettable'
لَا يُدْحَضُ, 'irrefutable'
لَا يُعَدُّ, 'countless'

The past (الماضِي)

The past is essentially expressed in Arabic by the perfect (الماضِي) tense (either with or without the addition of كان), while English has six past tenses: the **simple past** is used to denote a definite point in the past, or a past state; the **present perfect** reflects a period that started in the past and leading up to the present time; the **past perfect** denotes a past event taking place before another one in the past. The action in each of these can be stressed by the **progressive** aspect.

The Arabic-English correspondences may be presented as follows:

he did (Simple Past)	فَعَلَ	definite point in the past
he has done (Present Perfect)	(قَدْ/ لَقَدْ) فَعَلَ	period that started in the past and leads up to the present
he had done (Past Perfect)	كانَ (قَدْ) فَعَلَ	event taking place before another one in the past
he had been doing (Past Perfect Progressive)		
he was doing (Past Progressive)	كانَ يَفْعَلُ	stress on activity
he has been doing (Present Perfect Progressive)	يَفْعَلُ / كانَ يَفْعَلُ	

For the translator, the following points merit attention:

i. the **present perfect** and **present perfect progressive** can be expressed by means of the imperfect (indicative), especially with the particle مُنْذُ and a time adverbial, which denotes a period of time starting in the past and leading up to the present. e.g.

"I **have been saying** to him for a long time that he needs to study harder (be diligent in his studies)."

أَقُولُ لَهُ مُنْذُ وَقْتٍ طَوِيلٍ بِأَنَّهُ يَجِبُ أَنْ يَجْتَهِدَ في دِراسَتِه

The present perfect progressive is also often translated in Arabic by means of لَمْ يَزَلْ or ما زالَ, لا يَزالُ (also see 'KEEP ON ...'). e.g.

"The declaration has been awaited for two weeks."

ما زالَ البَيانُ مُتَوَقَّعاً مُنْذُ أُسْبُوعَيْنِ

"This issue has been causing division and controversy since the foundation of the organization."

لا تَزالُ هذِه المَسْأَلَةُ تُثِيرُ انْقِساماً وجَدَلاً مُنْذُ تَأْسِيسِ المُنَظَّمةِ

"He has been a revolutionary for forty years."

لَمْ يَزَلْ ثائِراً مُنْذُ أَرْبَعِينَ عاماً

مُنْذُ is also translated by a **present perfect** when it appears in a nominal sentence, often with an active participle. e.g.

"There **has been** much interest in voting in the elections **since** early morning."

إِنَّ هُناكَ إِقْبالٌ شَدِيدٌ عَلَى التَّصْوِيتِ في الانْتِخاباتِ مُنْذُ الصَّباحِ الباكِرِ

"The picture **has been** clear to us **for** more than two months."

لَقَدْ أَصْبَحَتِ الصُّورَةُ واضِحَةً لنا مُنْذُ أَكْثَرَ مِنْ شَهْرَيْنِ

ii. كانَ يَفْعَلُ is translated as '**used to**'. e.g.

كانَ يَكْتُبُ المَسْرَحِيَّاتِ الكُومِيدِيَّةَ في أَثْناءِ دِراسَتِه بِالجامِعَةِ
"During his university days, he **used to** write comedies."

iii. The **past progressive** can also be translated by كانَ and an active participle. e.g.

"He **was coming** from Alexandria, carrying a heavy suitcase."

كانَ قادِماً مِن الإسْكَنْدَرِيَّةِ حامِلاً حَقيبَةً ثَقيلَةً

iv. The past progressive often denotes **simultaneity**. e.g.

"He was lying when he said that he agreed to the request."

كانَ يَكْذِبُ عِنْدَما قالَ إنَّهُ وافَقَ عَلَى الطَّلَبِ

"The tank was destroying the centre of the town while two aircraft were circling over the suburbs."

دَمَّرَت الدَّبَّابةُ وَسَطَ المَدينةِ بَيْنَما كانَت طائِرتانِ تُحَلِّقانِ فَوقَ التُّخُومِ

"There is no doubt that the directors **knew** the predicament brought about by this type of production."

لا شَكَّ في أنَّ المُخْرِجينَ كانُوا يَعْرِفُونَ مَأزِقَ هذا النَّوْعِ مِنَ الإنْتاجِ

"He **realized** from the start that this operation was both unjust and tyrannical."

كانَ يُدْرِكُ مُنْذُ البِدايَةِ أنَّ العَمَلِيَّةَ جائِرةٌ وظالِمَةٌ

v. The Arabic perfect sometimes has to be translated by a **simple present** in English:

a. in certain **conditional** constructions (**q.v.**);

b. In the case of verbs expressing a state. e.g.

تَعِبَ, 'he is tired' (كانَ مُتْعَباً, 'he **was** tired')
عَطِشَ, 'he is thirsty' (كانَ عَطْشاناً, 'he **was** thirsty')
جاعَ, 'he is hungry' (كانَ جائعاً, 'he **was** hungry').

c. With verbs expressing a desire, wish or decision (resultative). e.g.

اِتَّفَقْنا, 'we **are** in agreement'
عَلِمْنا ذلكَ, 'we **know** this.'

vi. The Arabic perfect is translated by a **subjunctive (q.v.)** in English in certain wishing formulae. e.g.

بارَكَ الله فيكَ, '(May) God **bless** you'
رَعاهُ/حَفظَهُ الله, '(May) God **protect** him'
رَحَمَهُ الله, '(May) God **have** mercy on him'

vii. The **past perfect** can also be expressed by a periphrastic construction involving (قَدْ سَبَقَ أَنْ) ('*it preceded*'), followed by a perfect tense. e.g.

سَبَقَ أَنْ عَرَضْنا الأَهْدافَ الرَّئيسيّة للاسْتراتيجيّة في المَقال السَّابِق
"We **had put** forward the principal goals of the strategy in the previous article."

"The president referred to the fact that he **had demanded** that the Arabic summit be held at specific times every year."
أَشارَ الرَّئيسُ إلى أَنَّهُ قَدْ سَبَقَ أَنْ طالَبَ بِأَنْ تَكُونَ للقِمَّة العَرَبِيّة اجْتِماعاتُها المُحَدَّدَةُ سَنويّاً

viii. The particles قَدْ and لَقَدْ are often used with the past tense to denote aspectual differences and are rendered either by a **simple past** or a **present perfect**:

a. **near past.** e.g.

"I saw her (only) fifteen minutes ago."
قَدْ رَأَيْتُها قَبْلَ رُبْع ساعَةٍ

b. to stress the **completed** nature of the action, in which case one would often add the word 'indeed'. e.g.

"Egypt **(has) (indeed) achieved** a great victory in the African Nations Cup this year."

قَدْ حَقَّقَت مِصْرُ فَوْزاً عَظيماً في كَأْس الأُمَم الإفْريقيَّة هذا العام

"The new law **indeed** came into effect yesterday."

قَدْ دَخَلَ القانُونُ الجَديدُ في حَيِّز التَّنْفيذِ أَمْسِ

Prefixes

The translation of prefixes – as well as suffixes (**q.v.**) – constitutes a particular problem in English to Arabic translation, rather than the other way around. Indeed, though Arabic has prefixes, infixes (elements added within the word stem) and suffixes, these are derivational and inflectional morphemes, which are limited in number. Consider the following examples (the affixes are in bold) :

مَ : مَعْمَل (clitic denoting place) + عَمِلَ ('to work') à 'place where work is carried out' à a factory;

م : مِفْتاح (clitic denoting instrument) + فَتَحَ ('to open') à 'tool for opening' à key.

English does not have infixes (elements added within the word stem), while many of the affixes are of foreign origin, especially Latin and Greek, that are not always easily identifiable and/or translatable. There are many cases where the affixation process is a mere historical fact, such as 'diagnosis' (> Gr. dia, 'through' and gnosis, 'knowledge'), which is no longer considered an affixated compound since neither of its two constituent components has survived as an independent morpheme in English. The Arabic translation, تَشْخيص, is a wholly native construct, devoid of affixes. This example shows that the translation of prefixes is not merely a question of morpheme-for-morpheme rendition of the SL terms.

The translator should also be mindful of those cases where the same cluster is not, or ever has been, an affix, but is, rather, part of the root of the word. For instance, in 'epistle' (رسالة) the '**epi-**' is not an added morpheme, whereas it is one in a word like 'epicentre'.

One may identify several possible methods of translation of English prefixated compounds into Arabic:

1. as a simple word
   e.g. 'to recreate', جَدَّدَ;

2. genitive construction (إضافة)
   e.g. 'overproduction', إفْراط (فرط) الإنْتاج

3. prepositional phrase;
   e.g. 'subterranean', تَحْتَ سَطْح الأَرْضِ; 'supernatural', فَوْقَ الطَّبِيعَةِ

4. noun phrase (Adjective + Noun)
   e.g. 'low-born', وَضِيعُ النَّسَبِ

5. compound:
   e.g. 'decentralization', لامَرْكَزِيَّة

6. noun phrase: noun + preposition + DEF noun
   e.g. 'subspecies', فَرْع مِن الفَرْع

Generally speaking, most English prefixes are not rendered as clitics in Arabic, which is syntactically averse to compounding of this type, and instead prefers a genitive construction. A rule of thumb is that for recent coinings, there is a higher probability of the prefix being rendered by a separate morpheme in Arabic, than in words that are only etymologically affixated compounds, as in the case of 'eulogy'. In other words, if the prefix identifiably carries independent meaning, it is more likely that the Arabic translation will be a construct phrase (إضافة).

Several English prefixes may be rendered by the same Arabic term. e.g. 'contra-', 'counter-', 'anti-' all tend to be rendered by the noun مُضاد (in preference to ضِدّ).

The following table lists the principal ways to translate some common English prefixes:

	Variants	meaning	translation	example	translation
a-	-	privation	لا	'apolitical'	لا سِياسِيّ
anti-		against	مُضاد	'antibiotics'	مُضاد حَيَوِيّ
			ضِدّ	'antisocial'	ضِدّ النِّظام الاجْتِماعِيّ
ante-	-	before	قَبْل	'antenatal'	قَبْل الوِلادة
bi-	-	twofold, double	ثُنائِيّ	'bilingual'	ثُنائِيّ اللُّغة
contra-	-	against	مُضاد	'contraception'	مانِع الحَمْل (مُضاد للحَمْل)
counter-	-	against	ضِدّ	'counterrevolution'	ثَوْرة مُضادّة
cross-	-	through	عَبْر	'cross-dialectal'	عَبْر اللَّهَجات
de-	-	privation	لا	'decentralization'	اللامَرْكَزِيّة

	Variants	meaning	translation	example	translation
di-	-	twofold, double	شائي	'dicephalous'	شائي الرأس
			مزدوج (ازدواجي)	'diglossia'	ازدواج اللغة
dia-	-	through	خلال	'diachronic'	خلال التاريخ
dys-	-	bad	سيء (.adj)	'dyspeptic'	سيء/عسر الهضم
			سوء (nouns)	'dystrophy'	سوء تغذية
			عسر	'dysmenorrhoea'	عسر الطمث/الحيض
epi-	-	above, around	فوق	'epicranium'	ما فوق القحف
			خارج		
			حول		

	Variants	meaning	translation	example	translation
eu-		good	حَسَن	'euphemism'	حُسْنُ التَّعْبِير
			جَوْدَة		جَوْدَةُ اللَّفْظِ
extra-	-	very	مُتَناهٍ، خارِج، غَيْر	'extraordinary'	خارِقٌ لِلعادَةِ/غَيْرُ عادِيٍّ / خارِجَ العادَةِ
		outside	غَيْر، خارِق	'extracurricular'	خارِجَ البَرْنامِجِ الدِّراسِيِّ
hemi-	-	half	نِصْف	'hemisphere'	نِصْفُ الكُرَةِ
hyper-	-	extreme	فَرْط	'hypersensitivity'	فَرْطُ الحَساسِيَّةِ
			أَفْراط		إفْراطُ الإحْساسِ
in-	im-	deprived of	غَيْر	'insufficient'	غَيْرُ كافٍ
ir-			(nouns) عَدَم	'irresponsibility'	عَدَمُ المَسْؤُولِيَّةِ

	Variants	meaning	translation	example	translation
			غَيْرُ (.adj)	'incomparable'	غَيْرُ قابِلٍ لِلْمُقارَنَة
			لا	'irrevocable'	لا يُرَدّ
infra-	-	beneath	تَحْتِيّ	'infrastructure'	بِنْيَةٌ تَحْتِيَّة
			تَحْتَ	'infrared'	أَشِعَّة تَحْتَ الحَمْراء
intra-	-	inside	فِي	'intramuscular'	فِي العَضَلِ
meta-	-	beyond	ما وَراءَ	'metaphysical'	ما وَراءَ الطَبيعَة
mono-	-	single	وَحيد	'monodimensional'	وَحيدُ/أُحادِيُّ الأَبْعاد
			أُحادِيّ	'monovalent'	أُحادِيّ (التَكافُؤ) التَكافُؤ
multi-	-	several	مُتَعَدِّد	'multicultural'	مُتَعَدِّدُ الثَقافات

	Variants	meaning	translation	example	translation
non-	-	privation	غَيْر	'non-combatant'	غَيْرُ مُحارِبٍ
			عَدَم	'non-being'	عَدَمُ الوُجُود
			عَدِيم	'non-porous'	غير مَسامي، عَدِيمُ المَسامِ
omni-	-	all	كُلِّيّ	'omnipotent'	كُلِّيُّ القُدْرَةِ
poly-	-	numerous	تَعَدُّد (nouns)	'polygamy'	تَعَدُّدُ الزَّوْجات
			مُتَعَدِّد (adj.)	'polychromatic'	مُتَعَدِّدُ الأَلْوان
post-	-	after	بَعْد	'post-mortem'	بَعْدَ المَوْت
pre-	-	before	قَبْل	'prenuptial'	ما قَبْلَ الزَّواج
			ما قَبْل	'Prehistory'	ما قَبْلَ التّارِيخ
quadri-	-	of four parts	رُباعِيّ	'quadrilateral'	رُباعِيُّ الأَطْراف

	Variants	meaning	translation	example	translation
re-	-	again	إعادة + مضاف إليه	'reconstruction'	إعادة الإعمار/العمارة/البناء
super-	-	above	خارق	'supernatural'	خارق للطبيعة
			فوق	'supersonic'	فوق السمعيّ
supra-	-	above	فوق	'supranational'	فوق الوطنيّ
trans-	-	through	عبر	'trans-Atlantic'	عبر المحيط
tri-	-	of three parts	ثلاثيّ	'trilateral'	ثلاثيّ الأطراف
ultra-	-	beyond	فوق	'ultrasound'	فوق الصوتيّ
un-	-☒	privation	عديم	'unconnected'	غير مُتّصل/مُنْفَصِل
			لا	'unjustifiable'	لا يُبَرَّر

	Variants	meaning	translation	example	translation
			بلا	'undoubtedly'	بلا رَيْب
			سِيِّء	'unfortunate'	سِيِّء الحَظّ
			دُون	'unlicensed'	دُون رُخْصَة
uni-	-	single	وَحِيد	'uni-axial'	وَحِيد المِحْوَر
			أحَادِيّ	'unicellular'	أحَادِيّ الخَلِيَّة
vice-	-	deputy	نائِب	'vice-president'	نائِب الرَّئِيس

The main prefix-related issue in English is spelling inasmuch as prefixes are variously written together with the base, or with hyphenation:

e.g. **'nonsense', 'non-stop'**.

> ☞ **NOTE:**
>
> 1. Generally speaking, the more established the affixated word, the more likely it is that the prefix is attached to the base;
>
> 2. When the prefix ends in a vowel and the base starts with a vowel, a hyphen tends to be used in order to avoid ambiguity. e.g. *'pre-eminence'* (rather than *preeminence*).
>
> 3. When the base is a proper noun, or adjective derived from a proper noun, the affixated compound must always be hyphenated. e.g. 'trans-Siberian'.

The present (الحَاضِرُ)

The main present tense in English is the **Simple Present**, which is used in order to denote:

- a state. e.g.

"I am happy."
أنا سَعِيدٌ

- a general truth. e.g.

"The sun sets in the west."
تَأْفَلُ الشَّمْسُ في المَغْرِبِ

- an action taking place in he present, especially with non-action (stative) verbs. e.g.

"I **need** a car now."

أَحْتَاجُ إلى سَيَّارَةَ الآنَ

- An habitual action. e.g.

"She **drinks** tea every day."

تَشْرَبُ شاياً كُلَّ يَوْمٍ.

"Ahmad always eats dinner at home."

يَتَنَاوَلُ مُحَمَّدٌ العَشاءَ في البَيْتِ دائماً

The above examples reveal that the English **simple present** is generally rendered in Arabic by the imperfect or, in the case of a sentence containing the verb 'to be', by means of a nominal sentence.

The **Present Progressive** (also known as present continuous) denotes actions that are taking place at the moment of speaking or those that are considered to be temporary (e.g. 'You're smoking a lot'). It cannot be used with stative verbs. For instance, a sentence such as 'I'm owning a car' is grammatically incorrect. The present progressive is translated either by the imperfect or an **active participle (with intransitive verbs)**, or VN + بـ قامَ. e.g.

"We **are watching** television so we can't go to the shop."

نُشاهِدُ التِّلْفازَ ولذلِكَ لا نَسْتَطِيعُ الذَّهابَ إلى المَحَلِّ

"I am **coming**/on my way."

أنا قادِمٌ

"The company **is** (currently) **producing** pens in its new plant."

تُنْتِجُ الشَّرِكَةُ أَقْلاماً في مَصْنَعِها الجَدِيدة

"The opposition **are organizing** unprecedented demonstrations against the government."

تَقُومُ المُعارضةُ بِاحْتِجاجاتٍ غَيْرُ مَسْبُوقةٍ ضِدَّ الحُكومةِ

The present simple and present progressive can also be used to refer to a (near) future action. This is usually rendered by سَوْفَ/ـَسَ + IMPERFECT in Arabic. e.g.

"I **leave/am leaving** for London tomorrow."

سَأُسافِرُ إِلَى لَنْدَن غَداً

The imperfect is **negated** by means of لا. e.g.

"He is not writing/does not write."

لا يَكْتُبُ

The present progressive construction involving the active participle is negated by means of لَيْسَ. e.g.

"I am not travelling today

لَسْتُ مسافراً الْيَومَ

> ☞ **NOTE:** Arabic-speakers should take care that the English present progressive is usually not used with 'to have' when it involves possession or an illness, in which case the present simple should be used: e.g. 'I have a headache' (عَنْدِي صُداعٌ), NOT *'I am having a headache'; 'I have a car' (عَنْدِي سَيّارةٌ), NOT *'I'm having a car'.

Presently/at present

Presently means 'in a short while' while **at present** means 'now'. The former may be translated in Arabic by عَنْ/بَعْد قَليلٍ ,عَمّا/عَنْ/مِنْ قَريبٍ, which are used with the imperfect, either with or without سَوْفَ/ـَسَ. The latter is typically rendered by في الوَقْتِ الحاضِرِ or الآنَ. e.g.

"We will have a solution **presently**."

سَيَكُونُ لَدَيْنا حَلٌّ عَمَّا قَرِيب

"I'll go to school **presently**."

سَأَذْهَبُ إلى المَدْرَسَةِ بَعْد قَلِيلٍ

"She is leaving **at present**."

تُغادِرُ الآنَ

"**At present**, the Israeli army is among the most powerful, best-trained and most advanced armies in the Middle East."

إنَّ الجَيْشَ الإِسْرائيليَّ يُعَدُّ في الوَقْتِ الحاضِرِ من أَقْوَى الجُيُوش في الشَّرْقِ الأَوْسَطِ وأَفْضَلِها تَذْريباً وأَحْدَثِها تَسْليحاً

Price/prize

A '**price**' is the amount of money one pays for something (سِعْرٌ, pl. أَسْعارٌ; ثَمَنٌ, pl. أَثْمانٌ); a '**prize**' is something one wins in a competition, etc. (جائزةٌ, pl. جَوائزُ). '**Price**' collocates with the verbs '**to pay**' (دَفَعَ (a)) and in Arabic also with '**to cost**' (كَلَّفَ), whereas in English '**to cost**' is used without the noun '**price**'. '**Prize**' collocates with '**to award**' (مَنَحَ (a)), '**to win**' [(فازَ (يَفُوزُ), حازَ (يَحُوزُ), أَحْرَزَ)], and '**to receive**' (تَسَلَّمَ). e.g.

"He won/received the Nobel **Prize** for chemistry."

أَحْرَزَ/تَسَلَّمَ/حازَ عَلَى/فازَ بجائزةُ نُوبِل في الكِيمِياءِ

"No matter how much it **cost**."

مَهْما كَلَّف الثَّمَنُ

"She paid the asking **price**."

دَفَعَتِ الثَّمَنَ/السِّعْرَ المَطْلُوبَ

> ☞ **NOTE:** in the context of the stock exchange, سِعْر is used in preference to ثَمَن. e.g.

"Share **prices** have continued to rise at the stock exchange."
اسْتَمَرَّت أَسْعارُ الأَسْهُمِ في الارْتِفاعِ في البُورْصَةِ

Principal/principle

Principal as a noun denotes the person in charge of a school (US), college, etc. (مُدِيرٌ, pl. مُدَراءُ، مُدِيرُونَ); as an adjective, it is synonymous with 'chief', 'most important' (رَئِيسِيّ). **Principle**, on the other hand, can only act as a noun, meaning something on which one bases one's beliefs or actions (مَبْدَأً, pl. مَبادِئُ). e.g.

"The **principal** opposition parties decided on a plan to put forward two joint nominees."
أَقَرَّتِ الأَحْزابُ الرَّئِيسِيّةُ في المُعارَضَةِ خُطَّةً لِتَقْدِيمِ مُرَشَّحَيْنِ مُشْتَرَكَيْنِ

"There was an agreement on the **principle** of withdrawal."
كانَ هُناكَ اتِّفاقٌ حَوْلَ مَبْدَأ الإنْسِحابِ

Punctuation (عَلامَاتُ تَنْقِيطٍ)

In English, punctuation marks are extensively used to help convey meaning and grammatical function, and are, therefore, subject to a number of restrictions. In Arabic, on the other hand, Western-style punctuation is essentially a 20th-century invention, though some examples can already be found in the latter quarter of the 19th century.

In contemporary Arabic, punctuation is patterned on Western, especially English, principles, albeit with some permutations. The most striking observation with regard to punctuation in contemporary Standard Arabic is, however, its inconsistency, which at times borders on the chaotic as a result of idiosyncratic variations. Among the points that are relevant to the translator, one may mention:

- **quotation marks** (inverted commas, quotes; (عَلاماتُ اقْتِباسٍ) : in addition to enclosing the words quoted from someone else, these marks are used to enclose citation forms of words. In English, they tend to be represented by single or double inverted commas (' '/" ").

In Arabic, on the other hand, they are also used for emphasis, to enclose foreign proper nouns such as the names of companies (though not for cities, countries, etc.) or dialectal borrowings, where English would typically use italics, or nothing at all.

The form varies, ranging from angular double quotes of the type used in French («/»), to double English inverted commas, though the latter are increasingly rarely used for typographical reasons, i.e. the possible confusion with *tanwīn*. e.g.

قال رَئيسُ شَرِكَةٍ «إكسون موبيل»: يَجِبُ أَنْ يَتَراوَحَ سِعْرُ برميل النَّفْطِ بَيْنَ 60 وَ 70 دُولاراً

According to the CEO of Exxon Mobil the price of oil will have to be between 60 and 70 dollars per barrel.

قال عَضْوٌ آخِرٌ في جَيْشِ الثُّوارِ : « نَحْنُ مُسْتَعِدُّونَ للقتال»

Another member of the revolutionary army said: "We are ready to fight."

"There are two worlds: *us*/Us and *them*/Them."
هُناكَ عالَمانَ : «نَحْنُ» و «هُم»

أَنْتَ مُتَّهَمٌ بِأَنَّكَ سَرَقْتَ « وابور غاز»
You are accused of stealing a 'gas stove'.

حَضَرَتِ المَرْأَةُ المَضْرُوبةُ تَتَعَثَّرُ في «ملسها» الأَسْوَدِ الطَّويل
"The wife that had been beaten entered and tripped on her long black *malas*."

أَعْلَنَ النَّائِبُ بِدَوْرِهِ، دَعْم «الشَّعبي»، لاِسْتِجواب «الوطني» وَمُشارَكَةَ أَحَد أَعْضاء الكُتْلَةِ الحَديثِ مُؤَيِّداً لِلاِسْتِجواب

"The deputy in turn announced the support of al-Sha'bi to al-Watani's interpellation and the participation by one of the members of the new bloc that support it."

أَلْقَى مُدِيرُ الأَمْنِ بِاللَّوْمِ عَلَى الإِعْلامِ في الاِنْفِلاتِ الأَمْنِي قائلاً: «الإِعْلامُ فَهَّمَ الناسَ أَنَّ هُناكَ غِياباً أَمْنِياً كامِلاً، وَهُوَ ما شَجَّعَ العَديدَ عَلَى اِرْتِكابِ الجَرائمِ».

The head of the security services blamed the media for the breakdown insecurity: "the Media inform people that there is a total absence of security, which encourages many to commit crimes."

- **round brackets** (قَوْسانِ) : these are, confusingly, also used as quotation marks in Arabic for citations, even if the practice is these days restricted to religious references (especially Qur'anic). This usage also explains the expression بَيْنَ القَوْسَيْنِ, 'between brackets', which is actually equivalent to the English 'between quotation marks/inverted commas'. In present-day formal Arabic, round brackets are predominantly used for:
  (1) foreign proper nouns;
  (2) foreign borrowings;
  (3) titles of books, films, etc.;
  (4) (foreign) abbreviations;
  (5) parentheses, providing additional information, explanatory **NOTE**s, etc.

In translation, they are rendered as follows:

Arabic	English
foreign proper nouns	Omitted
foreign borrowings	Italics
titles of books, films, etc.	Omitted
(foreign) abbreviations	Omitted
parentheses	=

e.g.

And the Almighty said: "We have created all living things out of water."

ثُمَّ قَالَ تَعالَى : (وَخَلَقْنَا مِنَ الْمَاءِ كُلَ شَيٍ حَيْ)

ثُمَّ قَالَ تَعالَى : (وَخَلَقْنَا مِنَ الْمَاءِ كُلَ شَيٍّ حَيْ)

"We spoke with the actress during the shooting of the soap *Nur Maryam*."

تَحَدَّثْنا مَعَ الفَنَّانة في كَوالِيس مُسَلْسَل (نور مريم)/أَثْناءَ تَصْويرِ مُسَلْسَل (نور مريم)

"The Rec.Sport.Soccer Statistics Foundation (RSSSF), which belongs to the International Football Federation (FIFA), was set up in 1994."

أُنْشِئَت مُنَظَّمَةُ إِحْصاءاتِ وَأَرْقامِ كُرة القَدَم (RSSSF) التّابِعَةُ للاتِّحادِ الدُّوَلِيّ لِكُرة القَدَم (الفيفا) في سَنَةِ 1994

"We only managed to eradicate 71% of illiteracy at the end of 2010, whereas it was 40% in1980 and 25% in 1960, and probably even less in 1952."

فلم نقض إلا عَلَى 71% (واحَد وَسَبْعينَ في المائة) مِنْ الأُمِّيَّة حَتَّى نهايَة عام 2010 بَيْنَما كانت نسبَةُ الأُمِّيَّة 40% (أَرْبَعُونَ في المائة) عام 1980 و 25% (خَمْسَة وَعِشْرُونَ في المائة) عام 1960 وَرُبَّما أَقَلُّ عن ذلِكَ في عام 1952

وَنَظَرَ القاضِي في (الرول) وقالَ:
"The judge looked at the roll and said: '...' "

فيتامين (د)
"vitamine D'

- **Exclamation** (عَلامَةُ التَّعَجُّب) and **question marks** (عَلامَةُ الاسْتِفْهام) : according to English usage, these should not be used together, or only sparingly in cases where there is a genuine question and outcry. In Arabic, however, one finds that authors tend to correlate the intensity of the utterance with the number of punctuation marks. In translation, these must be reduced. e.g.

"Who is responsible, the police or the demonstrators?"

مَنْ المَسْئُولُ: الشُّرْطة أَمْ المُتَظاهِرونَ؟!

- **Suspension points** (ellipsis): consisting of three dots, these should be used only in literature in English to indicate a pause in speech or an unfinished thought. It should not be used as a replacement of 'etc.' ('and so on') at the end of a list. In contemporary Arabic, on the other hand, both form (number of dots) and usage differ dramatically in that they seem to be used at the end of lists or for emphasis, or, occasionally, even added to other punctuation marks (!). In English translation, the Arabic suspension points are generally omitted or replaced by another punctuation mark (typically a comma), except in cases where they comply with English usage. e.g.

"And so, at specific times, when I suffer these breakdowns, I stay in bed for a whole day."

وَهَكَذا ... في فَتْراتٍ مُعَيَّنَةٍ ... في فَتْراتٍ انهياري تِلْكَ ... أَبْقَى في فِراشي يَوْماً كامِلاً

"The reformers know what they want, whereas we..."

المُصْلِحُونَ يَعْرَفُونَ ما يُريدُون، أَمّا نَحْنُ ...

"Yes?"

نعم ؟!

Relative pronouns

The differences in usage and forms of relative pronouns in English and Arabic pose a number of problems in translation.

Essentially, a relative pronoun provides additional information about a noun (or a clause). In the case of a **defining relative clause** it involves essential information without which the sentence would not be clear. In English, the choice of relative pronoun is determined by

(1) whether it refers to a place, human(s) or non-human(s);
(2) the type of information it contains regarding the **antecedent** (the part of the sentence to which it refers);
(3) the grammatical function of the relative pronoun in the clause;
(4) the presence of a preposition.

This may be represented as follows:

	Subject	Object	Possessive	Prepositional Phrase (PP)
Human(s)	who/ that	whom/ who/that	whose	PREP+whom
Non-human(s)	which/ that	which/ that	whose	PREP+which
Place	where			

Consider, for instance, the following sentence:

"I saw the man, **who** was in the park, sitting outside the house."

رَأَيْتُ الرَّجُلَ الَّذِي كانَ في الحديقة وَهُوَ جالِسٌ خارج البَيْتِ

In this case, the **who** refers to a person ('man') and is the **subject** of the relative clause, which provides additional – but non-vital – information. This type of clause is commonly known as a **non-defining** or **non-restrictive** clause and can be easily identified because:

i.   omitting it still yields a grammatically correct and semantically sound construction ('I saw the man parked outside the house.');
ii. of the presence of **commas.**

Conversely, in 'The car **that/which** I saw in the park' the relative clause provides essential information, and is therefore known as **defining** or **restrictive**. Note that in this case, there is no **comma**, while the relative pronoun may be omitted. e.g.

"The man [person] **who/that/NO PRON** [= subject] was there."

الرَّجُلُ الَّذي كانَ هُناكَ

"The man [person] **whom/who/NO PRON** [= object] we saw."

الرَّجُلُ الَّذي رَأَيْناهُ

"The dog [non-person] **which/that/NO PRON** [= subject] is here."

الكَلْبُ الَّذي هُنا

"The dog [non-person] **which/that/NO PRON** [= object] we saw."

الكَلْبُ الَّذي رَأَيْناهُ

"The man **whose** dog [possession] I saw."

الرَّجُلُ الَّذي رَأَيْتُ كَلْبَهُ

"The man **in whose** house [PP] I lived."

الرَّجُلُ الَّذي سَكَنْتُ في بَيْتِهِ

"The dog **whose** paw [possession] was hurt."

الكَلْبُ الَّذي كانَ كَفُّهُ مَجْرُوحاً

"The man **to whom** [OBJECT] I gave the book."

الرَّجُلُ الَّذي أَعْطَيْتُهُ الكِتابَ

"The dog **with which** [PP] she came in."

الكَلْبُ الَّذي دَخَلَت مَعَهُ

Arabic, on the other hand, does not make a distinction in terms of (non-) humanness of the antecedent.

The basic distinction in Arabic relative clauses is based on whether the antecedent is grammatically **definite** or **indefinite**. Relative pronouns are used only for **definite antecedents**.

	Masculine	Feminine
Singular	الَّذي	الَّتي
Dual	اللَّذانِ	اللَّتانِ
	اللَّذَيْنِ	اللَّتَيْنِ
Plural	الَّذين	اللاتي، اللَّواتي

There are two further differences between Arabic and English relative clauses in that Arabic has:

i.   pronouns denoting the **dual**. e.g.

"The two men **who** are in the hotel."

الرَّجُلانِ اللَّذانِ في الفُنْدُق

"The two girls **who** are in the hotel."

البِنْتانِ اللَّتانِ في الفُنْدُق

"I saw the two men **who** are in the hotel."

رَأَيْتُ الرَّجُلَيْنِ اللَّذَيْنِ في الفُنْدُق

"I saw the two girls **who** are in the hotel."

رَأَيْتُ البِنتَيْنِ اللَّتَيْنِ في الفُنْدُق

ii.   pronouns denoting the **plural**. e.g.

"The men **who** were in the house."

الرِّجالُ الَّذينَ كانُوا في البَيْتِ

"The two girls **who** are in the hotel."

اِلبَناتُ اللّاتِي/اللّواتِي فِي الفُنْدُق

iii. the need for a so-called **resumptive pronoun** (known as عائِدٌ), which is necessary when the antecedent is the **object** of a **verb** or a **preposition**. e.g.

"I forgot the suitcase in the hotel (that) we are staying at."

نَسِيتُ الحَقِيبَةَ فِي الفُنْدُقِ الّذِي نُقِيمُ فِيهِ

The use of the resumptive pronoun also explains why Arabic speakers often make the mistake of adding a pronoun in English relative clauses. e.g. *"This was the house that I lived in **it**", rather than, simply, 'This was the house that I lived in.'

When the reference is to a place, English uses **where** (or **in which**) and Arabic حَيْثُ. e.g.

"The prison **where** the dissidents were held."

السِّجْنُ حَيْثُ اعْتُقِلَ المُعارِضون

> ☞ **NOTE** that حَيْثُ has a **fixed** case ending.

Another area of possible pitfalls is that of **indefinite relative clauses**. English does not make a distinction when it comes to relative pronouns between an antecedent that is definite or not. e.g. 'the/a man **who** was there.' In Arabic, however, an **antecedent** that is grammatically **indefinite** does **NOT** take a relative pronoun. e.g.

"A man **who** was there."

رَجُلٌ كانَ هُناكَ

"A man **that** we saw there."

رَجُلٌ رَأَيْناهُ هُناكَ

Non-specific relative pronouns are those that do not have a specified antecedent:

Whichever (أَيٌّ);
whatsoever (أَيٌّ/ما/ماذا/مَهْما);
whoever/whosoever (مَنْ).

e.g.

"Sports strengthen your bones, **whatever** your age/no matter how old you are."

الرِّياضةُ تُقَوِّي عِظامَكَ أَيّا كانَ عُمْرُكَ

"**Whoever** said that is a liar."

مَنْ قالَ هذا فَهُوَ كَذَّاب

"Take **whichever** books you like, it's going to be a long flight."

خُذْ مَعَكَ أَيَّ كتابٍ يُعجِبُكَ فَستكون الرِّحلةُ طَويلةً

"**Whichever** option you choose, it's still going to be difficult to win the contest."

أَيّا كانَ اختيارُكَ ،فَسَيظَلُّ الفَوْزُ في المُسابَقة صَعْباً

Rise/raise

To rise is 'to go up' (اِرْتَفَعَ), whereas to raise means 'to make something go up' (رَفَعَ (a)). An increase in salary is called a **rise** or a **raise** (!). e.g.

"The prices **rose** last week."

اِرْتَفَعَتِ الأَسعارُ الأُسْبُوعَ الماضِي

"The government **raised** prices last week."

رَفَعَتِ الحُكومَةُ الأَسْعارَ الأُسْبُوعَ الماضِي

Say/tell

In English, **say** is a transitive verb which does not have a personal object; **tell** is a transitive verb which is usually followed by a personal direct object. In Arabic, **say** is generally rendered by قالَ (+ إِنْ), tell by, for instance, حَكَى، تَحَدَّثَ، حَدَّثَ، أَخْبَرَ. e.g.

"I **said** that I was unhappy."

قُلْتُ لَها إِنِّي كُنْتُ مَهْمُوماً

"He only **said** a few words to me."

لَمْ يَتَحَدَّثْ مَعِي إلاَّ قَلِيلاً

"He was **telling** me what (had) happened to his family during the war."

كانَ يُخْبِرُنِي بِما حَصَلَ لِعائِلَتِهِ خِلالَ الحَرْبِ

"She **tells** us many stories about her childhood."

تَحْكِينا/تُحَدِّثُنا قِصَصاً كَثِيرَةً عَنْ طُفُولَتِها

☞ **NOTE:** only **say** can be followed by a 'that'-clause in English: e.g.

"She **said** (NOT *told) **that** he was going home."

قالَتْ إِنهُ كانَ ذاهِباً لِلْبَيْتِ

Self

In order to express reflexivity, English uses **self**, which is added to a pronoun. e.g. *myself, yourself, herself* ... In Arabic, this is conveyed through the word نَفْس (pl. أَنْفُس), which means 'soul, spirit'. However, when نَفْس is the first element in an إضافة construction, denotes **same**. e.g.

"I can't imagine **myself** in a world without paper, pens and books."

لا أَتَصَوَّرُ نَفْسِي في عالَمٍ مِنْ دُونِ أَوْراقٍ وَأَقْلامٍ وُكُتُبٍ

"She told **herself** that she was being truthful."

قالَت لِنَفْسِها إنَّها صادِقةٌ

"He was injecting **himself**."

كانَ يَحْقِنُ نَفْسَهُ بِنَفْسِه

"We deserve to do this for **ourselves**."

نَسْتَحِقُّ أَنْ نَفْعَلَ ذلِكَ مِن أَجْلِ أَنْفُسِنا

"Instead of criticizing others, you should take a look at **yourselves**!"

اِلْقَوا نَظْرَةً إلى أَنْفُسِكم بَدَلاً مِن لَوْمِ الآخَرِينَ !

"Don't be stingy on **yourselves** (f.pl.)."

لا تَبْخَلْنَ عَلَى أَنْفُسِكُنَّ

"They(, **themselves**,) elected **themselves**."

اِنْتَخَبُوا أَنْفُسَهُم بِأَنْفُسِهِم

"Don't disturb **yourself**."

لا تُزْعِجْ نَفْسَكَ

☞ **NOTE:**

- the use of ذات to render '**self**' in expressions such as:

الثِّقَةُ بالذَّات, 'self-confidence'

اِحْتِرامُ الذَّاتِ, 'self-respect'

الحُكْمُ الذَّاتِيُّ, 'self-determination'

- the expression '**in itself**, في (حَدّ) ذاتِه. e.g.

"This crisis, **in itself**, is harmful to the national interest."

هذِهِ الأَزْمَةُ في حَدِّ ذاتِها إِضْرارٌ بالمَصالِحَ الوَطَنِيّة

"The people are not against an amendment of the constitution, **in itself**,
but rather to the character of the changes."

الشَّعْبُ لَيْسَ ضِدَّ تَعْدِيلِ الدُّسْتُور في ذاتِهِ وإِنَّما ضِدَّ نَوْعِيّةِ التَّغَيُّرات

Sensible/sensitive

Sensible denotes intelligence (حَصِيف, حَكِيم) whereas **sensitive** (حَسّاس) involves
emotions. e.g.

"His father was a **sensible** man who realized the importance of education."

كانَ أَبُوهُ رَجُلاً حَصِيفاً يَعْرِفُ أَهَمِّيَةَ التَّعْلِيم

"One of the female colleagues asked this **sensitive** question which was
causing her great concern."

سَأَلَتْ إِحْدَى الزَّمِيلاتِ هذا السُّؤالَ الحَسّاسَ الذي أَقْلَقَها جِدًّا

"Jojoba oil is excellent for people with **sensitive** skins."

زَيْتُ الجُوجُوبا رائِعٌ خُصُوصاً للأَشْخاصِ الَّذِينَ يُعانُونَ مِن جِلْدٍ حَسّاسٍ

Shade/shadow

These words cannot be used interchangeably in English, as **shade** denotes a place out of the sun, while **shadow** is the shape cast by an object, person, etc. In Arabic, both are rendered by ظِلّ (pl. ظُلُول, ظِلال, أَظْلال). However, when it involves a living being (especially a person or animal), **shadow** may also be translated by شَبَح (pl. أشْباح, شُبُوح). e.g.

"I saw him sitting in the **shade** of a tree near his uncle's house."

رَأَيْتُهُ وَهُوَ جالِسٌ تَحْتَ/في ظِلّ شَجَرَةٍ بِقُرْبِ بَيْتِ عَمِّهِ

"I noticed a **shadow** moving outside the bedroom."

لاحَظْتُ شَبَحاً مُتَحَرِّكاً خارِجَ غُرْفةِ النَّوْمِ

"Women continue to live in the **shadow** of men."

قَدْ ظَلَّتِ المَرْأَةُ تَعيشُ في ظِلّ الرَّجُلِ

"The long **shadow** of the bear appeared suddenly."

بَدا الظِّلُّ الوارِفُ للدُّبِّ مُفاجَأَةً

In **figurative** context, ظَلام can also be used. e.g.

"Diplomacy should take place in the light of day/out in the open, not in the **shadows**."

تَجْدُرُ مُمارَسةُ الدِّبْلوماسِيَّةِ في النُّورِ وَلَيْسَ في الظَّلامِ

☞ **NOTE** the following expressions:

- تَحْتَ ظِلّ/في + NOUN (+ GEN)/PRON: '**under the auspices of**'. e.g.

"The project was completed under the auspices/patronage of the UN."

تَمَّ المَشْرُوعُ تَحْتَ ظِلِّ الأُمَمِ المُتَّحِدةِ

BUT: في ظِلّ can also mean '**in (the) light of**' (!) ('in view of', 'considering'). e.g.

"The pharmacists' union believed that an increase in the price of medicines was not justifiable, particularly **in light of** the difficult economic conditions
that people are living in."

اِعْتَبَرَتْ نِقابَةُ الصَّيادلةِ أَنَّ رَفْعَ أَسْعارِ الأَدْوِيةِ لَيْسَ لَهُ ما يُبَرِّرُهُ، خُصُوصاً في ظِلِّ الظُّرُوفِ الاِقْتِصادِيَّةِ الصَّعْبةِ الَّتِي يُعِيشُها المُواطِنُونَ

- تَقَلَّصَ ظِلُّهُ:'his authority faded/decreased/(was) diminished/ dwindled'

- وِزارَةُ الظِّلّ: 'shadow cabinet'

Some/any

Some is used in affirmative sentences, **any** in interrogative and negative sentences. e.g.

"I saw **some** of the students."
رَأَيْتُ بَعْضَ الطُّلَّابِ

"Did you see **any** of the students?"

هَلْ رَأَيْتَ أَيّاً مِنَ الطُّلَّاب

"I didn't' see **any** of the students."

لَمْ أَرَ أَيّاً مِنَ الطُّلَّاب

☞ NOTE: the English 'some' and 'some of' are translated identically in Arabic, without the use of مِن for the latter: e.g.

'some (of the) ministers'

بَعْضُ الْوُزَراءَ (NOT* بَعْض مِن الوزراءَ)

As the above sentences show, Arabic uses the same word, i.e. the noun بَعْضٌ, which can be the first term in an إضافة, or added with a pronoun:

"I have seen **some of** them."

رَأَيْتُ بَعْضَهُم

In Classical Arabic, بَعْض can also mean '**one of**'. e.g.

"**One of** the princes/a certain prince said this."

قالَ بَعْضُ الأُمَراءَ ذلِكَ

Often, **some/any** are not translated in Arabic. e.g.

'I'll bring you **some** coffee in a minute':

سَوْفَ أُحْضِرُ (أَجْلِبُ) لَكَ فِنْجاناً مِن الْقَهْوَة خِلالَ دَقيقَةٍ

[NOT* سَوْفَ أُحْضِرُ (أَجْلِبُ) لَكَ بعض الْقَهوة خِلالَ دَقيقَةٍ]

This is especially the case with negative and interrogative '**there was/were**' (see **THERE IS/ARE ...**) constructions. e.g.

هَلْ كانَ هناك أَيُّ طالِبٍ في المُتْحَفِ؟

"Were there **any** students in the museum?"

لَمْ يَكُنْ هناك أَيُّ سائِحٍ في الكَنيسةِ

"There weren't **any** tourists in the church."

☞ For the reciprocal use of بَعْض, see 'EACH OTHER/ONE ANOTHER'

The English non-specification construction with 'any' in the sense of 'whatever' is rendered into Arabic by the use of the verb كانَ, which occurs in the PER-FECT. e.g.

"The new British Foreign Minister is looking forward to working with the countries of the region **in any capacity**."

يَتَطَلَّعُ وَزِيرُ الخَارِجِيَّةِ البريطانيُّ الجَديدُ لِلعَمَلِ مَعَ الدُّوَلِ في المِنْطَقةِ بِأَيَّةِ صِفةٍ كانَتْ

"The new methodology will be implemented **in any way**."

سَيَتِمُّ تَطْبيقُ المَنْهَجِيَّةِ الجَديدةِ بِأَيَّةِ طَريقَةٍ كانَتْ

☞ NOTE: '**in any case**', which is equivalent to '**anyway**', is translated as عَلَى/في كُلِّ حالٍ/أَحْوالٍ. e.g.

"**In any case**, fanaticism affects individuals in all societies and religions."

في كُلِّ حالٍ التَّطَرُّفُ يُصيبُ أَفْرادَ كُلِّ المُجْتَمَعاتِ والأَدْيانِ

Sometime/sometimes

Sometimes means '*with intervals*'; **sometime** means '*at one time*'. e.g.

"He was a **sometime** professor at Harvard." (= at one point in his career, he was a professor at Harvard)

كانَ أُسْتاذاً في جامِعَةِ هارفارد سابِقاً

"He **sometimes** acted like a professor."

كانَ يَتَصَرَّفُ كَأُسْتاذٍ أَحْياناً

Note the following expressions, which all mean '**sometimes ... sometimes**', '**at times ... at other times ...**':

تارَةً ... تارَةً
تارَةً ... طَوْراً
e.g. تارَةً ... (تارَةً) أُخْرَى

"Things are **sometimes** conscious, **sometimes** unconscious."

الأُمُورُ تَكُونُ تارَةً شُعُورِيَّةً وتارَةً لا شُعُورِيَّةً

"**Sometimes/at times** she chides me, **other times** she turns to me for help."

تَلُومُني تارَةً وَتارَةً تَتَوَسَّلُني

"**Sometimes**, it was on the list of terrorist states, **and other times** it was on the list of renegade states."

كانَت الدَّوْلَةُ تارَةً في قائِمَةِ الدُّوَلِ الإرْهابِيَّةِ وتارَةً أُخْرَى في قائِمَةِ الدُّوَلِ المارِقَةِ

"He belittled him, **sometimes** openly, **sometimes** indirectly."

كانَ يقلِّلُ من شَأْنِهِ، عَلَناً/تَصْريحاً تارَةً وَتَلْميحاً طَوْراً

"He tried to hold on to power **sometimes** by using the sects, and **sometimes** by using the national identity."

حاوَلَ أَنْ يَقْبِضَ عَلَى أَزِمَّةِ الأَمْرِ تارَةً بِاسْتِخْدامِ الطَّوائِفِ وَطَوْراً بِاسْتِخْدامِ الهُوِيَّةِ الوَطَنِيَّةِ

Still

This adverb can have widely varying meanings, depending on context and use:

- *'now, or in the future as in the past'*: ما زالَ/لا يَزالُ ,(ما زالَ) ('to not cease be') which can be followed by an adjective, noun (in the accusative) or verb in the IMPERFECT. e.g.

"It was **still** difficult."

ما زالَ صَعْباً

"The chairs are **still** used."

ما زالَتْ الكَراسِي مُسْتَعْمَلةً

"She **still** loves me."

لا تَزالُ تُحِبُّني

"I'm **still** looking for you."

ما زِلْتُ أَبْحَثُ عَنكِ

- *'until now'*: حَتَّى/إلى الآنَ. e.g.

"I **still** don't know his name."

لا أَعْرِفُ اسْمَهُ حَتَّى الآن

- *'yet'*: مَعَ أنَّ/مَعَ ذلِكَ. e.g.

"The newspaper apologized about the mistakes in the article, but he **still** sued them."

اِعْتَذَرَت الجَريدةُ لَهُ عَنْ الأخطاء/الأغلاط في المَقالةِ وَمَعَ ذلِكَ رَفَعَ عَلَيْها دَعْوَى

Subjunctive (المضارع المنصوب)

This is a mood (like the indicative or imperative), which is used with certain verbs and phrases, mostly conveying commands, suggestions ... e.g.

to advise (that)	It is best (that)
to ask (that)	It is crucial (that)
to demand (that)	It is essential (that)
to insist (that)	It is imperative (that)
to propose (that)	It is important (that)
to recommend (that)	It is recommended (that)
to request (that)	It is vital (that)
to suggest (that)	to urge (that)

In English, it has its own conjugation, which is the simple form of the verb, i.e. the INFINTIVE form without **to** for all persons. e.g.

"It is imperative that you **be** there."

عَلَيْكَ أَنْ تَكُونَ هُناكَ

"They demanded (that) the government **release** the leader of the party."

طالَبوا الحُكومَةَ بِإِطْلاقِ سَراحِ زَعِيمِ الحِزْبِ

In very formal (British) English writing, the subjunctive form can also be constructed with **should + infinitive**. e.g.

"It is necessary that he (**should**) go home early."

يَجِبُ أَنْ يَذْهَبَ إلى البَيْتِ مُبَكِّراً

Although Arabic also has something which is also referred to as **subjunctive**, it has little in common with its English counterpart, either in meaning or in form. The Arabic **subjunctive** is used in the following cases:

- After particles denoting **purpose**: حَتَّى, لِكَيْ, كَيْ, لِـ, which are translated by **in order to, so that**;

- With لَنْ to negate the future (**q.v.**). e.g.

"**So that** the international community takes its responsibilities."

لِكَيْ يَتَحَمَّلَ الْمُجْتَمَعُ الدُّوَلِيُّ مَسْوُوْلِيّاتَهُ

"The time has come **for** the citizen to know and take part in making difficult decisions."

فَقَدْ آنَ الأَوانُ كَيْ يعرف الْمُواطِنُ وَيُشارِكَ في صُنْعِ القَرارِاتِ الصَّعْبَةِ

"What are the instruments that can be used **in order to** reach the required objective?"

ما هِيَ الآلِياتُ الَّتِي يُمْكِنُ استعمالَها لِنَصِلَ إِلى الهَدَفِ الْمَطْلُوبِ؟

- After the complementizer أَنْ, which introduces subordinating clauses with verbs or phrases expressing desire, intention, need, etc. (see **'AN/'ANNA/…**).

Suffixes

As Arabic does not have English-style derivational suffixes, their translation often poses problems, in that there is never a one-to-one correspondence…
The following are the usual methods employed in translating English suffixated compounds into Arabic:

1. **genitive construction** (إضافة). e.g.
   مُدَّةُ الرِّئاسة ,'presidency'

2. **noun phrase** e.g.
   مُنَزَّةٌ عَنْ الْخَطَأ ,'infallible'
   قابِلٌ للشُّرْبِ ,'drinkable'

Terms of address

The way one addresses people, or refers to them, is often highly culturally determined. Arabic not only has a greater variety of terms and references of address, they are also used in many more contexts than in English, where they are clearly in a state of decline. For instance, in contemporary English, it is quite common to address someone by their first name within minutes of meeting them (or even before!). This kind of familiarity is considered disrespectful in Arabic, especially if there is a difference in status and/or age. Conversely, English-speakers are often thrown or even embarrassed by the eulogic flourishes that are part and parcel of Arabic social intercourse...

At the same time, things are not uniform across the Arabic-speaking and English-speaking worlds either! For instance, while in Egypt it is obligatory to have some honorific, adapted to the person's perceived status, Tunisian practice is much closer to that of the West (France).

In translation, the rendering of honorifics is based on a number of things, the most important of which is the **context** (e.g. formal/informal) in which they are used, the **social relationship** between the participants and the **pragmatic intent** of the utterance (i.e. what is the intendent result on the part of the speaker).

When translating from Arabic into English, the honorifics will generally have to be toned down, or omitted altogether. Conversely, when translating from English into Arabic, these markers of respect must be added, so the target phrase will be an amplified version of the original.

Let us take, for instance, the generic حَضْرَتَك, which may sometimes be rendered as 'sir'. In most cases, however, it should simply be toned down to 'you', though in formal contexts an equivalent politeness formula may be required. e.g.

قالَتْ :هَلْ حَضْرَتَك قِبْطِيٌّ؟
"She asked: are you a Copt?"

ما اسْمُ حَضْرَتِكَ؟

"What is your name?" (e.g. a student to a fellow student)

"What is your name, please?" (e.g. a colleague one meets for the first time)

"Excuse me, sir, what is your name please?" (e.g. a hotel receptionist to a guest)

Honorifics may even contain titles, such as حاج (denoting someone who has been on the pilgrimage) or أُسْتاذ ('teacher, professor'), even if the person in question is not associated with the activity. e.g.

دَخَلَ الحاجُّ مُصْطَفى الغُرْفَةَ

"Hajj Mustafa came into the room."

يا أُسْتاذُ، أَيْنَ المَدْخَل مِنْ فَضْلِكَ؟

"Excuse me sir, where is the entrance(, please) ?"

Even where both languages employ an honorific, cultural usage must be observed; for instance, it is usual in Arabic to use a title with the **first name**, whereas in English this is reserved for the **last name**: for instance, the reference to someone called 'Dr Sarah Johnson' will differ in the two languages:

وافَقَت الدُّكْتورةُ سارة عَلَى هذا الأَمْرِ

"**Dr** Johnson agreed on this matter." (NOT * 'Dr Sarah...')

Arabic also has a wide range of **honorific formulae**, especially with persons of note. e.g.

حَضْرَةُ صاحِبَ الجَلالةِ السُّلْطانُ قابُوس بِن سَعيد المُعَظَّم/حَفَظَهُ الله وَرَعاهُ

When translating this sentence in official documents, it should appear as 'His Majesty, Sultan Qaboos bin Said al-Muazzam – may God preserve him and watch over him – '; in all other cases, it should be rendered as 'His Majesty, King Qaboos (bin Said al-Muazzam)'. Similarly, جَلالَةُ المَلِكِ ... المُفَدِّي should be translated as 'His Majesty the King', rather than 'His Majesty, the dearly beloved King'.

For deceased people, the name is always accompanied by رَحْمَةُ الله عَلَيْهِ ('<May>

the Mercy of God be upon him') or المَرْحُوم ('the late'), with the former following the name and the latter preceding it. e.g. (المَرْحُومُ) مُحَمَّدَ مُصْطَفَى (رَحْمَةُ اللهِ عَلَيْهِ).

In English these are translated at the first mention and subsequently omitted. There are also many expressions that are added to the names of historical figures – especially religious authorities – held in great esteem, such as رَضِيَ اللهُ عَنْهُ ('May God be pleased with him'), which accompanies the mention of the first four caliphs, i.e. the Rightly-guided or Righteous ones (الْخُلَفَاءُ الرَّاشِدُونَ): Abu Bakr (أَبُو بَكْرٍ), 'Umar Ibn al-Khattab (عُمَر بن الْخَطَّاب), 'Uthman Ibn Affan (عُثْمان بن عَفَّان)and 'Ali Ibn Abi Talib (عَلِي بن أَبِي طالِب).

In practice, these should simply be omitted in English translation. In the case of the Prophet Muhammad, however, the formula that is used when uttering his name, صَلَى اللهُ عَلَيْهِ وسَلَّم ('May God pray for him and grant him peace'), is increasingly rendered by 'Peace Be Upon Him', abbreviated to 'PBU': e.g. "The Prophet (PBU) ...".

This usage should, however, be restricted to Muslim texts as it remains a highly 'foreignizing' device, rendering a text unnecessarily exotic. And so, while one would recommend adding the formula in texts aimed specifically at a Muslim readership, it would not be appropriate in general media texts.

When it comes to **official titles** in formal documents, there are issues of protocol and etiquette, and the table below includes the correspondences between titles in common use in both languages:

His Majesty (the) Sultan	(حَضْرَةُ) صاحِب جلالة السلطان
His Majesty (the) King ...	(حَضْرَةُ) صاحِب الجلالة المَلِك ...
His/Her Majesty	(حَضْرَةُ) صاحِب/ـة الجَلالة
His/Her Royal Highness ...	(حَضْرَةُ) صاحِب/ـة السُمُو المَلَكي
His Excellency the President	فَخامةُ الرَّئِيس
His Excellency the Prime Minister	صاحِبُ السَّعادةِ رَئِيسُ الوُزَراءَ

His Highness, Shaykh ..., the Minister for ...	...سُمُو الشَّيْخ... وَزِيرُ
His Excellency, Shaykh ..., the Minister for ...	(حَضْرَةُ) مَعالي الشَّيْخ ... وَزِير ...
His Excellency, the Minister for ...	(حَضْرَةُ) مَعالي وَزِير ...
His Excellency, (the) Minister...	(حَضْرَةُ) مَعالي الوَزِير ...
His Excellency, the Ambassador	سَعادةُ السَّفِيرِ
His Grace the Duke	سُمُو الدُّوق
His Eminence... (Cardinal)	نِيافةُ (الْحَبرِ) ... (كَرْدِنال)
His Grace ... (Bishop)	نِيافةُ (الْحَبرِ) ... (أُسْقُف)
Shaykh ... (Islamic scholars)	فَضِيلةُ الشَّيْخ ...
Shaykh ... (high-ranking Islamic scholars, e.g. rector and shaykhs of al-Azhar)	صاحِبُ الفَضِيلةِ الشَّيْخِ ...
His Eminence the Mufti	سَماحةُ المُفْتِي

☞ **NOTE**: some of these titles are nominalised, in line with European usage. e.g.

سُمُوُّهُ, 'His Royal Highness';
معاليه, 'His Excellency' (for Ministers);
جلالَته, 'His Majesty';
سَعادَتُكم, 'Your Excellency' (for an ambassador)

There is/are ...

In view of the absence of a copula ('**to be**') in Arabic, these phrases sometimes pose problems in translation, as they can be rendered in a number of ways, depending on whether it involves a present, past or future, or whether the location is specified or not.

1. Present

- In **affirmative sentences** in the present tense, *there is/are* is usually rendered by هُناكَ or هُنالِكَ. e.g.

هُناكَ/هُنالِكَ مَدْرَسةٌ في وَسَطِ المَدينةِ
"**There is** a school in the centre of town."

- In **interrogative** sentences, '**there is/are**' is rendered by the particles هَلْ and أَ (**q.v.**). e.g.

أَ/هَلْ في البَيْتِ كُتُبٌ؟
"**Are there** books in the house?"

- In **negative sentences**, the verb لَيْسَ is used. e.g.

لَيْسَ هُناكَ خَشْبٌ في السِّرْدابِ
"**There is** no wood in the cellar."

- In **negative interrogative** sentences, لَيْسَ is preceded by the particle أَ. e.g.

أَلَيْسَتْ هُناكَ أَقْلامُ في المَكْتَبةِ؟
"**Are there** no pencils in the library?"

- When the place is not specified, هناك/هُنالِكَ must be added. e.g.

أَ/هَلْ هُناكَ/هُنالِكَ خَطَأٌ؟
"**Is there** a mistake?"

لَيْسَتْ هُناكَ/هُنالِكَ زُهورٌ
"**There are** no flowers."

أَلَيْسَتْ هُناكَ/هُنالِكَ قَهْوَةٌ؟
"**Is there** no coffee?"

☞ **NOTE**: the use in English of '**no**' rather than '**not**' in the above sentences.

2. Past

- In **affirmative** sentences, the verb كانَ is used. Remember that its subject noun (اسْم كانَ) is in the **nominative**, but its predicate (خَبَر كانَ) in the **accusative**. e.g.

كانَ في الصَّفِّ طالِبٌ
"**There was** a student in the classroom."

- In **interrogative** sentences, كانَ is preceded by هَل or أ. e.g.

هَلْ كانَ في المَطْعَم أَساتِذةٌ؟
"**Were there** any lecturers in the restaurant?'

- In **negative** sentences, the negative of كانَ, i.e. لَم يَكُنْ is used as a translation of '**there has/have not been**', and ما كانَ for '**there wasn't/there weren't**'. e.g.

لَمْ تَكُنْ هنَاكَ جَرائِدُ في غُرفة الانْتِظار
"**There were no**/have not been any newspapers in the waiting room."

- In **negative interrogative** sentences, لَم يَكُنْ is used, preceded by أ. e.g.

أَلَمْ تَكُنْ عَلَى الطَّاوِلة قَدَّاحةٌ؟
"**Was there** no lighter on the table?"

- When the place is not specified, كانَ (ما كانَ/لَمْ يَكُنْ) followed by هُناكَ/هُنالِكَ must be added. e.g.

كانَ هُناكَ/هُنالِكَ خُبْزٌ ولَحْمٌ
"**There was** bread and meat."

أَكانَ هُناكَ/هُنالِكَ مَحلّاتٌ؟
"**Were there** any shops there?"

لَمْ يَكُنْ/ما كانَ هُناكَ/هُنالِكَ دُخانٌ
"**There was** no/has not been any smoke."

أَلَمْ يَكُنْ هُناكَ/هُنالِكَ ثَلْجٌ؟
"**Was there** no/Wasn't there any snow?"

3. Future

- In **affirmative** sentences, the imperfect of the verb كانَ is used with the future particle سـ, i.e. سَيَكُونُ. e.g.

سَتَكُونُ هُناكَ خِدْمةُ الغُرَفِ في الفُنْدُق
سَتَجِدُ خِدْمةُ الغُرَفِ في الفُنْدُق
"**There will be** room service at the hotel."

- In **negative** sentences, the negative future of كانَ, i.e. لَنْ يَكُونَ is used as a translation of 'there will not be'. e.g.

لَنْ تَكُونَ هناكَ أَمْوالٌ في المَصرِف
"**There will not be** (any) money in the bank."

- In **interrogative** sentences, سيكون is preceded by أ. e.g.

أَسَيَكُونُ هُناكَ كَراسٍ في الصّالَة؟
"**Will there be** (any) chairs in the hall?"

- In **negative interrogative** sentences, the لَنْ يَكُونَ is preceded by أ. e.g.

أَلَنْ يَكُونَ هُناكَ أَحْزِمَة الأَمان في مَقاعِدَ الطَّائِرةِ؟

"**Will there not be** (any) safety belts in the airplane?"

- Whenever the place is not specified, هُناكَ/هُنالِكَ must be added. e.g.

سَتَكُونُ هُناكَ/هُنالِكَ مَشْرُوباتٌ

"**There will be** drinks there."

لَنْ تَكُونُ هُناكَ/هُنالِكَ أَيُّ كَرارِيسَ

"**There will not be** (any) NOTEbooks."

أَسَيَكُونُ هُناكَ/هُنالِكَ مِسْبَحٌ؟

"**Will there be** a swimming pool?"

أَلَنْ يَكُونَ هُناكَ/هُنالِكَ مَكْتَبٌ لِلاِسْتِعْلاماتِ؟

"**Will there not be** an information desk?"

- In cases where the place is '**there**', هُناكَ is put at the end of the clause in Arabic, whereas in English '**there**' must be repeated. e.g.

أَلَيْسَتْ قَهْوَةٌ هُناكَ؟

"**Is there no** coffee there?"

- In impersonal constructions, the noun of كانَ is the subject (not the object!), as a result of which it is put in the nominative since it is اِسْم كانَ, rather than خَبَر (predicate). Compare the following sentences:

كانَ هناكَ دَلْوٌ في الحَديقَة, 'There was a bucket in the garden.'
كانَ دَلْواً في الحَديقَةِ, 'It was a bucket in the garden.'

> ☞ **NOTE**: in negative and interrogative sentences, it is often necessary to add '**any**' in English.

Time

Arabic has a number of translations for the various meanings of the word 'time':

- As an abstract: زَمَن (pl. أَزْمان) or تَوْقيت. e.g.

"**Time** was one of the things that occupied people's minds."

إِنَّ الزَّمَنَ مِنَ الأَشياءِ التي شَغَلَت فِكرَ الإِنْسانِ

"The poll revealed that 80% of respondents supported the abolition of summer **time** in the country."

أَظْهَرَتْ نَتيجَةُ الاِسْتِطْلاعِ تَأْييدَ 80٪ مِنَ المُشارِكينَ لإِلْغاءِ التَّوْقيتِ الصَّيْفِيِّ في بِلادِنا

"The new episode of the (soap) series will be shown at 10 a.m. Greenwich Mean **Time**/GMT on Friday."

سَيَكونُ مَوْعِدُ عَرْضِ الحَلْقَةِ الجَديدةِ لِلْمُسَلْسَلِ عَلَى هذه القَناةِ حَسَب تَوْقيتِ غرينِتش الجُمْعَةَ السّاعَةُ التّاسِعَةُ صَباحاً

- Reference to a specific point or period: وَقْت (pl. أَوْقات) or, in the case of an appointed time, تَوْقيت, ميقات (pl. مَواقيتُ). Note that in some cases the English plural has to be translated by a singular in Arabic, or vice versa! e.g.

"He came in at the same **time**."

دَخَلَ في الوَقْتِ نَفْسِه/نَفْسِ الوَقْتِ

"I told you what happened at that **time**."

أَخبَرَتُكَ/قُلتُ لَكَ ما حَصَلَ في وَقْتِه

"I hope you arrive at the hotel **on time**."

أَتَمَنَّى أَنْ تَصِلَ إلى الفُنْدُقِ في الوَقْتِ المُناسِبِ

"There was an increase in the demand for hard currency at specific **times**, especially at the end of the year."

كانَت هُناكَ زِيادَةٌ في الطَّلَبِ عَلَى العُمْلاتِ الصَّعْبَةِ في بَعْضِ الأَوْقاتِ، خاصَّةً في نِهاية العامِ

ازدادَ الطَّلَبُ عَلَى العُمْلاتِ الصَّعْبَةِ في بَعْضِ الأَوْقاتِ، خاصَّةً في نِهايةِ العامِ

"The mothers were talking most of the **time**, without giving the child the opportunity to participate in the discussion."

كانَت الأُمَّهاتُ يَتَحَدَّثْنَ مُعْظَمَ الأَوْقاتِ دُونَ إِعْطاءِ الطِّفْلِ فُرْصَةً لِلمُشارَكَةِ في الحَديثِ

"The telephone guide provides a service for the prayer **times**."

دَليلُ التِّليفُونات يَشْتَمِلُ عَلَى خِدْمَةِ التَّعَرُّفِ لأَوْقاتِ/مَواقيت/مَواعيد الصَّلاةِ

"The post office opening **times** during Ramadan are from 8 a.m. until 5 p.m."

مَواقيتُ/أَوْقاتُ عَمَلِ مَكاتِبِ البَريدِ في شَهْرِ رَمضانِ مِنَ الثَّامِنةِ صَباحاً إِلَى الخامِسةِ مَساءً

"It didn't happen at a specific **time**."

لَمْ يَحْدُثْ في وَقْتٍ مُعَيَّنٍ

- • 'era', 'period', 'age', 'epoch': عَصر (pl. أَعْصار، أَعْصُر)، دَهْر (pl. دُهُور) عُصُور e.g. وَقْت or (pl. أَزْمِنة) أَدْهُر)، زَمَن، زَمان

"There is a lot of crime in modern **times**/the present day."

يَشْهَدُ العَصْرُ الحَديثُ حَوادِثَ إِجْرامِيَّةً كَثيرةً

"In Islamic cities in mediaeval **times**/during the Middle Ages, it was customary for the judge to go out to look at the New Moon."

جَرَت العادةُ في المُدُنِ الإِسْلامِيَّةِ خِلالَ العُصُورِ الوُسْطَى عَلَى خُرُوجِ القاضي لِرُؤْيَةِ الهِلالِ

"She was a great film star in her **time**."

كانَتْ نَجْمَةً سِنمائِيَّةً عَظيمَةً في وَقْتِها

"He was respected by the people of the **time**/his contemporaries."

كانَ أَهْلُ زَمانِه يَحْتَرِمونَهُ

"Ten years is not a long **time** in the history of a people."

عَشَرَ سَنَواتٍ في تارِيخِ الشُّعُوبِ لَيَسَتْ بِالزَّمَنِ الطَّوِيلِ

"My professor explained the benefits of geological knowledge which has contributed to human progress and civilizational development since ancient **times**/since **time** immemorial."

أَوْضَحَ أُسْتاذِي فائِدةَ المَعْرِفةِ الجِيُولُوجِيَّةِ الَّتِي ساهَمَتْ مُنْذُ أَقْدَم الأَزْمانِ في تَقَدُّمِ البَشَرِيَّةِ وَنُموها الحَضارِيِّ

"He was a minister in the **time** of Muhammad Ali Pasha."

كانَ وَزيراً في زَمانٍ/عَصْرِ مُحَمَّدٍ عَلِي باشا

☞ **NOTE:** دَهْر is also used to denote a long period of time. e.g.

"He has lived in exile **for a long time/for ages**.".

أَقامَ في بِلادِ الغُرْبةِ دَهْراً

زَمان is also used to translate the English '**tense**' (in grammar). e.g.

"You have to study the present **tense** before the past in French."

يَجِبُ أَنْ تَدْرُسَ الزَّمَنَ الحاضِرَ قَبْلَ الماضِي في اللُّغةِ الفَرَنْسِيّةِ

• A single occurrence or repetition of an event: مَرّة. e.g.

"This **time**, I'll forgive him."

سَأَغْفِرُ لَهُ هذِهِ المَرّةَ

"Many **times**/on many occasions, the government stressed that it needed more **time** to study the package of proposals."

أَكَّدَتِ الحُكُومةُ مَرّاتٍ عِدَّة أَنَّها بِحاجةٍ إِلَى المَزيدِ مِنَ الوَقْتِ لِدِراسة حُزْمة المُقْتَرَحاتِ

☞ **NOTE** the following expressions:

"What's the **time**?"

كَمِ السَّاعَةُ؟

"in the course of **time**"

عَلَى مَرِّ الزَّمانِ

"through the **ages**"

عِبْرَ/ عَلَى مَرِّ الْعُصُورِ وَالدُّهُورِ

"it's **time** to go"

حانَ وَقْتُ الذَّهابِ

"we had a **good time**."

قَضَيْنا وَقْتاً مُمْتِعاً

"next **time**"

الْمَرَّةُ القادِمةُ

"another **time**"

مَرَّةً أُخْرَى/جَديدةً/ثانيةً

"for the first/last **time**"

لِلْمَرَّةِ الأُولى/الأَخيرةِ

"time and again"

مَرَّةً عَن مَرَّةٍ

مَرَّاتٍ

Time can also be used as a verb, meaning 'to measure the duration' or 'to determine the appropriate moment': e.g.

"to **time** a race"

دَوَّنَ/سَجَّلَ وَقْتَ الْمُباراةِ/السِّباقِ

"He **timed** the attack perfectly."

لقد وفِقَ في إختياره وقتَ الهُجوم توفيقاً بالغاً/أَحْسَنَ التَّوْ فِيق

Too

The rendering of this adverb in Arabic can sometimes be very problematic, particularly since there is no single word that conveys the same meaning. The most common translations involve the use of:

- the **elative** أكْثر in the following constructions, all of which mean '*more than necessary*':

أكْثر من اللّازم
أكْثر مِمّا يَنْبَغِى
أكْثر مِمّا يَجبُ

- the verb أَفْرَطَ في ('to be excessive in') followed by a noun;

- the adverb جدّاً.

e.g.

"He is **too** young."
هُوَ صْغَيرٌ جِدًّا

"He drinks **too** much."
يُفْرِطُ في الشَّراب

"This car is two thousand pounds **too** expensive."
دَفَعَتْ ثَمَنَ هذِهِ السَّيَّارةِ أَلفَيْ جُنَيهٍ أكْثر مِمّا يَنْبَغِي

"It's **too** far."

هُوَ بَعيدٌ جِدّاً

BUT:

"Why did you park the car there? The restaurant is **too** far from here!"

لِماذا رَكَنتَ/وَقَّفْتَ السَّيَّارةَ في هذا المَكانِ؟ المَطْعَم بَعيدٌ جداً مِنْ هُنا

"She talked **too** much."

تَكَلَّمَتْ أَكْثَرَ مِمَّا يَنْبَغي

"We are **too** old."

نَحْنُ كِبارٌ في السِّنِ

"I clearly arrived **too** early."

مِنَ الواضِحِ أَنَّني وَصلتُ باكِراً جِدّاً/أَبْكَرُ مِمَّا يَنْبَغي

"He earns **too** little."

إنَّ راتِبَهُ أَقَلُّ مِمَّا يَجِبُ

"They're **too** close."

هُمْ أَقْرَبُ مِمَّا يَجِبُ

"There's **too** little food left."

ما بَقِيَ مِن الطَّعامِ أَقَلُّ مِنَ اللازِم

"It's **too** late."

إنَّ الوَقْتَ مُتَأَخِّرٌ جِدّاً

> ☞ **NOTE** the following idiomatic phrases with **too**:
>
> "It's not **too** bad."
> هُوَ بَيْنَ بَيْنَ
>
> "Not **too** much."
> لَيْسَ بِما فيهِ الكِفاية/قَليلاً
>
> "It's **too** good to be true."
> أَغْرَبُ مِن أَنْ يُصَدَّقَ

The construction **too + adjective + for/to+infinitive**, is usually rendered by 'elative + مِن + أَنْ'. e.g.

"He is **too** young **to** vote in the coming elections."
هُوَ أَصْغَرُ سِنّاً مِن أَنْ يُدْلِي بِصَوْتِهِ في الانْتِخاباتِ المُقْبِلِة

"This is **too** dangerous **for** us."
هذا أَخْطَرُ مِن أَن نَعْمَلَهُ
هذا خَطيرٌ جِدّاً لَنا

"The circumstances were **too** sensitive to be mentioned."
كانَت الظُّرُوفُ أَكْثر حَسّاسيَّةً مِن أَنْ نَسْتَطيعَ الكلامَ عَنْها

Bear in mind that in English you cannot add 'too' to an adjective+ noun phrase; instead, you must use the construction '**too + adjective + indefinite article + noun**'. e.g.

"This is **too** difficult **a** task for us to do." (**NOT** *this is too difficult task)
هذِهِ المَهَمّة أَصْعَبُ مِن أَنْ نَقُومَ بِها

It is important to highlight the common mistake made by Arabic speakers in the use of this adverb, when it is used as an intensifier. e.g.

"He loves her *too* much."
"She was *too* happy."

Unless the speaker wishes to convey a negative connotation, i.e. the love and happiness are excessive, the use of 'very' is more appropriate than 'too' in this context as what is meant is, respectively:

"He loves her **very** much." [= "He loves her greatly/a great deal."]

يُحِبُّها جِدًّا/كَثيراً

"She was **very/extremely** happy."

كانَتْ فَرِحَة جِدًّا/كَثيراً (فَرِحَتْ فَرَحاً عَظيماً)

Transliteration and transcription

Rendering characters from one script into another often gives rise to a raft of problems as in many cases there is no single accepted – and applied (!) – system. As like as not, scholars will use a different system from that employed in the media and non-specialized literature.

Arabic into English

Although **transliteration** and **transcription** are often used interchangeably, a distinction is sometimes made between the two, with **transliteration** referring to a one-on-one correspondence between the SL and TL characters, and **transcription** denoting the fact that sounds are rendered by characters in the target language that most closely resemble the original sounds. Either way, both are a form of **romanization**, i.e. the rendering of the symbols of another script in Roman characters (the Latin alphabet).

The above may be illustrated as follows. The 'scholarly' transliteration of نجيب محفوظ would be Najīb Maḥfūẓ (or Nagīb Maḥfūẓ, if one wished to reflect the Egyptian pronunciation of ج), whereas the **transcriptions** include *Naguib Mahf(o) uz* (English, French), *Nagib Machfus* (German), *Naguib Mahfuz* (Spanish), *Nadjib Mahfoez* (Dutch). Another example is the name محمد, rendered variously as *Muhammad, Mohammed, Mohamed* or *Mahomet*. These examples clearly reveal the problem of the 'rough-and-ready' phonetic transcriptions: each language chooses its own sounds, which can sometimes give rise to words being unintelligible to anyone who is not familiar with the sounds of the language. Whilst most people would be able to 'decipher' the various forms of the name of the famous Egyptian novelist mentioned above, the same cannot necessarily be said of, for instance, the Spanish rendering of أخبار, *ajbar*, or indeed whether 'Alaa Amir' is علاء/آلاء عامر/عامر/عمرو؟

Perhaps the most damning argument against the 'broad' transcription is its inconsistency, with, for instance, authors quite happily using 'Saeed' and 'Aziz' in the same line, thus rendering the same Arabic sound (and character) ي in two different ways!

In addition, there are occasions when the same symbol is used to represent two different phonemes, as is the case for ء and ع, both of which are sometimes confusingly represented by the apostrophe. The use of assimilation may also result in confusion for non-Arabic speakers, as in the case of *arihla*, for instance, for *al-rihla* (or *ar-rihla*).

However, when it comes to transcription, there is a school of thought which happily condones ambiguity of this type on the grounds that 'those who know the language will know what the word refers to, whereas it doesn't matter for those who do not know the language.' Proponents of this view further justify their approach by stating that transcribing 'correctly' is a labour-intensive task, which for the non-Arabic speaker is both difficult (if not impossible) and pointless. On the one hand, it is difficult to dismiss this view out of hand; for one thing, how is the non-Arabic speaker to know how to transcribe a word correctly (short of having it done by a specialist) ? On the other hand, it is difficult to see how inconsistency and lack of riguour can do anything but detract from the quality of a text. Indeed, if one takes this argument to its logical conclusion, it does not matter either if there are spelling mistakes in a word, since people who can read should be able to correct the mistakes anyway!

The above shows the extent to which every Unicode[1] recommendation is breached, as the guidelines state that any transliteration system should be:

▶ *standard:* follow established systems (standards, authorities, or *de facto*

---

1. = the computing industry encoding standard, set forth by the Unicode Consortium (see http:// www.unicode.org). For the transliteration guidelines, see http:// cldr.unicode.org/ index/cldr-spec/ transliteration-guidelines.

practice) where possible, deviating sometimes where necessary for reversibility;

▶ *complete*: every well-formed sequence of characters in the source script should transliterate to a sequence of characters from the target script, and vice versa.

▶ *predictable*: the letters themselves (without any knowledge of the languages written in that script) should be sufficient for the transliteration, based on a relatively small number of rules.

▶ *pronounceable*: the resulting characters have reasonable pronunciations in the target script. Simply mapping by alphabetic order could yield strings that might be complete and unambiguous, but the pronunciation would be completely unexpected.

▶ *reversible*: it is possible to recover the text in the source script from the transliteration in the target script. That is, someone that knows the transliteration rules would be able to recover the precise spelling of the original source text.

The main problem is that there does not seem to be an acceptable standard, despite very early attempts, such as those by the United Nations and the League of Arab States in 1972, which ensued from the first conference on Arabic transliteration held in Beirut.

'Narrow' transcription

It must be pointed out that the use of a given 'system' of transliteration/transcription in many cases depends on the **target audience**. Indeed, a narrow transliteration, with its use of diacritics, may well suit scholars, but is highly inappropriate for a newspaper article (if only for the typographical problems this choice would entail).

And then, there is the problem of **recognized transliterations** of words, which poses a problem even in scholarly texts. For instance, it is highly unlikely that even in technical studies, الامام would be transcribed as *imām*, rather than 'imam' in view of the fact that this word has been 'naturalized' in English, just as 'taco' or 'bikini', which were once as alien. The rule here would seem to be to let common sense prevail! One example is the transliteration of the name of the former Tunisian president (Habib) ***Bourguiba***, which ultimately goes back to ***Bū Ruqayba***, or even ***Abū Ruqayba***. However, it is safe to say that neither of these would be recognized as referring to the same man!

However, there is not even a single scholarly system for the romanization on which all agree and which is applied throughout the field. Instead, there are a number of competing systems, albeit with minor variations on the whole, as the table below reveals:

Table 1: competing transcriptions

Arabic Letter	Continental European	UK	US
ء	'		
ب	b		
ت	t		
ث	ṯ	th	th
ج	ǧ	j	j, dj, dj
ح	ḥ		
خ	ḫ	kh	kh
د	d		
ذ	ḏ	dh	dh
ر	r		
ز	z		

Arabic Letter	Continental European	UK	US
س	s		
ش	š	sh	s͟h
ص	ṣ		
ض	ḍ		
ط	ṭ		
ظ	ẓ		
ع	c		
غ	ġ	gh	g͟h
ف	f		
ق	ḳ	q	
ك	k		
ل	l		
م	m		
ن	n		
ه	h		
و	w		

Arabic Letter	Continental European	UK	US
ي	j	y	

In terms of the **vowels**, the following picture emerges:

i. **Short: a, i, u**
ii. **long:** ā/â, ī/î, ū/û

In the case of the long vowels, the symbols with the 'macron' (lengthening mark) tend to be used by English-speaking Arabists, whereas the symbols with the macron (i.e. lengthening mark) are those favoured mainly by French scholars.

It is worth pointing out that in many cases no distinction is made in transcription between ى and ١, in that both are represented by the same 'long a' symbol. Among the 'accepted' scholarly systems, it is only that of the American Library Association (ALA), which introduces such a distinction, i.e. 'ā' for 'standing *alif*', and 'á' for 'broken *alif*' (though it does not have a separate symbol for the so-called 'dagger alif', as in الله.

Finally, it is not as if the narrow transcriptions are without problems; indeed, the use of digraphs to represent one phoneme, such as '**sh**', '**gh**' and '**kh**', has rightly been called confusing to the reader who does not know Arabic, which runs counter the very principle of transcription since the object of the exercise is to make things accessible to the foreign reader. For instance, the reader might misinterpret *raghaba* as consisting of '*rag-haba*' (i.e. two phonemes instead of one), just as the foreign learner of English may misread the English word 'haphazard' as 'hafazard' (considering the 'ph' to be like that in 'apastrophe').

Recommended 'narrow' (scholarly) transcription

The table below lists the rcorrespondences for Standard Arabic characters.

ء	ʼ	ظ	ẓ
ب	b	ع	c

ت	t	غ	gh
ث	th	ق	q
ج	j	ك	k
ح	ḥ	ل	l
خ	kh	م	m
د	d	ن	n
ذ	dh	ه	h
ر	r	و	w
ز		ي	y
س	s		
ش	sh		
ص	ṣ		
ض	ḍ		
ط	ṭ		

☞ **NOTE:**

1. **Alif:** both ى and ا are transliterated ā.
2. **tā´ marbūṭa** (ة) is rendered as -a in pre-pausal form) and as **–at** if the word is the first element in a genitive (إضافة) construction. e.g. *mudarrisa* BUT *mudarrisat al-kulliyya.*
3. نسبة **suffix: ī-,** fem. **–iyya.** e.g. *qahrī, sirriyya.*
4. تَنوين: **-un, -an, -in:** *darsun, darsin, darsan.*
   !! In transcription, it is common not to transcribe the تنوين, except in certain cases (e.g. *jiddan*) !!
5. The so-called **diphthongs,** the following are the common ways of representing them in the scholarly systems: ـي **ay;** ـو, **aw.**
6. **Gemination** (تَشْديد), i.e. the doubling of sounds, is represented by a doubling of the relevant characters. e.g. *dubb.*
7. **Assimilation** (إدْغام) is not rendered. e.g. *al-shams.*
8. The **hyphen** is used to separate the article from its noun or adjective. e.g. *al-qamar.*
9. The **numerals** are rendered as 'Western' Arabic numerals: 1, 2, 3,... (rather than as ١,٢,٣).
10. When preceded by a particle or preposition ending in a vowel, the vowel in the article is replaced by an apostrophe. e.g. *bi 'l-qalam.*
11. When Arabic transcribed words appear at the beginning of a sentence, they are **capitalized**; if it involves a **proper noun,** this may entail capitalizing both the article, and the name. e.g. 'Al-Kindī...'; 'According to al-Kindī ...'

Transcribing the colloquial

Whilst the above applies to Standard Arabic, it stands to reason that transcription can and is also used to represent colloquial varieties of the language. In this case, the rule of thumb is that one should use the symbol which comes closest to the original pronunciation. For instance, in rendering a Palestinian pronunciation of *al-Quds* (Jerusalem), one may transcribe it as *al-ʾuds* (with the *hamza* symbol representing the pronunciation of 'q' as a glottal stop). Similarly, if it is important to render the Egyptian pronunciation, one would transcribe *najm* (نَجْم) as *nagm.*

The transcription of colloquial speech also involves the introduction of additional vowel characters. e.g.

Short vowels: **e, o** (for Standard Arabic 'a'/'i' and 'u', respectively)
Long vowels: **ē, ō** (for Standard Arabic 'ay' and 'aw', respectively)

Colloquial pronunciations can also affect personal names, sometimes to comic or embarrassing effect, as in the name '*Samina*', which reflects the vernacular pronunciation of ث as/s /, with a girl named ثَمِينة ('precious') becoming 'fat'![1]

'Broad' transcription

When it comes to the non-technical, non-scholarly 'broad' transcriptions – i.e. those without diacritical marks – the confusion increases exponentially. Indeed, one need only pick up a newspaper (or two!) to see the wide variety of inconsistent transliterations and transcriptions on offer. Nevertheless, it is the broad transcription which should be used if the text is aimed at what may conveniently be called a 'lay' audience, or the general public.

Here, too, simple rules may be proffered, in order of importance:

i.   recognized translation?

ii. select transcription that is closest to the Arabic. e.g. *Ahmad*, rather than *Ahmed*.

iii. economy of the number of characters, i.e. when possible choose one rather than several. e.g. *balid* (rather than '*baliid*' or '*baleed*'), *Hasan*, rather than *Hassan*.

iv. consistency in representing the same word and sounds.

The above steps appear in hierarchical order, which means that (1) overrides (2), (3) and (4). So, the fact that 'Harun' is a recognized form of this ruler does not necessarily rule out the transcription of 'Julnaar' with 'aa', *provided* all other instances of 'long a' are rendered in the same fashion, since this complies with the **consistency** rule. The table below lists the recommended and recognized

---

1.   cf. A. Schimmel, *Islamic Names*, Edinburgh University Press, 1989.

transliterations of some commonly encountered Arab first names:

Table 2: transliteration of common Arabic names

English Transliteration	Arabic
'Abd Manaf	عبد المناف
'Abd al-Hamid	عبد الحميد
'Abd al-Latif	عبد اللطيف
'Abd al-Muttalib	عبد المطلب
'Abd ar-Rahman	عبد الرحمن
'Abd as-Salam, 'Abd el-Salam, 'Abd al-Salam, 'Abd al-Salaam, Abdessalam	عبد السلام
'Abd-al-Wahhab	عبد الوهاب
'Abdul Aziz	عبد العزيز
'Abdul Halim	عبد الحليم
'Abdullah, Abdallah, Abdellah	عبد الله
'Adil, Adil, Adel	عادل
'Ali, Ali	علي
Amin, Ameen	أمين
Amir, Ameer	أمير

English Transliteration	Arabic
'Amir	عامر
Amr	عمرو
Ashraf	أشرف
Atif	عاطف
Badr	بدر
Bashar	بشار
Buthayna, Bouthaina, Boutheina	بثينة
Daoud, Daud	داوود
Fadil	فاضل
Faisal, Feisal	فيصل
Farid, Fareed	فريد
Hafsa	حفصى
Hamdan	حمدان
Hamid, Hameed	حميد
Hasan, Hassan	حسن
Hisham	هشام

English Transliteration	Arabic
Husayn, Husein, Hussein	حسين
Ibrahim	إبراهيم
Isa, 'Isa	عيسى
'Izz al-Din	عز الدين
Jaber, Jabir	جابر
Jamal	جمال
Jamila, Jameela	جميلة
Kamil, Kamel	كامل
Khaled, Khalid	خالد
Lamis, Lamees	لميس
Layla, Leila	ليلى
Majd	مجد
Maryam, Meryem	مريم
Mahmud, Mahmoud, Mahmood	محمود
Muhammad, Mohammad	محمد
Murad, Mourad	مراد

English Transliteration	Arabic
Musa, Moosa	موسى
Mustafa, Mostafa	مصطفى
Nadir, Nader	نادر
Nasir, Naser, Nasser	ناصر
Nawfal, Nofal	نوفل
Nesrin, Nesreen	نسرين
Nur, Noor	نور
Omar, Umar	عمر
Qasim	قاسم
Rashid, Rasheed	رشيد
Razan, Rezan	رزان
Ruqayya(h)	رقية
Saʿ ad, Saad	سعاد
Said, Saʿid	سعيد
Salman	سلمان
Samira, Sameera	سميرة

English Transliteration	Arabic
Suleiman, Sulayman	سليمان
Taha	طه
Tariq	طارق
Tawfiq	توفيق
'Ubayd, Obeid	عبيد
'Uday	عدي
Usama, Osama	أسامة
'Uthman, Othman	عثمان
Walid, Waleed	وليد
Yasir, Yaasir	ياسر
Yunis, Younis	يونس
Yusuf, Youssef, Youssif	يوسف
Zayd, Zeid	زيد
Zaynab, Zeinab, Zeineb	زينب
Zahra, Zohra	زهرة

Proper nouns: 'translation' vs transliteration

Most modern history books written in English still refer to past French rulers by their anglicized names, and students learn about the exploits of *Francis* or *John*, instead of *François* and *Jean*. Similarly, the traditional rendering of *Yaʿqūb* bears little resemblance to its English counterpart *James*!

In the case of Arabic, one could conceivably apply this principle to names that also appear in the Bible, and so one would talk about *Abraham*, rather than *Ibrahim*, or *Mary*, rather than *Maryam, Joseph*, rather than *Yusuf*. Another category are names that are similar to English ones in form, such as *Sawsan* ('lily-of-the-field'), which, depending on the individual is sometimes rendered as *Susan*.

The recommendation here is NOT to translate, whereas an 'anglicized' rendering should prevail if it is available, so that for instance سارة, should be rendered as 'Sarah'.

In the case of Arabic transliterations of originally English, or French names, it is the original that should be preferred in translation. e.g. ميشال, 'Michel', BUT ميخائيل, 'Mikha'il'.

Sometimes, convention and historical practice take precedence over the above points. This is the case, for instance, in a number of Spanish place-names, which date back to the Arab-Muslim occupation of part of the Peninsula (al-Andalus) : طُلَيْطُلة (Toledo), غَرْناطة (Grenada), لَشْبُونة (Lisbon), إشْبِيلية (Seville), قُرْطُبة (Cordoba), بَرْشَلونة (Barcelona), while the *Alhambra* is, of course, الحمراء! A particularly interesting example of 'translation' is الجَبَل الأَسْوَد, which is the Arabic translation of the Latin etymon *Montenegro*, even if increasingly the media are referring to منتينيغرو, instead!

English to Arabic transliteration

The issue of the transliteration of foreign words is just as much of an issue in Arabic, as it is in English, with what at times appears to be a 'free-for-all', with forms wavering between a transcription of the word as it is pronounced in the original language and a graphemic representation. e.g. انغاهم ('Ingham') and شنغهاي ('Shanghai'), vs درم ('Durham'). In many cases, the approach involves selecting the Arabic sound that best represents the original sound, though this is by no means the rule, as the above example of 'Ingham' shows, where the غ

renders a *silent* letter in English! If anything, variety seems to be the norm with
غواتيمال ('Guatemala') co-occurring happily with جواتيمالا.

Similarly, there may be differences depending on the source language as in
تشارلز vs. شارل, or برنارد vs برنار, which render 'Charles' and 'Bernard', respectively,
with the first in each set reflecting the French pronunciation, and the second the
English one. This also explains the existence of doublets, such as تياتر/تياترو, in
which one has its origin in the Italian *teatro*, and the other in the English *theatre*
(or French *théatre*).

In addition, transliterations, especially of proper nouns also vary according to
the region, with local pronunications of Arabic sounds playing a determining
role: for instance, in the case of 'English', which is usually rendered as إنكليزي,
the **form** إنجليزي reflects the realization in Egypt (and Oman) of ج as the first
sound in the word 'go', rather than as the first sound in 'John', whereas in the
case of 'Malaga', مالقة vs مالغة, the former reflects the pronunciation of ق as/**g** /, as
is common in the Gulf and many parts of North Africa.

The following practices can be observed in the transliteration of foreign
proper nouns (also see table below) :

- originally short vowels tend to be lengthened. e.g. دانيال, 'Daniel';

- acceptance of a succession of consonants not otherwise allowed in Arabic.
  e.g. شنغهاي, 'Shanghai';

- a significantly higher proportion of so-called 'emphatic' consonants. e.g.
  قنصل, 'consul'.

A particularly interesting case in modern usage is the increasing neglect of 'classical' transliterations – many of which go back to Christian names; for instance,
rather than بُطْرُس 'Peter' or لوقا 'Luke', one is more likely to find بيتر and لوك,
respectively, today.

One of the main problems in Arabic transliteration is that already
encountered for English, i.e. recognisability; while برايثوايت, may be deciphered
with some degree of ease as 'Braithwaite', other cases are far more obstruse. In
this case, the following strategies are generally applied:

285

1. in all cases, the foreign name should be placed in brackets. e.g.

كَتَبَ البروفسور (أَنْدِي سميث) مَقالةً حَوْلَ الأَمْراضِ الباطِنيَّةِ

"Professor Andy Smith wrote an article on internal medicine."

2. In scientific and technical texts, where it is important to specify technical terms or for sources to be recognized, the name is generally rendered in latin script within the Arabic text, either by itself, or in conjunction with an Arabic rendition. e.g.

هذه التوصية هي أهم ما تضمنته المراجعة الحديثة لتوصيات لجنة الخبراء في الكلية الأميركية لأطباء النساء والتوليد حول سفر الحوامل بالطائرات، والتي ستنشر تحت عنوان «السفر الجوي خلال الحمل» Air Travel During Pregnancy، ضمن عدد أكتوبر (تشرين الأول) لمجلة طب النساء والتوليد Obstetrics & Gynecology.

Table 3: transliteration of common English names

English	Arabic Transliteration
Anne	آن
Charles	تشارلز
Daniel	دانيال
David	دايفد
Edward	إدوارد
Elisabeth	إليزابيث
Francis	فرانسيس فرنسيس
George	جورج
Graham	غراهام جراهام
Henry	هنري
James	جيمس

English	Arabic Transliteration
John	جون
Lawrence	لورنس
Mary	ماري
Michael	مايكل
Oliver	أوليفر
Paul	بول
Peter	بطرس
Philip	فيليب
Sarah	سارا
Susan	سوسن سوزان
Thomas	توماس
William	وليم
Michaelangelo	ميكيلانجيلو
Napoleon Bonaparte	نابليون بونابرت
Picasso	بيكاسو

Until/till/by

The time adverb **until** and its less formal abbreviated form **till** are used to talk about an ongoing state, whereas **by** refers to an action taking place at, or before a point in the future. In Arabic, **until/till** are generally rendered by حَتَّى (+ genitive) or إلى and **by** through قَبْلَ. e.g.

"We'll stay here **until** the evening."

سَنَبْقَى هُنا حَتَّى المَساءِ

"Up **until** now, the bank is still not certain whether the economy was affected by the international crisis."

حَتَّى الآنَ لا يَزالُ البَنْكُ غَيْرَ مُتَأَكِّدٍ ما إذا كانَ الاِقْتِصادُ مُتَأَثِّراً بالأَزْمَةِ العالَمِيّةِ

"I hope you will be able to do it **by** Friday."

آمُلُ أَنْ تَعْمَلَهُ قَبْلَ يَوْمِ الجُمْعَةِ

"She finished reading the book **by** the time the lecture started."

اِنْتَهَتْ مِن قِراءةِ الكِتابِ قَبْلَ بِدايةِ المُحاضَرةِ

☞ **NOTE:** حَتَّى can have a number of other meanings:

▸ **'to the point of'**, **'up to'**, with the following noun being in the *genitive*. e.g.

"The investigators searched the building from the basement **up to** (including) the roof."

فَتَّشَ المُحَقِّقُونَ المَبْنَى مِن السرداب حَتَّى السَّقْفِ

In this meaning, it may sometimes be interchangeable with بِما في ذلك ('**including**'). e.g.

"The king called for the normalization of relations with Algeria, **including** the opening of borders."

يَدْعُو المَلِكُ إلى تَطْبِيعِ العَلاقاتِ مَعَ الجَزائِرِ بِما في ذلك فَتْحُ الحُدُودِ

▸ **'in order to'**, followed by a **subjunctive** (cf. لِ (كَي)). e.g.

"**In order to** realize the hopes and ambitions of the people in his country."

حَتَّى تَتَحَقَّقَ آمالُ شَعْبِ دَوْلَتِه وطُموحاتُهُ

▸ For '**even**', see 'EVEN/EVEN IF/...'

Wa (وَ) and fa (فَـ)

Both these two conjunctions can mean 'and', but are mutually exclusive in a number of instances:

i.   Only فَـ can be used in conditional constructions (with إِنْ) where it introduces the result clause [see '**AS/BECAUSE/SINCE/FOR**'];

ii. Only وَ can be used in the حال construction (circumstantial clause) (**q.v.**);

iii. Only وَ tends to be used when linking two (or more) **nouns**. e.g.

"I saw Salwa, Leila **and** Sally."

رَأَيْتُ سَلْوَى وَلَيْلَى وَسالي

[**NOT**: رَأَيْتُ سَلْوَى فَلَيْلَى]

> ☞ **NOTE**: when there are more than two nouns, English prefers commas with **and** before the last item in the series.

iv. فَـ is preferred to link cause and effect or a sequential series of events, when it can sometimes be replaced by وَبَعْدَ ذلِكَ, وَبَعْدَ هُ or ثُمَّ. In English, the former meaning is often rendered by '**and so**', '**and thus**', '**as a result**', '**therefore**'. e.g.

"He failed the exam **and** (**so he**) had to leave the university."

فَشَلَ في الاِمْتِحانِ فَيَجِبُ أَنْ يَتْرُكَ الجامِعَةَ

"He left his office, got on the bus **and/after which** he went to his mother's house."

خَرَجَ مِن مَكْتَبِهِ فَـ/ثُمَّ رَكِبَ الباصَ فَـ/وبَعْدَ ذلِكَ اتَّجَهَ إلى بَيْتِ أُمِّهِ

v. فَ often has **contrastive** meaning, in which case it may be rendered in English by **yet** or **however**. e.g.

رُغْمَ اِعْتِراف شَرِيكِها فَهِيَ تَنْفِي تَوَرُّطَها بِإِلْحاح

"Her accomplice confessed, **yet** she insists on denying her involvement."

When/if

Though both of these adverbs are used in conditional sentences (**q.v.**), **when** is used when there is a degree of *certainty*. In Arabic, **if** is rendered by إذا (or لَوْ), **when** by لَمَّا or حِينَ. e.g.

"**If** he gets here [it is not certain he will], I shall tell him what happened."
إذا جاءَ فَأَحْكِي لَهُ ما حَصَلَ

"**When** he becomes managing director [it is certain that he will be], he will make a few changes."
لَمَّا يُصْبِحُ مَدِيراً تَتَغَيَّرُ بَعْضَ الأَشْياءِ

"**When** the two astronauts return to earth from space."
حِينَ يَعُودُ الرَّائِدانِ مِنَ الفَضاءِ إلى الأَرْضِ

Whether (it be) ... or

This expression, which means *'irrespective, regardless of ...'* is translated into Arabic as:
لَوْ كانَ ... أوْ/أَمْ
إن كانَ ... أوْ/أَمْ

سَواءً كانَ ... أوْ/أمْ

e.g.

"The divorced wife observes *iddat* (the legally prescribed period waiting before contracting a new marriage) in her parents' home, **whether it be** close or far from the marital home."

تُعْتَدُّ الْمُطَلَّقَةُ في بَيْتِ أَهْلِها إنْ كان قَرِيباً أوْ نائياً مِن بَيْتِ الزَّوْجِيَّة

"There is no such thing as unimportant art, **whether it be** locally or internationally."

لا يُوجَدُ فَنٌّ بِلا أَهَمِّيَّةٍ سَواءٌ كانَ مَحَلِّياً أوْ عالَمِيّاً

In some cases, a simple coordinator can also be used. e.g.

"He will do it, **whether** he wants/likes to **or** not (willy-nilly)."

سَيَعْمَلُ غَصْباً أمْ طُوْعاً/مِنْ غَيْرِ غَصْبٍ

While/whereas

These two conjuncts both denote contrast between clauses and can often be used interchangeably; however, only **while** can also be used to express *simultaneity*, i.e. the co-occurrence of several actions. In Arabic, both may be translated by عَلَى/ في حين أن, بَيْنَما, which can also be used for simultaneity, or حَيْثُ. e.g.

"Foreign forces liberated the South, **whereas/while** the North was freed by domestic resistants.

تَوَلَّت القُوَّاتُ الأَجْنَبِيَّةُ تَحْرِيرَ الجَنُوبِ عَلَى حِينِ أَنَّ الشَّمالَ تَحَرَّرَ عَلَى يَدِ مُقاوِمِي الدَّاخِلِ

"It was said that the total weight of the container was 20 tons, **whereas/while** it can only contain 15 tons of goods."

يُقالُ إنَّ وَزْنَ الحاوِيَةِ 20 طُنّاً في حِينِ أَنَّها لاتَتَّسِعُ لأكْثَرِ مِن 15 طُنّاً

"He was reading **while** she was cooking dinner."

كانَ يَقْرَأُ بَيْنَما كانَتْ تُعِدُّ العَشاءَ

Will/shall

In traditional English grammar, **will** is used only with second and third persons, wheras **shall** is reserved for the first persons. In contemporary formal usage, however, this distinction is no longer maintained. Furthermore, the difference is often irrelevant as both are contracted to **'ll**. e.g.

سَنَكُونُ هُنا

"We **shall/'ll** be here."

يَذْهَبُ إلى المَكْتَبَةِ غَداً في الصَّباح

"He **will/'ll** go to the library tomorrow morning."

In legal language, **shall** is used to express obligation with second and third persons. e.g.

"The employee **shall** be deemed to have been appointed under probation for three months."

يُعْتَبَرُ الْمُوَظَّفُ مُعَيَّناً تَحْتَ الاِخْتِبارِ لِمُدَّةِ ثَلاثةِ شُهُورٍ

Wish

Though the translation of the concept does not necessarily pose any problems, its grammatical form often does in translation. In English, the verb '**to wish**' can occur in a number of constructions:

- + **to** + **infinitive**. e.g.

"I **wish** to see you."

أُرِيدُ أَنْ أَرَاكَ

أَتَمَنَّى أَنْ أَرَاكَ

- + **finite clause**. e.g.

"I **wish** we could afford to go to Paris."

أَتَمَنَّى لَوْ يُمْكِنُنَا تَحَمُّلَ نَفَقَاتِ الذَّهابِ إلى باريس

- + **that**. e.g.

"I **wish** that I (had) told them he wasn't going to be there."

أَوَدُّ لَوْ كُنْتُ أَخْبَرْتُهُم بِأَنَّهُ لَنْ يَكُونَ هُنَاكَ

- + **pronoun**. e.g.

"I **wish** you were here."

أَتَمَنَّى لَوْ كُنْتَ هُناكَ

- + **preposition**:

"I **wish** for you to be happy." [= "I want you to be happy."]

أَتَمَنَّى لَكَ (كُلَّ) السَّعَادةِ

The main thing to note in the English examples is the use of the hypothetical past-tense, or **subjunctive** (**q.v.**). When referring to the past or the present, the use of the hypothetical non-past indicates that the action to which reference is made is entirely hypothetical. e.g.

"I **wish** we knew how much they were making on the deal." [We don't know]

أَوَدُّ لَوْ عَرَفْنَا كَمْ سَيَكْسَبُونَ مِنْ هَذِهِ الصَّفْقَةِ

However, if the action refers to the future, it denotes possibility, even if it is unlikely. e.g.

"I **wish** you would go and visit your aunt next week on her birthday." [the visit may still take place]

أَتَمَنَّى لَو تَذْهَب لِزِيَارَةِ عَمَّتِكَ الأُسْبُوعَ المُقبِلَ في يومِ عيدِ مِيلادِهَا

In Arabic, '**to wish**' can be expressed in a number of ways, depending on the meaning; as a hypothetical '**if only...!**' (also expressed in very formal English by 'Would that...!'), or as an equivalent to '**like**' or '**want**'. e.g.

"Would that I knew/had known about his fraud!"
"If only I knew/had known..."
"I only wish I had known..."

لَو كُنتُ قَد عَرَفْتُ/أَعرِفُ عَن احْتِيالِه

Grammatically, this diversity can come in the guise of verbs and particles.

- The commonly used verbs are: رَغِبَ (يَرْغَبُ) في, تَمَنَّى, اِشتاقَ, رجا (يَرْجُو) ,اِرْتَجَى. Depending on the context, these may also do double duty for '*hope*' or '*look forward to*', or even '*want*'. One of the main blackspots in English-Arabic translation is the presence and choice of prepositions in Arabic, where English does not require any. e.g.

"Israel **wishes** to obtain US assistance to implement its project."

تَرْغَبُ إِسْرائيلُ في الحُصُولِ عَلَى مُساعدةِ الوِلاياتِ المُتَّحِدةِ مِن أَجْلِ تَطْبيقِ خُطَّتِها

"I **wished** (= had hoped) that the manager had/would have taken the necessary measures."

كُنْتُ أَتَمَنَّى مِن المُدِيرِ أَنْ يَأْخُذَ الإِجْراءاتِ الضَّرُورِيَّةِ

"I **wish** you hadn't said that."

أَتَمَنَّى لَو لَمْ تَكُنْ قُلْتَ ذلِكَ

"I **wish** I knew/had known what to say."

لَوْ كُنْتُ قَدْ عَرَفتُ/أَعرِفُ ماذا أَقُولُ

"She told me she **wished** you could come tomorrow."

لَقَد قَالَتْ لي إِنَّها تَتَمَنَّى لَو أَنَّكَ تَستَطِيعُ أَنْ تَأْتِي غَداً

"The minister is **looking forward to** more study of this proposal."

يَشْتَاقُ الوَزِيرُ إِلَى المَزِيدِ مِنَ المُطَالَعةِ لِهذا المَشْرُوعِ

The Public Prosecutor **hopes** that the new law will solve the matter..."

يَرْجُو المُدَّعِي العُمُومِيُّ أَنْ يَحُلَّ القانُونُ الجَدِيدَ المَسْأَلَةَ

"This was an alliance that the government neither **wished**/hoped for, nor expected..."

كانَ ذلِكَ حَلِيفاً لَمْ تَرْتَجِيهِ الحُكُومةُ أَوْ تَتَوَقَّعُهُ

☞ **NOTE:**

1. if a verb is required after رَغِبَ في do not forget to add أَنْ. e.g.

"According to the *New York Times*, America **wants** North Korea to acknowledge its nuclear capability."

"According to the *New York Times*, America **wishes** North Korea acknowledges its nuclear capability."

أَفادَت صَحِيفةٌ (نيويورك تايمز) أَنَّ أَمْرِيكا تَرْغَبُ في أَنْ تَعْتَرِفَ كُوريا الشَّمالِيَّةُ بِقُدْرَتِها النَّوَوِيَّةِ

2. رَغِبَ can have different meanings, depending on the prepositions with which it collocates:

a. في + عَلَى +: to **prefer** something over something else. e.g.

أَفَضِّلُ قِراءةَ الكُتُبِ عَلَى (مُشاهدة) الأَفْلام /
"I prefer reading to films."

b. عَنْ +: 'to dislike' (!). e.g.

لا تَرْغَبُ في الكلام عَنْ هذا المَوضوع
"She dislikes talking about this subject."

3. the fixed expression with the passive, used as an adjective:

لا يُرْغَبُ فيه, 'undesirable'

- the particle لَيْتَ, which is used for hypothesis only. e.g.

لَيْتَهُ كانَ هُنا
'I **wish** he were here!'

لَيْتَ شِعْري
'I **wish** I knew!'

لَيْتَ الأَمْر اقْتَصَرَ عَلَى هذا
"If only the order was restricted to this!"

لَيْتَ المُشْكِلة تَقِفُ عِنْدَ ذلكَ
"If only the problem ended there!"

لَيْتَني قُلْتُ لَهُ
"If only I had told him!"

لَيْتَني أَسْتَطِيعُ السَّفْرَ
"If only I could travel!"

☞ **NOTE:**

1. the noun following لَيْتَ is in the accusative.

2. لَيْتَ can be followed by لِ + suffix pronoun. e.g.

لَيْتَ لَكَ الوَقْتُ
"If only you had time!"

3. in formal English the use of the old subjunctive form '**were**' must be used in preference to 'was' as it involves a hypothesis. e.g.

"I wish I **were** a rich man."
لَيْتَني كُنْتُ غَنِيًّا

Appendix I: Tenses

Overview

Tense	English		Arabic	
	Form	Example	Form	Example
Present simple	PRESENT	'He has dinner at eight.'	IMPERF.	يَتَعَشَّى في السَّاعَةِ الثَّامِنَةِ مَساءً
Present progressive	TO BE+ ING	'He is drinking coffee.'	IMPERF	يَشْرَبُ قَهْوَةً
		'He is coming.'	AP [WITH INTRANS. VERBS]	هُوَ قادِمٌ
Past simple	PAST	'He went to the office.'	PERF.	ذَهَبَ إلى المَكْتَبِ
Past progressive	TO BE [PAST]+ING	'He was driving the car.'/'He used to drive the car.'	كانَ + IMPERF.	كانَ يَقُودُ السَّيّارَةَ
		'He was travelling.'	كانَ + AP [WITH INTRANS. VERBS]	كانَ مُسافِراً
		'I was going to say something'	كانَ + سَ/ سَوْفَ + IMPERF.	كُنْتُ سَأَقُولُ شَيئًا

Tense	English		Arabic	
	Form	Example	Form	Example
Present perfect	TO HAVE [PRESENT]+ PAST PARTICIPLE	'He has bought a house.'	قد + PERF.	قد اشْتَرَى بَيْتاً
Past perfect	TO HAVE [PAST]+ PAST PARTICIPLE	'He had told her.'	كان + قد + PERF.	كانَ قَدْ أَبْلَغَها
Future simple	WILL + INFINITIVE	'He will leave the country.'	سَ + IMPERF.	سَيُغادِرُ البِلادَ
			سَوْفَ + IMPERF.	سَوْفَ يُغادِرُ البِلادَ
Future perfect	WILL HAVE + PAST PARTICIPLE	'He will have finished the job.'	يَكُونُ+ قَدْ+ PERF.	يَكُونُ قَدْ انْتَهى العَمَلَ
Future progressive	WILL BE + ING	'He will be eating then.'	سَ/سَوْفَ IMPERF.	سَوْفَ/ سَيَأْكُلُ في هذا الوَقْتِ
		'He will be travelling."	يَكُونُ + PART. [WITH INTRANS. VERBS]	يَكُونُ مُسافِراً

Appendix II: Modality

Overview

TYPE	English		Arabic	
	Form	Example	Form	Example
OBLIGATION	MUST + [INF]	'You **must** tell him what he needs to know'	يَجِبُ + أَنْ + .SUBJ يَجِبُ عَلى + PRON + أَنْ + .SUBJ	يَجِبُ عَلَيْكَ أَنْ تَقُولَ لَهُ ما يَحْتاجُ إلى المَعْرِفَةِ
	HAVE TO + [INF]	'We **have to** work late tonight.'		يَجِبُ عَلَيْنا أَنْ نَعْمَلَ لِوَقْتٍ مُتَأَخِّرٍ اللَّيْلَةَ
	HAD TO + [INF]	'They **had to** fire him because he had stolen some money.'		كانَ عَلَيْهِمْ أَنْ يَفْصِلوهُ لِأَنَّهُ سَرَقَ بَعْضَ المالِ.

TYPE	English		Arabic	
	Form	Example	Form	Example
	SHOULD + [INF]	'I should get a haircut.'		يجب أن أقص شعري
	SHOULD HAVE + [PART]	'He should have behaved more politely.'	كان من الواجب + على + SUBJ. + أن + PRON	كان من الواجب أن يتصرف بأدب أكثر
	OUGHT TO + [INF]	'She ought to be more polite to her teacher.'		كان من الواجب أن تكون أكثر تهذيبا مع معلمها
	OUGHT TO HAVE + [PART]	'You ought to have helped your brother with his studies.'		كان من الواجب أن تساعد أخاك في دراسته
	MUST HAVE + [PART]	'He must have been here because his keys are on the table.'	لا بد أن + كان	لا بد أنه كان هنا لأن مفاتيحه ملقاة على الطاولة
POSSIBILITY	MAY + [INF]	'He may be the only one to applaud the lecturer.'	IMPERF. + قد	قد يكون الوحيد الذي يصفق للمحاضر
	MIGHT + [INF]	'We might do more harm than good.'	IMPERF. + قد	قد نضر أكثر مما ننفع

TYPE	English		Arabic	
	Form	Example	Form	Example
	MAY HAVE + [INF.] / [PART]	'We may have to pay them what they want.'	IMPERF. + قَدْ	قَدْ نَضْطَرُّ إلى أَنْ نَدْفَعَ لَهُمْ مَا يُرِيدُون
		'If he's seen her, he may have told her.'	PERF. + رُبَّمَا	رُبَّمَا، إِنْ كانَ قَدْ رَآها، أَخْبَرَها بِهِ
	MIGHT HAVE + [PART]	'He might have behaved differently, if he had known /had he known.'	IMPERF. + قَدْ + كانَ رُبَّمَا	رُبَّمَا كانَ قَدْ تَصَرَّفَ بِشَكْلٍ مُخْتَلِفٍ، لَوْ كانَ عَلى عِلْمٍ بذلك
ABILITY	CAN + [INF]	'You can pick up the books tomorrow.'	SUBJ. + أَنْ أَمْكَنَ · VN + يَسْتَطِيعُ	يُمْكِنُكَ أَنْ تَأْخُذَ الكُتُبَ غَدًا
		'You can walk around in the city.'	SUBJ. + أَنْ + يَسْتَطِيعُ	تَسْتَطِيعُ التَّجَوُّلَ في البَلَد
				تَسْتَطِيعُ أَنْ تَتَجَوَّلَ في البَلَد

TYPE	English		Arabic	
	Form	Example	Form	Example
COULD [INF]		"They could (were able to) solve their problems."	VN + قد تمكّن من (قد) تمكّن من أن .SUBJ +	قد تمكّنوا من حل مشكلاتهم
				قد تمكّنوا من أن يحلّوا مشكلاتهم
		"I couldn't walk after the accident."		لم أتمكّن أن أمشي من بعد وقوع الحادث
		"He could only save half of them."		أمكن بإنقاذ سوى نصفهم
		"I'm sure they could fund the project."	VN + يستطيع .SUBJ + أن + يستطيع	أنا متأكّد من أنّهم يستطيعون تمويل المشروع
COULD HAVE + [PART]		"We could have helped you, if you had told us about your problems."	كان من + أن .... كان من المُمكن أن	كان من المُمكن أن نساعدك لو كنت قد أخبرتنا عن مشاكلك

TYPE	English		Arabic	
	Form	Example	Form	Example
	WILL BE ABLE TO + [INF]	'He will be able to drive you to the airport.'	أ + قادر + يَكون + سـ/سوف + على	سوف/سـ يَكون قادراً على أن يوصِّلَك للمطار
			VN + يَستطيع سـ/سوف + على	سوف/سـ يَستطيع توصيلَك للمطار
			أن + يَستطيع سـ/سوف + SUBJ.	سوف/سـ يَستطيع أن يُوصِّلَك للمطار
			VN + يَقدِر على سـ/سوف	سيَقدِر على توصيلَك للمطار

English Index

Arabic Index